PUBLIC ENEMY NUMBER ONE

The True Story of the Brady Gang

Trudy Irene Scee

Down East Books

Camden, Maine

Published by Down East Books
A wholly owned subsidiary of The Rowman & Littlefield Publishing Group, Inc.
4501 Forbes Boulevard, Suite 200, Lanham, Maryland 20706
www.rowman.com

Unit A, Whitacre Mews, 26-34 Stannary Street, London SE11 4AB

Distributed by National Book Network
Copyright © 2015 by Trudy Irene Scee

British Library Cataloguing in Publication Information Available

Library of Congress Cataloging-in-Publication Data

Scee, Trudy Irene, author.
Public enemy #1 : the true story of the Brady Gang / Trudy Irene Scee.
pages cm
Includes bibliographical references and index.
ISBN 978-1-60893-511-6 (pbk.) -- ISBN 978-1-60893-512-3 (electronic)
1. Brady, Alfred, 1910-1937. 2. Criminals--United States--Biography. 3. Crime--United States--History--20th century. I. Title. II. Title: Public enemy number one.
HV6248.B71926S34 2015
364.1092--dc23
[B]
2015030375

∞™ The paper used in this publication meets the minimum requirements of American National Standard for Information Sciences Permanence of Paper for Printed Library Materials, ANSI/NISO Z39.48-1992.

Printed in the United States of America

For My Mother

Mary Louise Hemingway Taylor O'Sweeny Holland Scee Engelke

Whose early years overlapped a bit with those of the Brady Gang,
and whose travels overlapped more than a bit.

Happy Birthday Mom!
And you really should stop changing your name!
Love, Trudy Irene

CONTENTS

1

FOUR "MISSPENT YOUTHS" AND THE BEGINNINGS OF THE BRADY GANG, LATER IDENTIFIED AS THE "MOST VICIOUS" GANG IN AMERICA

About 150 to 200 robberies have been attributed to Alfred James Brady, Clarence Lee Shaffer Jr., and Rhuel James Dalhover, and a few of their associates, over the course of their reign as one of America's most prolific—or destructive—gangs of the Great Depression era. Known commonly as "The Brady Gang," the group was also deemed responsible for at least three murders (and considered guilty of a fourth, and possibly more), as well as committing a number of vicious assaults that had lasting repercussions for their victims. Much of their thievery and violence occurred before the Federal Bureau of Investigation, more limited in its jurisdiction in the early to mid-1930s than it would be by the end of the decade, became involved in hunting the gang down. The FBI did not become involved until the gang's crime spree was well underway, because, as far as was known or provable, the gang had not yet crossed state lines in the course of committing a single crime, nor committed another classification of crime then specifically under the jurisdiction of "Federal Bureau" as the department was called until mid-1935. Most cases of murder and robbery were state crimes, if committed within one state's borders.

The Brady Gang, as a gang, first became active in 1935. Their reign in the criminal world would last for only two years, but they would be a wild two years. The gang members would eventually be pursued by the

Federal Bureau, several state police departments, a plethora of local police and sheriff's departments, and even the Pinkerton National Detective Agency. They would be captured, and then escape; they would kill "in cold blood," and continue on, seemingly without feeling any sense of guilt. They would cross paths with other notorious thugs, and deceive the women in their lives. Al Brady would be named "Public Enemy No. 1, and "Public Rat No. 1" by J. Edger Hoover, who also identified the gang as the "most vicious" one then operating in America. And even before 1935, when the men formed their gang, each had already had numerous run-ins with the law. Each had what would sometimes be called a "misspent youth," including Al Brady, who was generally deemed the gang's leader.

Born in northwestern Indiana just outside of Kentland on October 25, 1910, Alfred James Brady seems to have enjoyed a fairly average childhood—at least, for a few years. He lived in the countryside and later attended elementary or grammar school in North Salem, Indiana. Kentland was and remains a small town, located in the flatlands of Jefferson Township of Newton County just a few miles from the Illinois border. It serves as the county seat, and was founded in 1860 as simply Kent, for Alexander J. Kent who acquired the then marshy site and helped prepare it for development. It was a farming and cattle town when Brady was born.

When Brady was just a few years old, however, his father Roy died in a farming accident. Young Alfred and his mother Clara Brady soon moved about 140 miles south to North Salem where Brady would attend school, and Clara remarried, to John A. Biddle. Brady would remain an only child.[1]

North Salem is located in more central Indiana, an even smaller town than Kentland, first settled in 1835 in Hendricks County in the Eel River Township, and incorporated as a town in 1899. The nearby Eel River and Big Walnut Creek offered fishing opportunities to its residents, and the surrounding area consisted of low flat farmland to the east when Brady's family moved there, and woodlands to the west of the town. North Salem is located northwest of Indianapolis.[2]

After the loss of his father a dozen years earlier, when Brady was just fourteen years old his stepfather died of gunshot wounds. The true story was never quite known to authorities, but the coroner ruled that the death was "probably accidental." Rumors had circulated, however, that either Clara or Al had killed Biddle, who was also rumored to have been abusive to young Al.[3]

Soon after his stepfather's death, Clara moved her son to Indianapolis in about 1925. By now, Brady had become a teenager with a quick temper, one allegedly experimenting with arson. The gray-eyed, light-brown-haired adult perhaps still had blonde hair into his teens as he had as a young child. Al Brady would never be a large man, and he was perhaps grown to his final height of five feet, six inches and weight of about 160 pounds by the time his mother died in December 1926. She was just thirty-seven years old, and Alfred only sixteen. Brady apparently received a guardian at this point, a man named Ira Wells.[4]

Brady worked in an Indianapolis clothing store for a short while, and later for a time for a hot tamale stand, running errands. A friend of his family owned the stand, and Brady worked there, during part of 1931–1932. After this, Brady left his job, and seems to have wandered around, as many people did during what were the early years of the Great Depression, the great Stock Market Crash having occurred in 1929 and an increasingly severe economic downturn setting in soon thereafter. Farmland such as that where Brady was born was already suffering before the 1929 stock market crash. Yet, Brady seems to have worked as an automobile mechanic in his hometown of Kentland, Indiana for a short time during this period.[5]

Around 1929, Al Brady set out to rob a grocer named Clifford Bernard in Indianapolis. He purportedly pretended that he had a gun in his pocket and demanded he be given all the money in the cashier's till, but was shot three times by a patrolman while fleeing the scene. He recovered, and received a suspended sentence.[6]

According to FBI records, Brady's former acquaintances saw little of him from when he left the tamale stand in 1932 until July 10, 1934, and then they heard of him again before they saw him. On July 10, Brady was arrested on a charge of vagrancy under the name James Reid. One of his old friends, with whom he had lived previously, intervened, and the charge was dismissed. The people with whom he had lived soon lost contact with Al Brady once more.[7] He was on the road, sometimes in jail, looking to find his place in the world.

Although his friends and acquaintances in Indianapolis did not know it, Alfred James Brady, described later as having been "pinch faced and hard muscled from his years on the farm and at a mechanic's bench," had already entered a life of crime, and one that went beyond that of vagrancy, with which thousands of people were charged during the Great Depression as they moved from town to town seeking work or merely sustenance.[8]

On July 21, 1934, Brady had been arrested on a charge of possession of stolen property—he had continued stealing automobiles—and was sentenced to serve 180 days at the state farm near Greencastle, Indiana. The following day, on July 22, 1934, Chicago police shot John Dillinger to death.[9]

Known as the Indiana State Farm from its establishment in 1914 for the next seventy years, the facility when young Brady served time there housed primarily male inmates convicted of minor crimes. The prisoners had to work on the farm growing crops or in its dairy operations. Brady would not have been exempt from such requirements. The prison would soon add a brickyard where prisoners would make, haul, and fire bricks in dome-shaped brick kilns, some parts of the work quite dangerous. Later on, more serious criminals would be housed at the Indiana State Farm, and its name changed to the Putman Correctional Facility.[10]

According to an early history of the FBI with an introduction by J. Edgar Hoover, Al Brady learned only to be a more cunning criminal while at the state farm. As the editors of *Look Magazine* put it, "The only lessons he learned from this experience were those taught him by other inmates. He boned up on crime techniques at the feet of masters, and determined not to mend his ways but to become a better criminal."[11] The same might be said of his two closest cohorts of following years.

Upon his release from the jail at Greencastle, Brady had visited a farm owned by his former guardian, Ira Wells, near Hanover, where he became acquainted with one James Dalhover. Dalhover had purchased—or was otherwise operating or working on—the neighboring farm in 1934–1935. Dalhover had also been in trouble with the law, and from an early age. By the time he met Brady, he had become a bootlegger operating in Kentucky, Indiana, and Ohio. Dalhover was four years older than Brady, and according to the FBI had been able to purchase the farm with the proceeds from his illegal liquor operations. Some sources, however, show that Dalhover was simply working the land, and making moonshine on the side, and did not actually own the property.

Considering Dalhover's past and future, this is quite likely true. Either way, the two men would maintain contact, however loosely, until they formed a gang.[12]

In the summer of 1935, probably in August, Brady returned to Indianapolis and secured a job at a mattress factory. He stayed at this job for only a short period, then found a job as a welder in an automobile factory. Brady would prove repeatedly in his life that he liked to work around cars, but often did so in less than legitimate ways. He decided to move on again, telling the people he had been living with that he was going to go on the road as an insurance inspector.[13] Brady went on the road all right, but not as an inspector.[14]

In January 1936, according to a Chicago policeman, Captain John Egan, Brady, recently released from the Indiana Reformatory at Pendleton after serving a five-month sentence for automobile theft, was at an Indianapolis poolhall when another man said to him, "Hey midget, you're nothing but a wise-crackin' punk. We don't want you 'round us. Why, you ain't even dry behind the ears." The man was backed up by several of his buddies, regulars at the poolroom that they used as their hangout, a gang of "toughs" Brady had purportedly sought to join. Brady supposedly blushed at first, but then, as the color drained from his face, retorted coolly, "Some day, I'll make John Dillinger look like a piker." Details of the story might vary, but the statement he—or one of his cohorts—made about making Dillinger look like a piker would be told time and time again, and become part of the increasingly tough gangster's legacy—if one may call it that. Brady had indeed been recently incarcerated for possessing stolen property, but had spent his sentence at the Indiana State Farm at Greencastle, Indiana. The date of the purported conversation may actually have been sometime in 1935, or perhaps Brady had served another jail stint, this time in Pendleton.[15] Either way, by January 1936, Alfred Brady had his own gang of "toughs," and one of *them* had served time in Pendleton, and that convict would be known as the braggart of the gang. Brady, although not immune to bragging, became more of a simple "show-off" as time progressed.

The Chicago police captain, writing in the mid-1930s, called Brady a "weak chinned former Sunday school teacher," who "made good on his boast," and "today is definitely this country's Public Rat Number One," a term coined by J. Edger Hoover. Brady had taken the "rat throne" from John Dillinger after Dillinger's shoot-out with police, only months after Brady made his infamous statement of his desires to occupy the "throne" of the underworld. The policeman referred to Brady as a "Midget Dillinger," noting that the slender man was five feet, seven inches tall—although other sources place him at closer to five feet, five inches.[16] In 1935, however, Brady had yet to attain the notoriety that would one day be his. He still needed to assemble his own gang of toughs, which he was indeed starting to do.

Brady lived in the Indianapolis region during most of 1935, seemingly doing factory work during at least part of the week and visiting the farm near Hanover on occasion. Although one of his "earliest sweethearts" would say that he was "too sweet to hurt anyone," during this time period he purportedly told some of his acquaintances that he had formed a gang—not the one with which he would later become notorious, but one composed of young boys. The boys would burglarize grocery stores and various businesses, and steal and sell or strip automobiles. Brady would skim off much of the proceeds of the boys' vandalism. Brady was looking for a scam with greater profit margins, however, and would soon make plans to that end with James Dalhover, who it seems did help Brady strip stolen automobiles and fence the parts during the winter of 1935–1936.[17]

Brady's second comrade in crime, as he would become known, was born Rhuel James Dalhover in Madison, Indiana, on August 24, 1906. Madison is located almost exactly across the state—both southerly and easterly, from Brady's hometown of Kentland. Situated along the Ohio River in Jefferson County, Madison was much larger in the early 1900s than was Kentland, and would become the largest city along the Ohio River between Cincinnati, Ohio (roughly seventy-five miles away), and Louisville, Kentucky (roughly fifty miles away), and have the largest downtown area registered on the National Register of Historic Places later in the century, encompassing some 133 city blocks. In 1910, four years after Dalhover's birth and the year in which Al Brady was born, Madison had a population of almost 7,000 people, a decline from the mid-1800s that would not rebound until the mid-1900s. The city had first seen Caucasian settlement about 1808 with a fairly rapid growth due to its location on the then busy Ohio River, as settlers headed into what was then known as the Indiana Territory and the Northwest Territory of the Midwest. Railroads soon augmented river travel, and by the early 1920s the various local lines would be consolidated into the larger

Pennsylvania Railroad system. However, as time progressed, Madison's growth would slow, while regional cities like Louisville and Cincinnati continued to grow.[18] The summer weather in Madison for young Dalhover would generally have been warmer and more humid than that of Kentland for Brady, with milder winters.

A few decades after the Brady Gang coalesced, Madison—with a population of just over 10,000 people—would be described by journalist Irving Leibowitz as "the loveliest town in Indiana, calm and quiet and nestled in the green and grassy hills that circle it along the gravelly bank that sweeps down to the beautiful Ohio River." The town would be selected during World War II by the nation's Office of War information as a "typical American town." Moreover, movies were produced in more than thirty-two languages extolling the virtues of America and reminding American military members of the life back home that they were fighting for, as well as showing the rest of the world what America life was like.[19] Unfortunately, the Brady Gang would not be such an icon of pride for the nation or the town, and would not be highlighted in the "typical town" film.

Dalhover lived in Madison, amidst its riverbanks and rolling hills until the age of eleven, attending grammar school there. He was later described as "a farm boy [like Brady]—raw boned and scrawny." His parents divorced, and Dalhover found himself in trouble early on, with his brother George, and the two were sent to a reformatory school in Plainfield, Indiana. They had robbed a grocery store in Plowhandle Point in 1917, securing about $10 for their efforts. James stayed at the reform school for sixteen months, then returned to live with his mother, who had since moved to Cincinnati, Ohio. James returned to school there for a time, and he did some odd jobs. The family soon moved to Kentucky, however. James finished school in 1920, and then went to work at the National Biscuit Company (later Nabisco) at its Cincinnati plant for two years. After leaving the job, Dalhover moved to Douglas, Arizona, with another one of his brothers. He worked at a few different manual labor jobs until 1924, when he returned to Indiana to live with his father, a cabinetmaker, in Madison for about a year. In July 1925, James Dalhover returned to Cincinnati and worked for the Standard Service Company until the spring of 1926. In 1925, he married Anna Moore of Cincinnati. The couple would have two children together, a son and then a daughter, the children two years apart in age.[20]

James Dalhover, like Al Brady, was a rather slight man, identified as being just five feet, five inches (some sources say five feet, four inches) tall as an adult and weighing 134 pounds with a medium build and blue eyes, light brown hair, and a ruddy complexion. In 1926, in spite of his family responsibilities, or perhaps, in some way, because of them, Dalhover stepped outside of the law again. He started making moonshine whiskey for his wife's grandfather. His brother George joined him, and the two were caught with a load of moonshine in Union, Kentucky. The brothers again served time together, this time in Kentucky, sentenced to one hundred days in jail, as well as having to pay a $100 fine. This was during National Prohibition, passed under the Eighteenth Amendment on January 16, 1920, and not repealed until 1933. However, after just three weeks in jail for running whiskey, James and George escaped and fled to Cincinnati. They then went to Madison, Indiana, where they picked up a car and started to drive to Arizona. On the way, at Roswell, New Mexico, their car broke down. In order to continue their flight from the law, the brothers stole a 1926 Ford coupe. The new car perhaps attracted more attention than an older model might have, and the two were soon captured. They were sentenced in 1927 to one-and-one-half to two years in the New Mexico State Penitentiary for the automobile theft.[21]

The Penitentiary of New Mexico at Santa Fe, where the brothers were incarcerated, had opened in 1885, although the U.S. Congress had authorized the construction of the jail in 1853. The prison was designed based on the architectural plans used to build the more notorious prisons of Sing Sing and Joliet. Like most of the other prisons in which the Brady Gang members would be sentenced to at various junctures, the New Mexico penitentiary put its inmates to work. In the late 1800s, prisoners made bricks, probably adobe bricks as no kilns were indicated on prison records. Starting in 1903, they also began to build roads, Arizona being the first western state to so employ its prisoners. The Santa Fe institution in the years during which the Dalhover brothers reached its cells were not good ones, although they were perhaps somewhat better than those in the early 1920s. In 1922, the inmates had rioted against the facility's poor food, overcrowding, and the excessive use of force by prison staff. The guards had opened fire from the prison towers after the rioters refused to return to their cells, killing one prisoner and wounding five others. A subsequent investigation blamed prison authorities for most aspects of the riot. However, although things may have improved by the time the Dalhovers arrived in 1927, prison inmates would riot again against the use of excessive force by prison guards and other conditions in 1953, with two inmates being killed and several more wounded. This riot would result in the original building being abandoned for a new structure in 1956, but it too would have problems, and one of America's most violent prison riots would occur there in 1980, and then the carnage would be much worse, with men decapitated and burned alive as well as other atrocities taking place.[22] The prison was a troubled one for most of its existence, including during the late 1920s and in the 1930s.

The Dalhover brothers would have been put to work in the New Mexico prison during their time there, and would no doubt have been unhappy about conditions at the prison. The brothers spent thirteen months there, and were then sentenced for their crime in escaping in Kentucky, charged specifically with assault with intent to kill during their escape. With the newest conviction against them, James and George Dalhover were sent to serve a two-year sentence in Kentucky's State Reformatory in Frankfort. This was Kentucky's first state prison, opened in 1798, and originally called the Kentucky State Prison, re-named after the Kentucky State Penitentiary in Eddyville along the Cumberland River opened in 1889. Inmates at both facilities in the 1920s wore loose denim pants and jackets, as well as cloth shirts and hats. Numbers were stenciled on the backs of their shirts and jackets. Offenders up until the 1940s were sometimes subjected to the chain-and-ball as punishment, and conditions overall were tough.[23]

James was released from the Kentucky State Reformatory on November 25, 1929, and returned to Cincinnati. He worked at a few odd jobs there, then started to make moonshine again, this time near Richmond, Ohio. Once again, Rhuel James Dalhover did not learn his lessons through incarceration or other experiences, and the early 1930s would see him again making poor choices, critically poor choices.[24]

By 1930, moreover, America was a changed nation. During 1930, after the stock market crash of 1929, the Great Depression began to settle in for its long run in America. Cities across the nation faced numerous economic hardships and social dislocations. Some of these issues resulted in various social ills and crimes, and Indiana would not be alone in facing an upswing in crime.

James moved again in January 1931, this time with his brother John to California. He found work at the Needles Gas and Electric Company, worked there for just two months, then took a job with the Santa Fe Railroad. He worked with the railroad until June 1932. Then, ever restless, Dalhover returned to his hometown of Madison, Indiana. There he worked part-time with his father making furniture. For the remainder of his time, he made moonshine once again. In summer 1933, his whiskey work was going so well that he gave up his work with his father to make whiskey full-time. Prohibition being repealed (although moonshine was still often illegal, and some places remained "dry," forbidding the sale of any alcohol), Dalhover bought—or worked on—the farm near Hanover and continued making whiskey through 1934. Early the following year, 1935, he would meet Alfred Brady when Brady was visiting at the neighboring farm. By this time, Dalhover had become greatly interested in firearms, something that would form a bond between the two thugs and then grow into a near obsession for them over the next couple of years.[25]

Later, Dalhover would state that Al Brady would bring yeast to him from Indianapolis, as the state and federal governments were attempting to cut off the yeast supply he used to make his illegal moonshine. In March 1935, revenue agents raided Dalhover's farm and destroyed his whiskey operation. They smashed his still. Tried in July 1935 in Madison, on July 6, Rhuel James Dalhover was sentenced in the Jefferson Circuit Court to sixty days in jail and fined $500.[26]

Dalhover served his time at the Indiana State Farm at Greencastle. After his sixty-day stint, Dalhover was released on September 8, 1935, and went back to his Hanover farm. There, he said years later, Al Brady asked him to join him in holdups and robberies.[27]

Dalhover refused at first, but Brady returned in a stolen automobile and renewed the offer. This time, Dalhover apparently agreed to partner in crime with Brady, and the two robbed a motion picture theater in Crothersville, Indiana, about fifty miles south of Indianapolis, on October 12, 1935. James received $4 as his cut from the $18 they had stolen. They had robbed the theater on a Monday night, so the till contained less money than it might have on a weekend. Expenses were subtracted from the money before Dalhover received his cut. The two did better, in terms of their take, when the following Saturday night, October 19, they held up a grocery store in Sellersburg, Indiana, and obtained about

$180.[28] And thus was formed part of the soon-to-be infamous Brady Gang.

Within a few weeks, Clarence Lee Shaffer Jr., age twenty and about five feet, five inches tall, was brought into the alliance. Brady purportedly brought Shaffer to Dalhover's farm, introducing him to his crime partner. (Dalhover, however, would later say that Shaffer had been working with him on the farm already when they met Brady.) At the time, Shaffer was using the name Lee Jackson. Brady supposedly introduced Dalhover and Shaffer on October 26, 1935. But, perhaps it was the other way around.[29]

Shaffer, too, had a history in crime before the Brady Gang came into being, and was referred to by one contemporary source as "an Indianapolis and Chicago outlaw" before the young men formed their gang.[30] The three convicts started pulling jobs together, and soon brought a fourth man into their gang.

Clarence Lee Shaffer Jr. had been born in 1916 in Indianapolis, Indiana. He would be the youngest member of the Brady Gang, but by his birth also the "big city" boy of the gang. His parents separated when he was about two years old. His mother obtained a divorce from his father a short time later. Clarence then went to live with his grandparents in Indianapolis. He would soon attend elementary school in Ben Davis, Indiana—located essentially within the urban sprawl of Indianapolis.[31]

At some point in his youth, Shaffer's mother remarried, to a John Bailey, who would serve as a stepfather to at least some degree to young Clarence. They would live on a forty-acre farm near Noblesville, Indiana by the time Clarence undertook his adult life of crime.[32]

At about age twelve, Clarence started stealing cars and stripping them, something that he continued to do for some time. He eventually started doing various odd jobs, including cutting grass and hauling coal. He worked for a time hauling coal with one Charles Geiseking, with whom he would become criminally involved in the future. He also served time at Pendleton, Indiana.[33]

Pendleton Correctional facility, originally known as the Indiana Reformatory, is located in Madison County south of Pendleton and approximately twenty-five miles northeast of Indianapolis. It was the newest of the prisons the gang members would serve in to date, having been built in 1923 after the original Indiana State Reformatory first located in Jeffersonville and then moved to Clarksville was destroyed by fire in 1918. By that time, the state prison system was divided into the Indiana State Prison South at Clarksville which housed inmates between ages sixteen and thirty, and Indiana State Prison North, in Michigan City, which would also hold one Brady Gang member.[34]

The newer prison, which held Clarence Lee Shaffer Jr., would be constructed on some thirty-one acres and eventually be surrounded by a concrete wall. The cellblocks fanned out from a central point at the new facility, as a "radial plan" prison, with an architect basing the overall design on the Spanish Revival style, with green spaces, as well as maximum light and air available. The prison originally contained three cellblocks, a dormitory, and an administrative building in the 1920s. Construction was ongoing in 1924, but in March of that year the superintendent of the prison decided to use convict labor to work on the site. This saved a substantial amount of money, and also created a means by which inmates could learn such trades as roofing, plumbing, bricklaying, electrical installation, and painting. Other jobs would be created in the 1920s, including a shirt-making factory.[35]

The Pendleton facility would be renamed in later years, but, in the meantime, as well as jailing at least one member of the Brady Gang, it had also held John Dillinger after his 1924 robbery of a grocery store and the beating of its owner in Mooresville, Indiana. Dillinger was sentenced to ten to twenty years in jail—the maximum sentence for the crime—and worked in the shirt factory at Pendleton, generally doubling his production quota. Dillinger's wife soon divorced him, and he was denied parole in 1929. Soon thereafter, he requested and received a transfer to the state prison at Michigan City. The State paroled Dillinger in May 1933, and, continuing with his career in crime, Dillinger was shot to death on July 22, 1934.[36]

Clarence Lee Shaffer Jr. as an adult was described as being five feet, five inches tall and weighing about 125 pounds with, like Brady, gray eyes, brown hair, and a medium build, but with a dark complexion instead of Brady's "ruddy one." In 1936, he was described as being "the loudmouth" of the Brady Gang. When he met Brady in 1935, Shaffer was described by the editors of *Look* in a monograph of the history of the FBI as being "like his new-found pals" a "product of his misspent youth . . . a cocky 19-year-old petty thief who bragged about a fancied relationship with John Dillinger." Dillinger, along with noted criminals of the era such as "Ma" and "Doc" Barker, and "Baby Face" Nelson, however, were now dead, and

> had left a bad taste behind them. The days of gangster worship were over. Harboring criminals was [now] a Federal offense, and those likely to be guilty of it had been well warned by the FBI. The Bureau in fact, had made it exceedingly difficult for big-time criminals. The Brady Gang, young and brash, [however] had not yet learned this.[37]

While working with Geiseking hauling coal, Shaffer had met a young woman whom he saw fairly frequently up until November 1935. During this time, late in the summer of 1935, he also opened a hamburger stand in Indianapolis, a business he operated for only three or four weeks. By late autumn, Shaffer had met Al Brady and James Dalhover. Shaffer purportedly told the girl, Christine Puckett of Indianapolis, that he was a truck driver. Soon thereafter, the young woman—actually a high school student—had a baby boy, which the girl claimed was Shaffer's. Both the girl and Shaffer's mother wanted Clarence to marry her, and Shaffer's mother also pleaded with her son to stop his criminal activities, but Shaffer did neither. In October 1937, Christine Puckett, still living with her parents, would assert in the press that her son, Russell Lee Puckett, born fourteen months earlier, was indeed the son of Clarence Lee Shaffer Jr. She had given her child Shaffer's middle name. The dark-haired young woman was photographed with her son wearing a white top with a plaid skirt, the toddler seems to have been wearing a t-shirt and shorts, both mother and son looking off to the side.[38] By this time, Shaffer had long left them for good, and Charles Geiseking had become a short-term, but crucial, fourth member of the Brady Gang. Charles Geiseking—an Indianapolis resident for some time by the time the gang formed—also had a prior criminal record before the four men embarked on their crimes together,[39] and escaped the final fate of the other three men because he was kept incarcerated during some of their most deadly actions.

And after the four met up, as J. Edgar Hoover would later describe it, "In the fall of 1935 and the spring of 1936, an epidemic of motorcar and grocery-store robberies broke forth in Indiana and Illinois." Dalhover would later say that while he, Brady, and Shaffer were staging robberies out of his farm, using it as their base of operations, that

Brady, Shaffer, and Geiseking were also robbing various places during the weekdays in late 1935.[40]

Dalhover would also later boast that the gang had pulled off about 150 robberies by the spring of 1936. These included grocery stores, gas stations, and drugstores in Indiana and Ohio.[41] Of course, Brady had already been well into theft by autumn 1935, as were his fellow gang members. Their united crime spree, however, would not be limited to robbery, it would also include armed bank robberies, violent assaults, and murders spreading from the Midwest to the East Coast. The members of the Brady Gang were in some ways products of their time, but they had had other choices, had seen fellow Hoosiers make other choices, some of them likewise gaining national attention, and many of those in a more positive light. But it was the Dillingers, the Nelsons, the Barkers—the slime on the underbelly of the Midwest—that the four young men from Indiana would decide to emulate.

NOTES

1. General sources on the towns, and "The Brady Gang," *FBI History: Famous Cases*. Federal Bureau of Investigation, FBI website as posted in 2014. Some errors or confusion exists on the website, and facts have been substantiated throughout this work by other sources where possible. Also see *Rushville [Indiana] Republication*, 4 October 1937, possible source for some of the later FBI coverage on the gangsters as young men; and *Bangor Daily News*, 13 October 1937, for supporting materials.

2. Ibid. And see Information on Kentland and North Salem from general sources including Indiana Government websites and Wikipedia.

3. Ibid. Also *Rushville [Indiana] Republication*, 4 October 1937; and Dick Shaw, "Last Days of the Brady Gang," *BDN*, 4–5 October 1997, on suspicions about the death and possible abuse.

4. "The Brady Gang," *FBI History: Famous Cases*. Federal Bureau of Investigation, FBI website as posted in 2014; J. Edgar Hoover, June 1937 "Wanted" Notice for the Brady Gang; also see *Rushville [Indiana] Republication*, 4 October 1937.

5. "The Brady Gang," *FBI History: Famous Cases.* FBI, 2104 website; *Rushville [Indiana] Republication*, 4 October 1937; *New York Times*, from Chicago Press, 12 October 1937, printed October 13, 1937; and *BDN* and Indiana Wire Service, Logansport, 18–19 July 1936.

6. Ibid. And see Dick Shaw, "Last Days of the Brady Gang," *BDN*, 4–5 October 1997.

7. FBI-National Archives Case Records 87-257; "The Brady Gang," *FBI History: Famous Cases*, FBI.

8. Quote from the editors of *Look Magazine, The Story of the FBI*, with an introduction by J. Edgar Hoover (New York: E. P. Dutton & Co., 1947, revised edition, 1954).

9. *Rushville [Indiana] Republication*, 4 October 1937, for quote; "The Brady Gang," *FBI History: Famous Cases*, FBI; and see related documents.

10. Information taken from general sources including the Indiana Department of Corrections and Wikipedia.

11. The editors of *Look Magazine, The Story of the FBI*, with an introduction by J. Edgar Hoover. The coverage of the gang on the later FBI website closely covered some of the same facts presented by the earlier book.

12. "The Brady Gang," *FBI History: Famous Cases*, FBI; FBI-National Archives Case Records 87–257. The FBI's later website had Dalhover owning the land, although he would later say that he was working there, as would a 1936 Indiana article which credited the FBI with much of its information: *Rushville [Indiana] Republication*, 4 October 1936. Also see *New York Times*, from Chicago Press, 12 October 1937, printed October 13, 1937, on quote about Dalhover.

13. FBI-National Archives Case Records 87-257; "The Brady Gang," *FBI History: Famous Cases*, FBI.

14. "The Brady Gang," *FBI History: Famous Cases*, FBI.

15. Captain John Egan (another source has him as Eagon), Chicago PD, as told to Douglas Hunt, "The Second Dillinger," written for *Official Detective Magazine* for November 1937 publication with excerpts printed in the *Bangor Daily News* (*BDN*), Maine, 13 October 1937; and "The Brady Gang," *FBI History: Famous Cases*, FBI.

16. Captain John Egan and Douglas Hunt, "The Second Dillinger."

17. *Rushville [Indiana] Republication*, 4 October 1937; and "The Brady Gang," *FBI History: Famous Cases*, FBI.

18. Information taken from general sources including the Indiana Government and Correctional Department and Wikipedia.

19. Irving Leibowitz, *My Indiana* (Englewood Cliffs, NJ: Prentice Hall, Inc., 1964).

20. FBI-National Archives Case Records 87-257; *Rushville [Indiana] Republication*, 4 October 1936; and "The Brady Gang," *FBI History: Famous Cases*, FBI. Also see the editors of *Look Magazine, The Story of the FBI*, with an introduction by J. Edgar Hoover (New York: E. P. Dutton & Co., 1947,

revised edition, 1954). On the money see Dick Shaw, "Last Days of the Brady Gang," *BDN*, 4–5 October 1997.

21. Description from John Edgar Hoover, "Wanted List," FBI, June 1937. For balance see "The Brady Gang," *FBI History: Famous Cases*, FBI; FBI-National Archives Case Records 87-257; *Rushville [Indiana] Republication*, 4 October 1936; and UP article based on state records, from Detroit, Michigan, as printed in the *Greenfield Daily Reporter*, Indiana, evening edition, 14 October 1936.

22. Taken from general sources including the New Mexico Corrections Department websites and reports and Wikipedia. Also see for information on prison conditions and riots: Judith R. Johnson, "A Mighty Fortress Is the Pen: The Development of the New Mexico Penitentiary," in Judith Boyce DeMark, ed., *Essays in Twentieth-Century New Mexico History* (Albuquerque, NM: University of New Mexico Press, 1994).

23. "The Brady Gang," *FBI History: Famous Cases*, FBI; Kentucky Department of Corrections websites and Wikipedia for general information on the prisons; and UP article from Detroit, Michigan, as printed in the *Greenfield Daily Reporter*, evening edition, 14 October 1936.

24. "The Brady Gang," *FBI History: Famous Cases*, FBI.

25. "The Brady Gang," *FBI History: Famous Cases*, FBI; J. Edgar Hoover, 1938 quote; and *Rushville [Indiana] Republication*, 4 October 1936.

26. "The Brady Gang," *FBI History: Famous Cases*, FBI; UP article from Detroit, Michigan, as printed in the *Greenfield Daily Reporter*, evening edition, 14 October 1936.

27. FBI-National Archives Case Records 87-257; "The Brady Gang," *FBI History: Famous Cases*, FBI. One source has him serving his time at Greencastle, the other at Newcastle.

28. Ibid.

29. Ibid. *Baltimore News-Post*, 13 October 1937, on Dalhover's statement, and for the October date see Dick Shaw, "Last days of the Brady Gang," *BDN*, 4–5 October 1997.

30. "The Brady Gang," *FBI History: Famous Cases*, FBI; *Rushville [Indiana] Republication*, 4 October 1936; and *NYT*, AP article printed October 13, 1937, for quote.

31. *Rushville [Indiana] Republication*, October 4, 1936; and "The Brady Gang," *FBI History: Famous Cases*, FBI. Shaffer's name is also spelled Schaffer in some sources, and Dalhover's as Delhover.

32. *BDN*, 14 October 1937, 2nd edition.

33. "The Brady Gang," *FBI History: Famous Cases*, FBI. The editors of *Look Magazine*, *The Story of the FBI*, with an introduction by J. Edgar Hoover. The coverage of the gang on the later website closely covered some of

the same facts presented by the earlier book. Also see *Rushville [Indiana] Republication*, 4 October 1936, which carried some of the other information used on the later website.

34. Information taken from general sources including the Indiana Government and Indiana Department of Corrections and Wikipedia.

35. Ibid.

36. Ibid. For more information on Dillinger see the following chapter.

37. Description of Shaffer from J. Edgar Hoover, "Wanted List," June 1937 and from *Rushville [Indiana] Republication*, 4 October 1936; and quotes from the editors of *Look Magazine*, *The Story of the FBI*, with an introduction by J. Edgar Hoover.

38. "The Brady Gang," *FBI History: Famous Cases*, FBI; Associated Press interview as carried in the *BDN*, 13 October 1937; and *BDN*, 14 October 1937.

39. FBI-National Archives Case Records 87-257.

40. J. Edgar Hoover, quote from 1938; and see "The Brady Gang," *FBI History: Famous Cases*, FBI and related documents.

41. See Baltimore, Indianapolis, and Bangor, Maine, press for October–November 1937.

2

OTHER OPTIONS

Indiana in the 1920s and 1930s, Its Economic Plight,
Its More Unique Leaders, and the Midwestern
Villains of the Era

Crime was on the rise in the Midwest as the Depression set in. In Indiana, the "Hoosier State" as it was nicknamed, robberies reached "epidemic proportions" even before John Dillinger engineered the state's so-called "greatest prison break" at Michigan City in 1933, and thereby "swash buckled into the nation's headlines," according to journalist Irving Leibowitz. Not just small robberies like those at gas stations and grocery stores were on the rise, but also bank robberies. Three bank robberies a day was not unusual in the early 1930s, and newspapers had a banner day when nine Indiana banks were heldup in one single day. According to Leibowitz, "The bold robberies of Dillinger held a bizarre fascination for a public disillusioned by the Depression."[1]

So, too, would the doings of the gang Alfred Brady assembled have a "bizarre fascination" for Indiana, the Midwest, and the nation, in following years. But the Brady Gang members did have other options, other possible role models, even if their own poor beginnings in life might have made these paths more difficult during the Great Depression. Their poor choices, had, however, started before the stock market crash of 1929. And the 1920s and 1930s would produce some of the most infamous gangsters

and mobsters in history in the American Midwest, and these would prove
the more alluring role models for the Brady Gang.

Indiana had seen various social, political, and economic experiments
or movements before Al Brady came to the forefront in the state's
public eye. Scottish industrialist Robert Owen, after implementing
sweeping reforms in his own mills in Scotland, decided to start a new
society in America—where he saw a greater potential for a new order.
He started a utopian community in Indiana in 1825, named New Harmony. Located on the banks of the Wabash River, New Harmony
aimed to have all of its inhabitants share in the community's wealth,
including food, clothing, work, and education. A committee oversaw the
running of the community and assigned men and women their jobs.
Planned social activities occurred at least three times a week. The early
experiment in communism or socialism soon faltered, however, as many
community members failed to live up to the ideals and work standards
set by Owen. Yet, New Harmony set a standard for free schools and
public libraries, and started other people, including some of its members, on a search for social progress elsewhere in Indiana and America.
One of Owen's sons, Robert Dale Owen, has been credited with being
one of the people who most influenced Abraham Lincoln—who had
spent part of his youth in Indiana—to free the slaves of America. Both
Owens and Lincoln would be highly revered by later generations of
Indianans.[2]

Closer to Brady, Shaffer, Dalhover, and Geiseking's time in Indiana,
indeed overlapping with it, Eugene Debs also tried to remake the state
and nation into a more egalitarian one. Debs, a socialist from Terre
Haute, Indiana, ran for the presidency of the United States five times.
Born in 1855, the Indianan became a railroad worker and the secretary
of his local brotherhood of Locomotive Firemen. He also clerked at a
grocery store, and then organized the American Railway Union (ARU)
in 1893. In spite of protests about the new and separate labor organization by other unions and labor leaders, Debs became ARU's president,
and the organization grew rapidly. It was originally a whites-only union.
The ARU participated in a major strike against the Pullman Railroad
Company of Pullman, Illinois, in 1894, and U.S. President Cleveland
had troops sent in. Debs was arrested and jailed for six months for
contempt, and left prison a devoted socialist. In 1897, he reorganized
the now faltering American Railway Union into the Social Democratic

Party and later fused that with the Socialist Labor Party. In 1900 in Indianapolis, he was nominated for the U.S. presidency on a socialist ticket, and ran for the office again in 1904, 1908, 1912, and 1920. As a vocal pacifist, Debs was jailed during World War I for attacking the Wilson administration's policies. President Harding pardoned Debs in 1921, and he returned to Terre Haute to great fanfare. His funeral in 1926 drew about 10,000 people.[3] By 1926, the Brady Gang members had started on the path to fame also, but not via the routes chosen by Debs and the Owens.

Indianapolis, the capital of the state and its largest city in the 1900s, would hold a special place in the dealings of the Brady Gang—who at various times would live, work, steal, hide, and kill there. Indianapolis, however, would see other negative influences during the era in addition to the rise of gangs like theirs. The city, seat of the state government, had experienced its share of political scandals over the years, including the influence of a Ku Klux Klansman, Grand Dragon D. C. (David Curtis) Stephenson who led perhaps half of the estimated six million Klan members in America in the mid-1920s. (The "New Klan" of the 1920s and 1930s generally advocated nativism and Protestant white supremacy.) Stephenson was given charge of organizing the KKK in Indiana in 1922, and then given responsibility for twenty states in the East. He first started his KKK campaign in a hotel in Evansville, Indiana, having emigrated there from Texas and Oklahoma in 1920 at age twenty-nine. Soon after moving to Indiana, he had run for the U.S. Congress as an anti-Prohibition Democrat, then, soundly beaten, he became an anti-liquor or "dry" Republican. He moved his KKK headquarters to Indianapolis in 1923, where he also entered the gravel and coal businesses. The KKK in Indiana at its peak had an estimated 100,000–200,000 members, with the Klan claiming membership of up to 500,000 Indiana members.[4]

Stephenson successfully campaigned for Edward Jackson for the state's governorship in 1924 and well as making and breaking other prominent politicians during the 1920s. Utilities and various business and trade groups came under his influence, and many paid him bribes. He also secured licenses for bootleggers, and raided the stills of those who refused to pay him tribute. John Duval, another pro-Klan politician, was elected mayor of Indianapolis with Stephenson's support, as were several city council members. Duval was indicted on charges of violating the Corrupt Practices Act in 1931 and served thirty days in jail. Stephenson had collected evidence against politicians he corrupted, and several city and state politicians went before the Marion County Grand Jury (which would later be scheduled, but not carry out, a hearing into the Brady Gang) in the late 1920s and early 1930s. Governor Jackson was indicted—but saved from jail due to a statute of limitations—and former Governor Warren McCray went to prison on charges related to banking fraud. He had also served time for mail fraud.[5] Such scandals, along with several other racketing and other charges, including illegal liquor sales, both put the city and state in a bind in the early 1930s, and essentially destroyed what remained of the KKK in the state. Democrats also took over the governorship and several other prominent positions in the state in the years Al Brady and his later cohorts were committing their lesser crimes.

D. C. Stephenson, meanwhile had broken away from the national Klan in the mid-1920s, but had tried to keep control over the Indiana branch of it. He ultimately went to prison on murder charges (specifically for withholding medical treatment from a dying person—a woman he had brutally sexually assaulted in 1925 and held captive on a trip to and from Chicago). Stephenson thought Governor Jackson would pardon him, but it turned out that Jackson was in no position by then to save him, as Stephenson had become too "hot" and Jackson himself would soon be in hot water. Stephenson would later be paroled, then reconvicted on another assault charge.[6]

Indiana saw perhaps a more virulent tie between the KKK and politics than did some states, and elsewhere the Klan had more quietly ebbed away, such as in Maine—where the Brady Gang would meet the full force of the law, eventually—and New England, although there had been political and legal issues there also in the 1920s. Interestingly, Stephenson was found to have been skimming funds from the KKK pot, as was the King Kleagle of Maine's KKK, F. Eugene Farnsworth. Both men were forced out of the KKK but left trying to hold on to local converts, Farnsworth even starting a rival, but unsuccessful, group.[7] Meanwhile, during the 1920s rivalry between Republicans—often with KKK support—and the Democrats, Debs was making his last runs at the U.S. presidency, and another man would try a different political platform, running for the presidency both during the mid- to late 1920s—difficult years for Midwestern farmers, and during the early

1930s—difficult years for urban areas as well as of ongoing problems for rural populations. The Brady Gang would strike urban and rural areas alike.

Indiana like other states saw severe agricultural and industrial downturns during the Great Depression. Much of Indiana's industry was located in the northern part of the state. By 1930, many natives of the state considered northwestern Gary, Indiana—and, also, East Chicago, Indiana—as being more a part of Chicago, Illinois, than the rest of Indiana, so developed was Gary's industry compared to the rest of the state, and with its location on Lake Michigan just a few miles from Illinois.[8]

Gary grew up after the United States Steel Company decided it could produce more effectively with a new facility and purchased land along Lake Michigan including a strip between the Calumet River in Indiana and the lake, about seven miles along the lakeshore. U.S. Steel then established the Indiana Steel Company to construct and operate its steel mills. Indiana Steel in turn established the Gary Land Company (named for the chairman of U.S. Steel) to lay out a town for the workers.[9]

Steel production began at Gary in 1908, with the steel company hoping to surpass the production of Pittsburgh. A major strike occurred for the Chicago district of the American Federation of Labor with Gary at the center of the events during WWI. William Z. Foster had come to the area in 1917 as secretary of the AFL, and after the strike and the war he joined the Communist Party. He ran for president of the United States in 1924, 1928, and 1932. In Gary as in Indianapolis, political corruption was rampant, in Gary primarily in the form of Prohibition violations, and some convicted politicians would retake office after serving time.[10]

Besides steel and iron manufacturing, the limestone and coal industries were especially hard hit in the north, with only two of the larger companies remaining open during much of the Great Depression. (Before World War I, the iron-based or -related industries had taken over the major economic role previously held in the economy by production based on the soil and timber. Indianans left the farms for the newer factories, and many natives of southern Indiana moved to the north, thus making the 1930s more difficult than they might otherwise have been.) Gary suffered more than most northern cities, and Lake County actually went bankrupt from the nation's economic collapse. Fortunately, by about 1936 the federal government assumed much of the region's relief burden.[11]

While the members of the Brady Gang were starting on their lives of crime, and amidst the angst of the Great Depression, zoologist Alfred C. Kinsey switched his focus from animals to relationships between men and women, and started a sexual inquiry revolution. Kinsey did so at Indiana University at the Bloomington campus. His studies caused massive debates in Indiana and across the country. Kinsey and his researchers traveled extensively to gather various research materials, with their research centered at Indiana's Kinsey Institute for Sex Research. Kinsey established the center after co-teaching a college course on marriage and discovering how little his students knew about and how little scientific research there was on human sexuality. Kinsey and his work did not remain highbrow and hidden from the general public. Although she did not go so far as to call him Public Enemy No. 1, Rose La Rose, a "striptease" dancer who performed at the Fox Burlesque in Indianapolis for a time, called Kinsey "a literary Peeping Tom."[12]

Kinsey was born in New Jersey in 1894, attended Bowdoin College in Maine, moved on to Harvard for graduate studies, and in 1920 became an assistant professor of zoology at Indiana University, originally focusing his research on the gall wasp. Al Brady would come from Indiana, and later end his career close to where Kinsey started his. Both men upset and enraged parts of America, and traveled sometimes in close to the same circles geographically.[13]

Regardless of one's political standpoint, Kinsey contributed substantively to the known psychology of sex in the Unites States in the early twentieth century, while—like Owens had earlier—people like Foster and Debs tried to share some of America's prosperity—even when times were harsh—with the less fortunate. During the same era, the KKK and D. C. Stephens sought to shut some people off from America's opportunities as best they could. Likewise, the members of the Brady Gang contributed little to societal knowledge, and simply sought the opportunity to steal some of America's prosperity for themselves. And although they may have come from impoverished backgrounds, the members of the Brady Gang did not seek to share the booty they acquired with other struggling people.

Moreover, it was not the researchers and the idealists who wanted to contribute something unique to the world, even if they created fervor in the process, who garnered the most press in the era of the 1920s and 1930s. It was the gangsters and mobsters who did so.

One gangster or mobster who led up to the gangster years of the 1930s and who overlapped with Brady spent much of his time just over the border from Indiana, in Chicago, where Brady and his men would travel more than once. Chicago and other parts of Illinois had seen intense gang violence in the 1910s and early 1920s, with Chicago known as the Crime Capital of the World. Race riots also erupted in the state. The most intense single incident of violence was the "Saint Valentine's Day Massacre" of 1929. And, between just 1929 and 1930, over two hundred men were killed in gang killings. Labor violence was also rampant in the larger cities of the state and in the coalfields. Government seemed unable to stem to the tide of violence.[14]

As the 1910s and 1920s had progressed, ethnicity played a major role in crime in some parts of the state, according to Richard J. Jensen in *Illinois, A History*. Jensen asserted that there was a 1920s milieu in Chicago that involved a disproportionate amount of crime being committed or organized by a few different ethnic groups, one of them being Italians. Jensen stated—although he noted that the vast majority of Italians and Italian-Americans in the state were law-abiding citizens—that, "the Italian milieu proved conducive to the operations of bootleggers and gangsters. The intensely family-centered particularism of the Italian community facilitated recruitment of kinfolk into large-scale criminal operations, known to outsiders as "the Mafia." The crimes of the gangs and syndicates in the 1920s in Illinois, especially Chicago, ranged from petty crimes to kidnapping and extortion; some gangs developed political power. Al Capone would later claim that he was behind the election of Chicago's mayor in 1927, and would prove influential in other elections as well. Much of the crime was based on bootlegging or illegal liquor sales, a major moneymaker during Prohibition.[15]

Specifically, Alphonse Capone, born in 1889 in Brooklyn, New York, of immigrant parents, joined a notorious street gang in New York as a youth. He worked in a bar for a time, and was given the name "Scarface" in 1917 after a customer attacked him with a stiletto knife. He married in 1918, and was later invited by his gang's former leader, Johnny Torrio, to join him in Chicago, where Torrio had moved and become a lieutenant in the Jim Colosimo mob. The Colosimo mob engaged in illegal brewing and distilling, and selling the beer and liquor so created, as well as controlling prostitution in a large portion of the city. They also participated in some legal businesses. Torrio seized control of the mob when Colosimo suffered a violent death, and Capone became his second in command.[16]

In turn, after Torrio received a serious wound in 1925, Capone gained charge of the mob, by which time he had purportedly, through threats of violence, heavily influenced elections in Cicero, located west of the city. The Capone mob then proceeded to use extreme violence and intimidation to gain control of the Chicago underworld, and to further extend Capone's political influence. Al Capone brought his brothers and a cousin into the mob—such family ties generally differentiate era "mobs" from "gangs." Then, on February 14, 1929, although Capone himself was in Florida where he purchased a home at Miami Beach, members of a rival gang were machine-gunned to death against a garage wall by men disguised as policemen who had had them line up, seemingly under threat of arrest. The deaths of the seven gangsters or mobsters in the St. Valentine's Day Massacre were ascribed to the Capone mob, although not proven.[17]

Despite its many transgressions against current state laws, the mob had not yet fallen under the era's more limited Bureau of Investigation jurisdiction. The Bureau of Investigation was formally created in 1908 by Attorney General Charles B. Bonaparte. The Bureau was initially charged with detecting and prosecuting only crimes that threatened the United States—at the time defined as transporting liquor into dry states, taking certain stolen goods across state lines (which would come to include automobiles), and intercepting such items as "obscene" books and materials. Over the next dozen years or so, other crimes became part of its jurisdiction, including transporting women across state lines for "immoral purposes." In 1932, kidnapping cases were added. Agents were forbidden to carry guns until 1933, however. J. Edgar Hoover had assumed control of the Bureau in 1924 with fifty-three officers, undertook a reorganization of the Bureau which at some junctures was highly politicized, and would use some mob and gang events of the 1930s to strengthen the power of the Bureau, and of himself as its leader. In 1932, Hoover had twenty-two officers, but was adding to new skills to their arsenal, such as fingerprinting for identification of criminals, no matter where they might turn up in the country. The Bureau would even undertake publicity on its own behalf. For example, not only did the Bureau produce some of its own pro-Bureau materials, it also exerted pressure on the way the Bureau and "gangsters" and the like were portrayed in the film industry, which was becoming increasing popular in the late 1920s and in the 1930s.[18]

Capone's Chicago-area crimes had yet to bring him under the jurisdiction of the Bureau of Investigation, but when he attempted to avoid appearing before a federal grand jury in March 1929 stating that his health was too poor for him to travel, at the request of the U.S. attorney's office, the Bureau became involved in investigating his medical claims and recent activities, disproved his contentions, and Capone was made to appear. Upon leaving the courtroom, he was arrested on charges of contempt of court. Released on bond, he and his bodyguard were rearrested in May 1929 for carrying concealed deadly weapons, and Capone was sentenced to a year in prison, a term for which he served nine months, and was released in March 1930.[19]

Capone was also found guilty of the contempt charge, but perhaps more importantly, the U.S. Treasury Department had been investigating possible tax evasion charges, charges for which Al Capone, his brother Ralph, and a few other mobsters of his were eventually convicted. Al Capone was also prosecuted for violations of federal Prohibition laws; apparently some of that liquor had passed state lines. In November 1931, Capone was sentenced to eleven years in federal prison, plus fines and court charges. He served time at the U.S. Penitentiary in Atlanta and was then transferred to Alcatraz Prison, "The Rock," in August 1934, a few months after it opened. He was released after some seven and a half years in prison, but by that time he had suffered severe brain deterioration as a result of syphilis, retired to his home in Miami with his wife and son, and before his death in January 1947 was determined to have the brain capacity or mentality of a child.[20] And so ended the life and career of one criminal whose path Al Brady and his cohorts would cross.

While Capone was on his way out of control of the crime scene in Chicago, or anywhere, the Great Depression hit in autumn 1929, with the lowest economic point in the state and Chicago, if not the nation, being 1932–1933, with industry spiraling downward, and the large industry-based Chicago suffering immense cutbacks in payrolls. "Gangsters in Chicago were still shooting each other," Illinois historian Jensen wrote, but violence was generally not seen on the city streets. Beer and liquor were once again legalized in 1933, and Chicago authorities undertook a crackdown on the city's extensive gambling underworld that year. Meanwhile, violence in the coalmines was "endemic," "as rival miners' unions used their knowledge of dynamite to blast each other into oblivion." About one-half the population of the state received some form of government relief between 1929 and 1932, with about 20 percent of the population being on the rolls at any given time.[21] Conditions started to improve in the mid-1930s in Illinois and in its neighboring state Indiana, but when the Brady Gang crossed over into Chicago, they entered a city with a still sizable underworld and with a population still feeling the effects of the Great Depression.

Meanwhile, another notorious criminal, Charles Arthur Floyd, a.k.a. "Pretty Boy Floyd," and his associates, kept the media attention turned to events a bit further west in the "Kansas City Massacre," a multiple murder committed on June 17, 1933, in front of the Union Railway Station in the Missouri section of Kansas City. Floyd, along with his cohorts Adam Richetti and Vernon Miller, were purportedly trying to free fellow gangster Frank Nash, who was being returned to the federal Fort Leavenworth Prison after a 1930 escape and a subsequent intense manhunt for him by the Bureau of Investigation and other agencies. Nash had a long history of crime, including a murder conviction, and the events surrounding the Kansas City massacre are credited with starting the Bureau's 1930s "War on Crime" which in turn led to its transition into the more modern Federal Bureau of Investigation, along with its related name change.[22]

Research by the Bureau of Investigation tied Nash to a number of escapes from the penitentiary and to various gangsters. Nash was captured on June 16, 1933, in Arkansas; then officers headed with their prisoner back to Kansas City on a Missouri Pacific train. Pretty Boy Floyd and Adam Richetti supposedly agreed to help a number of associates of Nash to help free him when the lawmen and Nash arrived in the city, although both men denied being involved in the Kansas City events up to the end of their lives, even while admitting to other serious crimes.[23]

When the lawmen and Nash arrived at the station, after checking out the surrounding area, the federal agents and other officers—seven to-

tal—escorted a handcuffed Nash to a waiting sedan. As they were getting in, three or four men opened fire. Five people were killed, including Nash, and two others wounded. However, later records would show
that it was one of the lawmen, not the gangsters, who had killed the
men: a federal agent trying to use an unfamiliar (1897) shotgun had
fired the fatal shots. Pretty Boy Floyd was supposedly shot after engaging in the gunfire, but limped along and escaped. The Bureau then
began an intensive hunt for Floyd and Richetti. After John Dillinger's
death in 1934, Pretty Boy Floyd became Public Enemy No. 1, an appellation both men would share with Alfred Brady, each in their own short
time.[24]

Floyd was about twenty-nine years old at the time of the Kansa City
Massacre, had been convicted of numerous charges, and had escaped
while being taken to the Ohio State Penitentiary. He was thus himself a
fugitive when the Kansas City Massacre occurred. He had started his
life out in Georgia and Oklahoma, and had engaged in bootlegging,
gambling, and theft by 1922. He married in 1924, and his wife soon
bore a son. The two would divorce, then reunite. He committed bank
robberies in Kentucky, Ohio, Oklahoma, Missouri, and Mississippi—
thus overlapping in a couple of the states with the Brady Gang. (He may
also have committed a bank robbery in South Bend, Indiana, right in
the Brady Gang's turf.) Floyd was also wanted for a few police murders—another shared bit of history. Floyd had spent time in the Jefferson City (Missouri) Penitentiary before the Kansas City Massacre. He
was nicknamed "Pretty Boy" by a Kansas City madam.[25]

Adam Richetti was twenty-three, had also been arrested in the past,
and like Clarence Lee Shaffer Jr., had been incarcerated at the Indiana
State Reformatory at Pendleton. Richetti was paroled in 1930. He was
convicted of other crimes, jumped parole, and with Floyd fled to Buffalo, New York, after the Kansas City killings to meet up with a couple of
women friends, and the group posed as two married couples.[26]

The foursome had an automobile accident in Ohio, and were pursued by the police. Noted Federal Agent Melvin Purvis lead the chase
for the FBI. Richetti was captured first. Pretty Boy Floyd fled again,
only to be shot again, after being discovered accidentally at a farm, and
died fifteen minutes later. Before he died, Purvis purportedly said to
him, "You are Pretty Boy Floyd," to which the dying man supposedly
replied, "I am Charles Arthur Floyd." Some people would assert that it

was not actually Floyd who had been killed, or state that he was shot again after identifying himself.[27]

Adam Richetti was returned to Kansas City and was subsequently tried and convicted for murder. He was sentenced to death by hanging, appealed on the grounds of insanity, lost his appeal, and was resentenced to death, this time by the gas chamber. He was executed on October 7, 1938, at the Missouri State Penitentiary at Jefferson City, Missouri.[28] Other thugs involved in the Kansas City Massacre were also pursued and prosecuted. Moreover, one of the Brady Gang members would meet his own death just weeks after Adam Richetti met his.

Other gangsters—also a bit westerly—likewise kept police busy during the era. Just as the Brady Gang was getting started, one of the most infamous duos of the era was ending its career, also a fairly short one. Bonnie Parker was married and her husband jailed for robbery before she encountered Clyde "Champion" Chestnut Barrow in Texas in January 1930. Bonnie was nineteen at the time, Clyde was twenty-one and single. Clyde had already been in trouble with the law, and soon after the two met he was arrested again, for burglary, and—probably using a gun Bonnie smuggled into him—escaped. He was recaptured and returned to jail. He spent his term then at Eastham State Prison Farm at Waldo, Texas, and said that he would rather die than go back to a place like that again. Yet, once he was paroled in February 1932, he returned to Bonnie, a former award-winning student and would-be poet, and the young duo embarked on a life of crime together, eventually gaining national notoriety.[29]

Bonnie and Clyde were suspected of committing some thirteen murders—including police officers and other lawmen—plus kidnapping, bank robberies, and automobile thefts. They ventured into New Mexico, Louisiana, Oklahoma, Missouri, Arkansas, and Iowa. They were eventually joined by Clyde's brother, Ivan M. "Buck" Barrow, his wife Blanche, and a gunman named Raymond Hamilton. William Daniel Jones—who was sometimes mistaken for "Pretty Boy" Floyd—replaced Jones in the gang in November 1932. Ivan Barrow died in a gunfight with police in Iowa in July 1933, and Blanche was captured. In November 1933, the Houston, Texas, sheriff's department captured Jones, and Bonnie and Clyde were once again on their own. Law enforcement tried to capture the couple, but they eluded escape and continued with their crime spree, including springing Raymond Hamilton and four other prisoners from the Eastham State Prison Farm. The couple, however, eventually came under the Bureau of Investigation's jurisdiction not for murder or their other more serious crimes, but for transporting an automobile across state lines.[30]

The Bureau traced the young couple to Ruston, Louisiana, in April 1933. It was suspected that Bonnie and Clyde and a few of their associates were to hold a party at Black Lake, Louisiana, on May 21 and return to the Ruston area soon thereafter. On May 23, Louisiana and Texas lawmen, including a noted Texas Ranger, hid along a highway near Sailes, Louisiana. Bonnie and Clyde came along, and tried to escape capture. They were fired upon and supposedly died instantly. Some 167 rounds of ammunition were fired into their car.[31]

It was only a few months after the deaths of Bonnie and Clyde that the Bureau agents received their more popular name of "G-men." According to J. Edgar Hoover, the name "G-men" came out of an incident in September 1933. Bureau agents had surrounded the hideout of gangster George "Machine Gun" Kelley, in Tennessee, and Kelly had cowered in a corner pleading, "'Don't shoot, G-men; don't shoot!'" giving Bureau agents the catchy "Government Men" appellation, which quickly spread. Some people, however, asserted that Machine Gun Kelly had not said that, and that the term G-men or Government Men had been in use years earlier, and applied indiscriminately to various types of federal officials.[32] Either way, along with co-opting the title G-men, the Bureau would continue to evolve in the early 1930s.

Another infamous gang would survive Bonnie and Clyde by a couple of years, but not past of the years the Brady Gang's crime spree. Their story would also captivate America.

In January 1935, more than a dozen G-men surrounded an old two-story home in Lake Weir, Florida, and gunfire erupted. The year before, the agency had taken down—among others—Pretty Boy Floyd and Baby Face Nelson. Bonnie and Clyde had been killed by a group of lawmen including Bureau's men, the year before that. Now, the largest manhunt on was for the "Barker-Karpis" Gang, led by Alvin "Creepy" Karpis, and brothers Fred and Arthur "Doc" Barker. Two other Barker brothers were also known and convicted criminals. The siblings' mother, Kate "Ma" Barker, had purportedly encouraged and aided her sons along the way. She did, at the least, die with one of them.

The Barker brothers engaged in numerous criminal activities during the 1920s and early 1930s, and had been jailed a number of times. While serving a stint in the Kansas State Penitentiary for burglary and larceny, Fred Barker had become acquainted with Creepy Karpis, and the two had spoken of committing various crimes together in the future. They met again and participated in several crimes, including shooting a Missouri sheriff during a store robbery. They fled to Kansas City, robbed a bank, and were forced to flee once again when the FBI discovered their hideout. In 1932, Arthur "Doc" Barker was released from the Oklahoma State Penitentiary, and with him the gang committed a number of robberies and killings.[33]

Then with several other men, and purportedly as conceived by Ma Barker, the Barker-Karpis Gang committed two high-profile abductions. The first kidnapping was of a wealthy St. Paul brewer, William A. Hamm Jr., who was freed after meeting a $100,000 ransom. The second of the high-profile abductions was that of banker Edward George Bremer Jr. in early January 1934. His family paid the demanded $200,000 ransom—an immense amount of money at the time. Brenner was released, but could not identify his kidnappers. He was, however, able to provide numerous clues to authorities, and a fingerprint of Doc Barker was discovered by police along the kidnappers' route.[34]

Other evidence soon linked Fred Barker to the case, as well as Karpis and others. Fred Barker and one of his co-kidnappers, Harry Campbell, registered in a Miami hotel under assumed names, and Ma Barker eventually joined them. The Barkers soon thereafter relocated to a cottage on Lake Weir in November.[35]

The Bureau tracked Doc Barker to a Chicago home and arrested him on January 8 without a struggle. Later that night, other gang members would be arrested without major incident, but one tried to fight it out and was killed. Doc's brother and mother would also not go out easy. When the FBI surrounded their lake rental on January 16 at 5:00 a.m., silence ensued. Agents called out for the pair to surrender, but were met by more silence. The same thing happened again fifteen minutes later, and yet again after that. The agents then shot tear gas into the house, with some or all of it erupting not in but against the building. Someone—seemingly a female—in the home yelled, "All right go ahead," and machine-gun fire erupted from an upstairs window. A shoot-out ensued, with Ma and Fred Barker pronounced dead by 10:30

a.m. Ma Barker had only one bullet wound, giving rise to numerous questions about what had happened in the house.[36]

Other members of the gang and their associates were later captured, including, eventually, Creepy Karpis. By that time, however, the Brady Gang was attracting increased attention. In 1939, Doc Barker was shot dead during an escape attempt at Alcatraz. Karpis remained in jail.

Of the various "good" or "bad" characters living in or passing through Indiana in the 1910s–1930s, however, it was John Dillinger with whom the Brady Gang would become most linked in the public eye, in part because of their numerous geographical and time-line overlaps, in part because of the oft quoted statement made by at least one member of the Brady Gang that they would "make Dillinger look like a piker," "out-Dillinger Dillinger," and related paraphrases.

John Herbert Dillinger was born on June 22, 1903, in Indianapolis, Indiana, into a middle-class family. His father was a strict man, a grocer, and his mother died when he was three. His father remarried, and seeing the young boy getting into trouble during his adolescence, moved him out of the city, to Mooresville, but to no avail. He was soon into trouble, although he did work for a short periods in a furniture factory and a machine shop. After enlisting in, and then deserting, the Navy in 1923, John Dillinger married a sixteen-year-old girl in 1924. He soon moved to Indianapolis, robbed a grocer, and was quickly captured by police. Dillinger pled guilty, and received conjoint sentences of two to fourteen and ten to twenty years in the Indiana State Prison after being convicted of assault and battery with intent to rob. Dillinger was purportedly stunned by what he deemed a harsh sentence, and became a bitter man while in prison. His wife divorced him, and soon remarried. He served eight-and-one-half years at the Indiana Reformatory in Pendleton, Indiana, and then at the state prison at Michigan City, Indiana. Both institutions would see members of the Brady Gang incarcerated within their walls. Dillinger was paroled in May 1933, and proceeded to rob a number of banks: one in New Castle, Ohio, one at Bluffton, Ohio, plus three in Indiana—Indianapolis, Daleville, and Montpelier. He was arrested on September 22, and held at the Allen County Jail in Lima, Ohio, while awaiting trial.[37]

A few days after his arrest, eight of Dillinger's associates broke out of the Indiana State Prison, shooting two guards in the process. Three of the fugitives, plus a friend on parole went to the jail in Lima, and told the sheriff they had come to the jail to transport Dillinger back to the Indiana State Prison for parole violation. The sheriff asked to see their credentials, and one of the convicts shot and beat him until he was unconscious. The men then removed the keys to the jail from the fatally wounded sheriff, locked up the lawman and his wife, and freed Dillinger. Indiana authorities requested that the FBI aid them in identifying and locating all the men involved in the breakout and assault, although they had not yet been deemed responsible for committing any violations under the Bureau's jurisdiction.[38]

Dillinger's gang terrorized the Midwest in the early 1930s, especially from September 1933 until July 1934. Among the list of their crimes were the murders of at least ten men, "only" one of them purportedly directly caused by Dillinger—Dillinger shooting an East Chicago, Indiana, patrolman in January 1934 following a $20,000 bank robbery there. The gang also injured at least another seven men, plus committed raids on police arsenals and committed a rash of bank robberies. They also staged three jailbreaks, committing one of their numerous murders in the process and wounding two guards. Dillinger and some of his cohorts were arrested following a fire at a hotel in Tucson, Arizona, where firemen recognized them. Dillinger was extradited to Indiana and held at the Crown Point County Jail, on the charge of murder of the East Chicago police officer, but escaped in March 1934, using a wooden gun he had carved in prison and blackened with shoe polish. Then, like Bonnie and Clyde, he brought the full force of the FBI down on him and his gang by stealing a sheriff's car and taking it across state lines (abandoning it in Chicago), in violation of the National Vehicle Theft Act. Dillinger was indicted for the crime, and the Bureau's search spread across the nation, headed by the aforementioned Melvin Purvis. In the meantime, three of his cohorts were convicted for the murder of the Lima sheriff, and two were sentenced to death. They attempted to escape, but one was killed in the attempt and the other executed a month later.[39]

Dillinger joined his girlfriend, Evelyn Frechette in St. Paul, Minnesota, and joined up with a number of other gangsters including Baby Face Nelson, and continued robbing banks. Alerted to some suspicious activity at a St. Paul apartment in late March 1934, an FBI agent and a local police officer went to the address, gunfire was exchanged, and Dillinger and his girlfriend escaped out the back, Dillinger having been

wounded. The couple fled to Mooresville, Indiana (one of their associates had been shot and eventually died during the St. Paul events) and
holed up with Dillinger's father. Frechette, however, decided to make a
trip to Chicago. She was arrested there and sentenced to two years in
prison. Dillinger, however, continued with crime, and raided the arsenal at Warsaw, Indiana, then fled, eventually holing up in Wisconsin. The
Bureau tracked him there, but during a shootout he escaped yet again.
He, Baby Face Nelson, and other gangsters were soon indicted in Wisconsin on conspiracy charges, and rewards issued for their capture.
Other charges followed. [40]

Dillinger's end came when a Gary, Indiana, madam facing deporta-
tion contacted a policeman to offer to help capture Dillinger in return
for a cash reward and their recommendation that she not be deported.
Ana Cumpanas, known as Anna Sage, informed the police that one of
her friends (a waitress) had come to visit her with Dillinger. Sage set up
Dillinger, telling agents and East Chicago, Indiana, police that Dillinger
and her friend, Polly Hamilton, would be attending one of two local
theaters. She would go with them, wearing an orange dress or skirt—
although the press would generally refer to her as "The Lady in Red"—
so they could identify her. She would call police when she knew just
what cinema they would attend. [41]

Sage, Hamilton, and Dillinger went to see Clark Gable in *Manhat-
tan* on July 22, to an evening show, and J. Edgar Hoover advised his
men to wait until the trio left the theater rather than risk a shoot-out in
a crowded public theater. Melvin Purvis was again in charge. Dillinger
and the two women exited the building at 10:30 p.m., and Purvis sig-
naled the other law officers. Dillinger realized what was happening,
reached for his gun and ran for an alleyway, and was shot three or four
times, the fatal bullet entering through the back of his neck. It smashed
one of his vertebrae, severed his spinal cord, entered his brain, and
exited through his right eye. Dillinger died at a local hospital at 10:50
p.m. if not at the scene, thereby fulfilling his assertion that he "would
never be taken alive." Some people asserted that it was not really Dillinger who had died, but no substantive proof of this exists, and Dillinger—his face and fingerprints a bit different than they had been years
before, purportedly due to plastic surgery to disguise his identity—was
buried in a cement vault, supposedly to prevent the looting of his body
or effects. [42]

J. Edgar Hoover used Dillinger as well as the other notorious gangsters and mobsters as a tool to gain greater strength and funding for the Bureau, which officially became the Federal Bureau of Investigation in March 1935, eight months after Dillinger's death. Melvin Purvis, who had become the most recognized FBI agent, retired in June 1935, supposedly after being harassed or mistreated by the Bureau. The reinforced federal agency would not bode well for Al Brady and his cohorts. However, although the newly renamed FBI would state that, "The events of that sultry July night in Chicago [when Dillinger died] marked the beginning of the end of the Gangster Era," the era had not yet ended. The "War on Crime" might just have some "mopping up to do" as one source called it, but the Brady Gang would make quite the mess over the next few years. [43]

NOTES

1. Irving Leibowitz, *My Indiana* (Englewood Cliffs, NJ: Prentice Hall, Inc., 1964).

2. General historical sources; Leibowitz, *My Indiana*, on Robert Dale Owens's letter to Lincoln.

3. General historical sources; Howard H. Peckham, *Indiana, A History* (New York: W. W. Norton & Company, Inc., 1978), for further information on Debs's popularity in Indiana.

4. General historical sources. See especially Howard H. Peckham, *Indiana, A History*, on membership statistics for Indiana.

5. General historical sources; Leibowitz, *My Indiana*, on the political figures, as well as Peckham, *Indiana, A History*.

6. Ibid.

7. Trudy Irene Scee, *Rogues, Rascals, and Other Villainous Mainers* (Camden, ME: Down East Books, 2014).

8. Leibowitz, *My Indiana*.

9. General historical sources.

10. Peckham, *Indiana, A History*.

11. General historical sources. See especially Howard H. Peckham, *Indiana, A History*, on Gary and Lake County.

12. General historical sources; Irving Leibowitz, *My Indiana*, on Rose La Rose.

13. General historical sources.

14. General historical sources; Richard J. Jensen, *Illinois, A History* (New York: W. W. Norton & Company, Inc., 1978), on the number of killings.

15. Jensen, *Illinois, A History*.

16. General historical sources; "Al Capone," *FBI History: Famous Cases*, FBI; and William Beverly, *On the Lam: Narratives of Flight in J. Edgar Hoover's America* (Jackson: University Press of Mississippi, 2003).

17. Ibid.

18. General historical sources; Beverly, *On the Lam: Narratives of Flight in J. Edgar Hoover's America*; and William J. Helmer and Rick Mattix, *Public Enemies: America's Criminal Past, 1919–1940* (New York: Facts on File, 1998).

19. General historical sources; "Al Capone," *FBI History: Famous Cases*, FBI.

20. "Al Capone," *FBI History: Famous Cases*, FBI; Beverly, *On the Lam: Narratives of Flight in J. Edgar Hoover's America*; and Lawrence Block, editor, *Gangsters, Swindlers, Killers, and Thieves: The Lives and Crimes of Fifty American Villains* (Oxford: Oxford University Press, 2004).

21. General historical sources; J. Jensen, *Illinois, A History*, on conditions in Chicago and state welfare demographics and miners' violence.

22. "Pretty Boy Floyd, The Kansas City Massacre," *FBI History: Famous Cases*. Federal Bureau of Investigation, FBI website, 2105; and Bryan Burrough, *Public Enemies: America's Greatest Crime Wave and the Birth of the FBI, 1933–1934* (New York: Penguin Press, 2009).

23. Ibid. And see Lawrence Block, editor, *Gangsters, Swindlers, Killers, and Thieves: The Lives and Crimes of Fifty American Villains*.

24. Ibid.

25. Ibid.

26. Ibid.

27. Ibid. And see Helmer and Mattix, *Public Enemies: America's Criminal Past, 1919–1940*.

28. Ibid.

29. General historical sources; "Bonnie and Clyde," *FBI History: Famous Cases*, Federal Bureau of Investigation, FBI website, 2015; Burrough, *Public Enemies: America's Greatest Crime Wave and the Birth of the FBI, 1933–1934*; and Block, editor, *Gangsters, Swindlers, Killers, and Thieves: The Lives and Crimes of Fifty American Villains*.

30. Ibid.

31. Ibid.

32. Quote from Hoover from the editors of *Look Magazine, The Story of the FBI*, with an introduction by J. Edgar Hoover. Also see Beverly, *On the Lam: Narratives of Flight in J. Edgar Hoover's America*.

33. "A Byte Out of History, Closing in on the Barker/Karpis Gang," *FBI History: Famous Cases*, Federal Bureau of Investigation, FBI website, 2012 posting; The editors of *Look Magazine, The Story of the FBI*, with an introduction by J. Edgar Hoover; and Burrough, *Public Enemies: America's Greatest Crime Wave and the Birth of the FBI, 1933–1934*. The gang is referred to also as the Karpis-Barker Gang.

34. Ibid.

35. General historical sources; "A Byte Out of History, Closing in on the Barker/Karpis Gang," *FBI History: Famous Cases*, FBI.

36. "A Byte Out of History, Closing in on the Barker/Karpis Gang," *FBI History: Famous Cases*, FBI; The editors of *Look Magazine, The Story of the FBI*; and Burrough, *Public Enemies: America's Greatest Crime Wave and the Birth of the FBI, 1933–1934*.

37. General historical sources; "John Dillinger," *FBI History: Famous Cases*, Federal Bureau of Investigation, FBI website, 2015; Burrough, *Public Enemies: America's Greatest Crime Wave and the Birth of the FBI, 1933–1934*; and Block, editor, *Gangsters, Swindlers, Killers, and Thieves: The Lives and Crimes of Fifty American Villains*.

38. Ibid.

39. Ibid.

40. Ibid.

41. Ibid.

42. Ibid.

43. Main quote from "John Dillinger," *FBI History: Famous Cases*, FBI; also see Burrough, *Public Enemies: America's Greatest Crime Wave and the Birth of the FBI, 1933–1934*.

3

THE BRADY GANG COALESCES AND STARTS ITS NOTORIOUS CRIME SPREE

In late 1935, four members of the Brady Gang, as they would soon be known, had banded together for the purposes of robbing theaters, stores, gas stations, and eventually banks. Composed initially of Alfred James Brady and Rhuel James Dalhover; Clarence Lee Shaffer Jr. and Charles Geiseking soon joined the pair, making their heists easier to pull off and allowing them to take on more challenging robberies.

Charles Geiseking did not long remain an active member of the Brady Gang, however. This was because he had the misfortune—or fortune, depending on one's vantage point—of being the first one incapacitated after they stepped up their criminal activities as a gang, be it all four of them at a time or a combination of two or three of them, as was often the case.

The gang purportedly, early on, spent much of their time planning their crimes in the back rooms of a honky-tonk in Indianapolis, a central location for the men, where a Victrola record player covered their conversations from any prying ears. The large city did at the minimum provide them more privacy than they might have found in any of the state's smaller towns and cities. According to one account, Brady did much of the talking, bragging to the others that they could get "any babes we want," with the big bankrolls their crimes would give them, and "kill any coppers" who got in their way, as "that's the only way to handle them."[1]

Shaffer, the youngest wannabe villain when the plans were being laid, supposedly went along with the other ideas, except that of getting "floozies," as he said that that was what had done Dillinger in: "a skirt." Brady then supposedly told him that he was only nineteen, too young to know anything about "broads." "Twenty," Shaffer instantly corrected him.[2] This information comes from a reliable—in general terms—police source, but the language and conversations may have been dramatized or sensationalized a bit.

Brady also supposedly warned the other three men that, "If any one in this gang turns stool, he'll get"—the natural ending for the statement might have been "whacked." But, they each agreed to the condition, and the men decided to start out small, as the "big guys" all advised, and work their way up.[3]

Some of the stories of the men and Brady in particular may have been exaggerated, but the four men did take on the life of outlaws, and they did stand out in places like their honky-tonk headquarters as they were each slender and under five feet-six or so and they each dressed quite well, looking respectable, perhaps sometimes too respectable or dressed up for their surroundings.

By the close of 1935, after committing a number of robberies—one of them purportedly a grocery store holdup in Crawfordsville, Indiana, in which two policemen were wounded when gunfire broke out—the men decided that they should have an automobile at their disposal that was legally theirs and registered. They decided that Dalhover should be the one to make the purchase, and to buy a larger vehicle than the borrowed or stolen Ford coupe they were currently using.[4] Thus they would have both more room and less of a chance of being stopped for a stolen vehicle while en route to perpetrate larger crimes, generally holdups and robberies.

However, before purchasing a car legally, they first chose the criminal path once more. On January 14, 1936, Brady, Geiseking, and Dalhover traveled to Anderson, Indiana, where—after driving the roads looking for just the right car—they held up a man and woman at gunpoint, after forcing their car off the road at Brady's orders, and stole their Buick sedan, searching them for other valuables as well as stealing their car. Geiseking had been driving the gang's stolen or borrowed Ford, which Geiseking then drove away, perhaps with Shaffer, although the youngest gang member may have been deliberately left out of the robbery. The gang left the couple they had robbed stranded along the roadway, went for a drive, then transported the newly stolen Buick to a garage, where they hid it for future use. Either before or after they stored the Buick, they spent a few days robbing grocery stores and filling stations near Indianapolis, taking in about $1,000.[5] As the gang would soon learn, Anderson had recently lost one of its officers to murder, and their actions would only bring them under close scrutiny not just for automobile theft but also for murder.

The gang had discussed needing new "hardware"—rifles, shotguns, revolvers, and hopefully a machine gun—and after the smaller holdups the gang apparently decided that they had enough money to buy some of the hardware they needed and to move on to some bigger heists. One of the first purchases Brady supposedly made was that of a Winchester .30 carbine for Geiseking, who had said that he could "shoot the eyes off a squirrel with one."[6]

Clarence Lee Shaffer Jr. was indeed the junior member of the group, and tended to drink too much and then start talking. Brady and Dalhover decided that Shaffer was too much of a risk with his drinking and bragging, so they decided to use Geiseking more and Shaffer less— if at all—in their crimes. They had decided this just before Christmas 1935, and thereafter it seems that it was Brady, Dalhover, and Geiseking who initially went on a crime spree throughout Indiana without Shaffer. However, they also decided to cross into Illinois, and in Danville on one trip they robbed two grocery stores on the same night. On another trip to Danville, also in January 1936, they took Shaffer with them. While making their escape, police officers gave pursuit. Brady opened fire on them with an automatic rifle. This seems to have been the first crime known to have been directly tied to them, as following one store robbery in Robinson, Illinois, witnesses were eventually able to identify Alfred Brady as one of the two men who went into the establishment. This identification would come sometime later, however, by which time the crimes of the gang far exceeded the heist of $320 they secured in the Robinson robbery.[7] Yet, the stakes had just risen dramatically for police throughout the region.

With winter upon them and frozen roads making it problematic to continue with their robberies and avoid capture should they be pursued, Brady organized a gang of youth in Indianapolis to steal cars for him. The boys would drive the cars to various garages, where Brady and

Dalhover would strip them and sell the parts.[8] This business, however, was not as profitable as hoped, just as Brady's earlier foray into the business had not been.

Instead of a bigger car, the gang now decided that they needed bigger guns to stage more profitable holdups and other crimes. The gang thus drove to Newport, Kentucky, where they drove to a local bar to meet with a bartender. The bartender agreed to get them a machine gun. He made arrangements to secure one from an Ohio police officer. He then introduced Brady and Dalhover to the officer, under fictitious names. The police officer and the gang members agreed on a welding job on the machine gun. (They ultimately, however, arranged to purchase more than one gun from the officer, as well as ammunition.) The police officer would later lose his job over this sale, and he also took them out to a relative's farm, perhaps to test out the machine guns, as one Chicago police offer would report that the gang had spent four hours in the woods firing the machine gun, plus rifles and shotguns. According to the same source, that night in a saloon Brady told the gang of his plans to hold up six jewelry stores, all in different towns in Ohio. Asked why they were to do just jewelry stores and not banks, Brady purportedly said that Dillinger had "ruined that racket," and now the banks were too heavily guarded to pull off a robbery without a major battle.[9] But, Brady and his men would indeed rob more than one bank in the future.

In early February 1936, Brady, Dalhover, and Geiseking drove to Springfield, Ohio and robbed two grocery stores, one after the other, and robbed them of close to $600. Soon after this, learning that they were being accused of murdering a policeman named Frank M. Levy in Anderson, Indiana, they decided that they needed to lay low for a while. According to a Chicago report, on November 25, 1935, the gang had killed Levy when he interrupted the gang while they were engaged in or about to commit a robbery. To avoid arrest, they took the stolen Buick out of the garage and drove it to New Orleans, Louisiana. They stayed there for about a week.[10] The death of Frank Levy in Anderson, however, would follow the gang thereafter.

Anderson was a "gas boom" town of the late 1800s that had declined by the 1930s, although some gas production would continue into the mid-1900s. According to one journalist, the city—although it had many fine citizens—was a depressing one, and, "Anderson . . . is not as bad as its downtown looks. It's worse."[11] Certainly, the events of November 1935 were "bad" ones, but it remains unclear as to the participation of the Brady Gang in them. Certainly they would pass through the city during their reign of crime, at a minimum stealing a car there.

Authorities were not able to ascertain ultimately if the gang had killed the police officer, or if the story later circulated—which could only have been circulated by someone involved in the shooting or have been fabricated in parts—was true. In 1935, the city had a population of some 48,000 people.

What is known is that Frank Levy had been making his regular rounds in Anderson. The fifty-seven-year-old patrol officer was near the end of his shift when he stopped to investigate a parked car at 10th and John Streets, a car that he apparently thought looked suspicious. He was shot to death before he ever had a chance to pull out his gun.[12]

What is unknown was exactly who killed him, or the truth of a story circulated later. According to that story, when one of the Brady Gang members was later in prison, a fellow prisoner asked him about the killing of Frank Levy and he purportedly answered that the gang had been sleeping when Levy approached the automobile they were in and he had asked them what they were doing. One of them then quipped "Killing coppers! That's what we're doing!" and shot Levy. No charges, however, were ever filed against his murderer or murderers.[13]

The events surrounding the shooting were widely covered by the local media, and the search for his killers an intense one. Suspicion would first fall elsewhere, and then come to rest on the Brady Gang.

The *Anderson Daily Bulletin* for November 25, 1935, carried the banner "PATROLMAN KILLED BY UNKNOWN GUNMAN," as its lead, with the subtitle "Frank M. Levy Shot Dead Shortly After Midnight, Officer is Slain as he Approaches Parked Car to Question Occupants." Levy had been shot that morning at 12:15 a.m. He had pulled up alongside a car believed to have been a black sedan left with its lights and engine running for some time in front of a private home. Levy had not even unfastened the flap of his gun holster to reach for his revolver. A resident of the house, a Mrs. Blythe Johnson, called police to report the shooting, and responding officers found Levy lying in the street, gasping for breath. They called for an ambulance, and he was taken to St. John's Hospital. When the ambulance arrived at the hospital, Levy was pronounced dead.[14]

The black car had disappeared before the officers had reached the scene of the shooting. Witnesses told police that it appeared that there had been a man and a woman in the vehicle. Anderson Police Chief Joseph Carney sent the entire city night patrol on a search for the automobile. Local police also sent word about the shooting to nearby cities via police radio. As reported to the local press, the patrolman had "apparently stepped out of his machine and was walking over towards the parked car" when he was shot "by the occupant of the other automobile. After the shooting, the dark car sped away." That same day, the *Anderson Daily Bulletin* carried a photograph of Frank M. "Pete" Levy, who had served on the local police force for six years, standing in his dress uniform in front of a large bush or tree.[15]

Police Chief Carney indicated to the local paper that the fact that the murderer had shot Carney "without giving the officer a chance to defend himself," indicated that "the murderer was a degenerate character and feared apprehension for some grave offense."[16] Certainly members of the Brady Gang would prove to be both, but no mention of their names appeared immediately after the shooting.

The sedan had been left running for some time, possibly hours it was believed, so that the occupants might make a quick getaway should they need to do so. Perhaps, police or others suspected, they had been preparing to pull off a robbery. Mr. and Mrs. Johnson both stated that the car had pulled up at about 10:45 p.m. the night before, a Sunday night, and that it was either a black or very dark blue car resembling a Chevrolet or Oldsmobile. They could not see anyone in the car. Their son came home a little after midnight, and said the car was still there but that he could not tell who was in it. He later said that a few minutes after he retired that he had heard another car pull up alongside the parked vehicle, had heard a few words being exchanged but could not tell just what they were, and then four shots rang out and the dark car drove away "hurridley." He went to a window, looked out, and saw the fallen officer. Mrs. Johnson called the police, the family dressed to go out to the patrolman, and police arrived at about the same time as the family headed outside. The family thought the car was a black 1935 model sedan, but did not see its license plates. Police found burn marks in the road from when the car had sped away. They also recovered an empty .45 caliber revolver shell near where Levy had fallen.[17]

Frank Levy had been shot four times. Two bullets had entered his abdomen, while another passed through his groin and one had entered his heart. The one that had passed through his groin was quickly identified as having been shot by a .45 automatic pistol. Experts were to examine the bullets and the tire burn marks to see if additional information could be obtained. The fact that three of the bullets did exit Levy's body was ascribed to his being shot at close range. Levy left behind a wife and ten children.[18]

Within two days of the shooting, State Police Captain Matt Leach, who would one day head a search for the Brady Gang, stated that the shooting of Frank Levy was similar to killings by a thirty-three-year-old, Liberty, Indiana, murderer named Willard Carson, who had killed his father and perhaps two other people, one a policeman. He was a "vicious killer" and determined not to be apprehended. He had fled previously, but might have returned to the Anderson region. He had purportedly been spotted in Indianapolis and Muncie. Police had been searching for him for nine years.[19]

In a statement that would prove to foreshadow later events, Leach told members of an American Legion post in Anderson that their offer to provide a reward for the capture of Levy's murderer was a welcome one. He told those assembled in honor of Levy:

> The Indiana State Police are not confined to the restriction of city limits, but when a case such as the wanton murder of Patrolman Levy or any other major crime is turned over to us, to carry on additional investigation outside the city we assign a specialist to that line of crime detection to go on the case and remain on the trail, regardless of where it may lead, until the criminal is brought to justice or the last vestige of a trail and clue has been run down.[20]

Moreover, Leach told those assembled that the reward fund that they were offering "is unique in the annals of Indiana crime. It is the first time any Legion post in Indiana has arisen to such an emergency." It gave Leach "the greatest possible encouragement."[21] Leach did not know it yet, but he would soon embark on a long search for the Brady Gang, a very discouraging search. And, he had already undergone one of those: he had helped in the search for John Dillinger.

While the search for Carson continued, a woman came forward and stated that she had come to the area with two men who had been involved in jewelry and clothing thefts in the Midwest, and that they said that they had been in "a jam" with police in Anderson. She knew the men only by the nicknames "Tony" and "Foots." Moreover, while the local American Legion was putting together its $1,000 reward money, a third, as yet undisclosed, theory of the crime was being explored. When it was disclosed to the public, the theory involved a former prisoner who had purportedly made threats against Levy. His involvement in the case was later discredited. Meanwhile, the various leads took police attention in various directions.[22]

The woman, Jeannette Hamilton, who said she had gone to Indianapolis with the two men, plus a woman she knew as "Dot," had been arrested earlier, and was questioned further. She was given a Keeler lie detector test in Indianapolis, and questioned by Leach. Her story was largely dismissed as irrelevant to the Levy shooting by October 29. Her true name was later identified, and a relative testified that she suffered from a mental disorder.[23]

By December 9, two new suspects had emerged in the case, Paul Pierce and Donald Joseph. The men had served time at the Indiana State Prison, and were currently wanted for shooting two Indianapolis detectives just a couple of days earlier. The men had been connected with an automobile theft in Anderson, as well as a grocery store robbery on Thanksgiving Day. One of the men had previously lived in Anderson, and the pair had just escaped from an Indianapolis apartment after wounding the two detectives sent to interview them about the Levy murder.[24]

State police soon apprehended the two men. They were indeed in Anderson on the night of the shooting, but had firm alibis for the time of the shooting. Matt Leach interviewed the men, who claimed to have left the city for a motel in Hamilton, Ohio, early in the evening. Both men had been wounded in the shootout with the police, and they had also escaped from the Michigan City State Prison early that October. One of the men had also spent time in the Indiana Reformatory in 1929, where Al Brady had spent a bit of his youth. The men had been registered at the Ohio hotel, but it was initially unclear if they had indeed been there during the evening hours of November 25. However, police soon determined that the two had indeed been some one hundred miles away from Anderson in Ohio at the time Levy was killed. In following days, while local police awaited ballistic results in the Levy shooting, local police and Leach interviewed the former inmates, a youth was also questioned for driving them around Anderson, and a man was arrested for harboring them in Indianapolis as well as for parole violations.[25]

Next, four young men implicated in numerous Indiana robberies were arrested and investigated as to their possible involvement in the Levy murder. They were held in Rochester, Indiana, and insisted that they had nothing to do with the killing of the lawman. The young men were known under various names.[26] The arrested men were not the members of the Brady Gang, although the timing fit.

The trail then went cold for some time. However, in spring 1936 the press reported that the Brady Gang was wanted in connection with the murder. The *Daily Times Tribune* of Alexandria, Indiana, reported on May 19, 1936 that police expected the Levy mystery to be solved with the arrests of Alfred Brady, Clarence Lee Shaffer Jr., and James Dalhover, in connection with the murder of another police officer.[27] Before then, however, the Brady Gang went on to other adventures—or misadventures.

Upon learning in February 1936 that they were wanted on possible murder charges for the Frank Levy shooting in Anderson, the group, as stated, decided to travel to New Orleans. Before they went south, however, the Brady Gang seemingly had something of a fling in the North. According to one story, they held up three jewelry stores, robbing them of $55,000 of goods altogether. Brady then went off to meet a fence, and returned from selling their jewelry only to have to explain to the other men that he had only received a portion of what the jewelry was really worth because the fence needed to make money, too. Apparently, however, he had secured enough money that, added to their other funds, allowed them to have quite a celebration.[28]

Brady ordered up a "large supply of liquor," to their accommodations in an Indianapolis hotel, and sent for a few women from a "call flat." He supposedly asked for a blonde woman for himself, one who was, "Not too hefty. . . . I like'm slim." Dalhover asked for the same type of woman, while Geiseking wanted a redhead. When Brady asked Shaffer what type of woman he wanted, Shaffer purportedly became furious and "snarled," at the others: "You dummies! Won't you learn that guns and women don't mix!" He then stormed out. The party lasted until

Brady threw the women out three days later. He sent them off with perhaps $1,000 stuffed in their stockings.[29]

After the women left, Brady started reading an article about Mardi Gras in New Orleans. The gang decided to go, filled up their vehicle with gasoline, and, by taking turns at the wheel, reached New Orleans in nineteen hours. They set out to have a fine time and attended balls, wore elaborate costumes, mixed with a few noted artists and wealthy people, and attended various theatrical performances. Then, Al Brady disappeared for twenty-four hours. Afraid that their leader had been arrested, the others prepared to flee the city. Then Brady walked into the hotel, escorting a dark-haired woman, and told them to "Meet Margaret. She's all mine." However, Margaret Larson was a married woman. She supposedly said that she and Brady would get married as soon as she could get a divorce. The gang was shocked at this turn of events, but on February 26, 1936, Margaret and Brady showed up at her house, and while her three-year-old son clung to her dress and her legs, she told her husband that she had fallen in love with Brady, who—he had ironically claimed—was an agent of the Federal Department of Justice. Margaret's husband did not want her to leave or to grant her a divorce, and told her that she should stay there for at least a month so that she could be certain that she was not making a mistake. Brady supposedly told the man that if in a month Margaret still wanted to be with him, that he, Lester, had to give Margaret a divorce.[30]

While laying low—each in their own way—in New Orleans, the gang members, not just Brady, had met some women and began taking them out. At least one of the women, Margaret and perhaps another woman, supposedly saw some of the guns, and the men responded that they had the firearms because they were federal officers.[31] Hence Brady, under the name Ernest Gentry, had told Margaret he was a government agent.

NOTES

1. Captain John Egan, Chicago PD, as told to Douglas Hunt, "The Second Dillinger," written for *Official Detective Magazine* for November 1937 publication with excerpts printed in the *BDN*, 13 October 1937.

2. Egan and Hunt, "The Second Dillinger."

3. Ibid.

4. "The Brady Gang," *FBI History: Famous Cases*, FBI. Also see Egan and Hunt, "The Second Dillinger," on the Ford having been borrowed by Brady. See Helmer and Mattix, *Public Enemies: America's Criminal Past, 1919–1940*, on the November robbery.

5. "The Brady Gang," *FBI History: Famous Cases*, FBI; and Egan and Hunt, "The Second Dillinger."

6. Egan and Hunt, "The Second Dillinger."

7. "The Brady Gang," *FBI History: Famous Cases*, FBI; *Rushville [Indiana] Republication*, 4 October 1937, on the Robinson holdup.

8. "The Brady Gang," *FBI History: Famous Cases*, FBI.

9. Ibid. Also see Egan and Hunt, "The Second Dillinger."

10. "The Brady Gang," *FBI History: Famous Cases*, FBI; *NYT*, from Chicago Press, 12 October 1937, printed October 13, 1937, on the murder.

11. Leibowitz, *My Indiana*.

12. The "Officer Down Memorial Page" website and "The Brady Gang," *FBI History: Famous Cases*, Federal Bureau of Investigation, FBI.

13. Ibid. Dalhover would later deny the story and the murder.

14. *Anderson Daily Bulletin*, 25 November 1935.

15. Ibid.

16. Ibid.

17. Ibid.

18. Ibid.

19. *Anderson Daily Bulletin*, 27 November 1935.

20. Ibid.

21. Ibid. And see *Anderson Daily Bulletin*, 29 November and 3 December 1935.

22. *Anderson Daily Bulletin*, 28 November 1935.

23. *Anderson Daily Bulletin*, 29 and 30 November 1935.

24. *Anderson Daily Bulletin*, 9 December 1935.

25. *Anderson Daily Bulletin*, 10–12 December 1935. Also see AP articles of the same day printed in the local paper.

26. AP article from Rochester, Indiana, as printed in the *Anderson Daily Bulletin*, 24 December 1935.

27. *Daily Times Tribune*, 19 May 1936.

28. Egan and Hunt, "The Second Dillinger," 1937.

29. Ibid.

30. Egan and Hunt, "The Second Dillinger."

31. "The Brady Gang," *FBI History: Famous Cases*, FBI.

4

DEATH OF A SALES CLERK

The Gang Moves in for Bigger Loot and Takes a Life in the Process

In spite of Al Brady's love affair in New Orleans, the gang decided to return to their home region as planned, and to move on to bigger, more lucrative, crimes. Once back in Indiana, the gang quickly embarked on their prime jewelry-store robbing spree. On March 4, 1936, they drove a stolen automobile to a jewelry store in Greenville, Ohio. Site of the signing of the 1795 Treaty of Greenville that brought peace to the region and opened up the Northwest Territory for settlement, the community of Greenville, Ohio, was a fairly small one in the mid-1930s, with about 7,500 residents.[1]

The Brady Gang members brought several sacks or "pillowcases" with them to Greenville, prepared to make off with as many valuables as possible. They—or, rather, two of them—entered the store on March 4, the Roy O. Wieland Jewelry Store, and held up the employees who were preparing to close for the day. Before robbing the store, one of the men, purportedly Brady but also identified as Dalhover, had gone in and asked to look at some diamond engagement rings. It was a little before 5:00 p.m. He asked what time the store closed. It closed at 5:30. He told the proprietor—or one of the clerks, Robert Gray who had assisted him in choosing a ring—that he would be back soon, as he wanted to consult his girlfriend and verify her ring size and perhaps her preferred style of ring.[2]

When the young man returned as promised, he had his accomplice with him, Roy Wieland later stated. The men entered the store at about 5:20 p.m., and the clerk who had helped the first man select a ring came forward with the paperwork, only to meet a rude surprise. One of the robbers made the proprietor and his three clerks lie on the floor, holding an automatic pistol aimed at them, while the second robber gathered up the store's jewelry and other items in the "pillowcases," the first man ordering him what to take and what to leave, leading authorities to believe that he was knowledgeable about jewelry. The thieves also removed $350–$500 from the safe, and drove off in their stolen car. They had spent about fifteen to twenty minutes in the store, leaving the premises by 5:35. The value of their jewelry hoist was approximately $8,000 according to most sources, closer to $25,000 by another, either amount a significant value in the Great Depression. The later source, the one with the highest estimated value of the jewelry, reported that the gang stole some 431 diamond rings, close to 100 watches, plus numerous other items of value. An extant list of the missing items indeed shows them to have numbered in the hundreds. The difference in the estimated values may have been due to calculations of retail versus wholesale values.[3]

The store had made its unique mark in all of its own rings—most of the rings made of white or yellow gold and having inlaid diamonds or other valuable stones—as well as having identifying marks in some of the other stolen items. The jewelry store compiled its stolen items list, at the bottom of which was noted a $500 reward being offered for the recovery of the stolen items as well as separate rewards for the capture of the thieves. Included in the list of stolen goods were not only rings and watches of all types, but also pins, necklaces, pen sets, and black plush ring trays with metal frames. The gang had stolen jewelry left for repairs as well as the new jewelry and other items, plus, any trays or cases they had touched, seemingly to avoid leaving fingerprints or other evidence. They also looted the store of all of its higher-quality fountain pens. The gang had indeed been thorough.[4]

The local authorities—and the press—were also thorough. Suspecting that the robbers were "professional talent" as the local newspaper, the *Greenville Daily Advocate*, described it, the authorities reported the heist to the FBI, and on March 17, 1936, FBI director John Edgar Hoover sent a letter to the special agent in charge of the Cincinnati,

Ohio, division stating that he was in receipt of a news item about the robbery, and that the proprietor had therein reported the loss to be between $7,000 and $8,000. Hoover "suggested" that the Cincinnati agent investigate the heist to determine the descriptions of the robbers and the items stolen, and to determine if the robbery fell under the jurisdiction of the Bureau. The agent was also "directed to submit a closing report in connection with this matter," should the agent fail to determine that the robbery was within the FBI's jurisdiction. The store's list of its stolen goods may have been made after the FBI made contact with them; the date of the list, printed on the store's stationary, was not indicated. The press described the robbers as "two young, well-dressed bandits." According to reports sent to the FBI by the Indiana State Police, the car used was a gun-metal gray, 1935, Oldsmobile sedan. It had been parked across the street from the store (the store was located on a corner) during the robbery. The bandits had been spotted heading south on Road 121, and the FBI in return pondered where the men were going and if they might be in violation of the National Stolen Property Act.[5]

The FBI continued to look into the matter, and filing an internal report using the Stolen Property Act as its basis, stated that the robbers had not yet been identified as of April 4, 1936, even though Mr. Wieland had been given photographs of various suspects to peruse. According to descriptions obtained from those in the store, the robber with the automatic pistol and who gave the orders on what to steal was about thirty to thirty-four years old, weighed roughly 150 pounds, and stood five feet, six inches. He had a square jaw and was smooth-shaven. He had dark hair and wore a dark overcoat and a dark hat. The other robber had carried a sawed-off shotgun. He was described as being of about the same age, height, and weight as the first robber, but having blond hair, a narrow forehead, and having a heavy square jaw. He had worn a blue shirt, brown overcoat, and a tan hat. The third robber was not observed, so the FBI secured no description of him.[6]

Local sources stated that the only descriptions the police could obtain were rather vague, seeing that the men had acted so quickly. The crime was purportedly "one of the few major nature crimes engineered" in the Greenville area in recent years. It "was carried out with clock-work precision, a definite indication that the fugitives are professional talent. Their method of approach verifies that belief." When the clerk

Robert Gray had come forward to help the first man, thinking he had come back with the ring size verified to complete the sale, the man had pulled out a gun while the clerk was looking at the paperwork, and ordered him to join the proprietor and the other two clerks at the back of the store. It was at that moment that the second man, who, the locals seemed to think, was the "brains of the gang" entered the store and held the clerks and owner at gunpoint. Then, the two thieves—primarily the "pseudo customer" under the direction of the second man, had "rifled a safe, counter cases, and even the display windows of all valuables." The "brains" had seemed to have "a keen sense of jewelry values," Wieland stated. The man "at various times would call to his companion, 'Leave that alone—it's of little value.'" The loot thus obtained— "virtually completely stripping the place"—was then "brazenly carried to the auto under the eyes of several persons, who unknowingly witnessed the theft." The first man had apparently made three trips to the car with a large sack, then, "on the fourth trip, both men fled."[7]

Local police initially focused their search on the Hamilton-Cincinnati area, and nearby Indiana, the Indiana State Line being just about twenty miles from Greenville. The locals knew that there had been a third accomplice both from street witnesses and from the fact that the third man seemingly used the car's horn to regularly send signals to the two robbers in the store. The storeowner, Wieland, promised to restock his store soon, and to replace any items left at the store for repairs or other reasons. [8]

No sightings were made of the car once it pulled away from the Greenland store, although police searched roads both on the Ohio and the Indiana side of the border. There were few clues of any sort. Then, the Jeweler's Security Alliance of New York brought the Pinkerton National Detective Agency into the case—an historic organization by the mid-1930s, having been established in 1850 and early on known for its investigations into a planned assassination of President Abraham Lincoln (not the one which ultimately took Lincoln's life), various railroad robberies, and later into labor unrest and its leaders. C. H. Brutus, a representative from the Pinkerton's Cincinnati office, went to Greenville to help local authorities and to advise the store owner. He soon reported to local officers that "there was but little tangible evidence that might lead to the definite identification of the hunted men."[9] The agency would stay with the case, however.

On March 7, 1936, just days after the robbery, the *Greenville Daily Advocate* announced in its headlines, "Probe of Wieland Hold-Up Has Reached [A] Blank Wall." Even with the Pinkerton Agency involved, the only definite clues established thus far were that "the two men who entered the store were comparatively young and well-dressed, and that the car in which they made their escape was a gun-metal gray, two-door sedan believed to have been a Pontiac." There was still no description of the third man.[10]

Although local authorities would continue to pursue the case, and the FBI would also begin to look into it, the trail did indeed seem to have gone cold. Other robberies in different states would follow, many of them similar to the one in Greenville in a number of ways, but the "Blank Wall" would continue to be an issue for law enforcement agencies for some time. Time would eventually link several jewelry robberies to the Brady Gang.

Meanwhile, the thieves needed to dispose of their loot. Shaffer had purportedly complained after the Greenville robbery that Brady's fence would probably give them just a few C-notes for their haul, to which Brady had supposedly responded, "The Hell with that guy. I'm gonna find a new fence." He knew a guy from a few years back, a George Klotter, a man in his early twenties, who might be able to set them up with someone for the job. The gang met with Klotter in a poolroom on Leland Avenue on the north side of Chicago. Klotter told them that he could set them up with someone who might know someone who could fence their goods. They met with that man, and he, William "Mickey" Masonlick, set them up with yet another man. They went to the home of this man, Jack Becker, a loop-jewelry salesman, who told them that their loot was just junk. A verbal argument ensued, and Becker finally agreed to give them perhaps $5,000, perhaps not, but to come back the next day so that he could get the money together. When the men returned, Becker gave them about $325, told them to leave all the goods with him, and said that he would pay them up to $1,000 for all of it, eventually, and told them that the next time they should steal better stuff. Brady, unhappy with the deal but wanting the money, took it.[11]

Then, in Chicago, Brady pulled a stunt that put the gang further on the police radar: he held up U.S. Internal Revenue Agent Oliver J. Salinger on March 16, 1936. He did it in front of the man's home on Lunt Avenue. Brady stepped out of gang's car—parked that night parked behind a large leafy tree—just as Salinger was getting out of his own car. Salinger had a gun, but it was in a shoulder holster, so when Brady ordered him to put his hands up, he did. Brady frisked him, and stole his gun, $35 in cash, and his car keys, and taunted the agent with, "You'll never catch me. . . . You guys got Dillinger, but you ain't going to get me." He made Salinger walk in the middle of the road, then stole his car, specially equipped to run at up to 110 mph, and roared off.[12]

Apparently thinking that jewelry heists were the way to go, in spite of the small returns in terms of percentages they apparently had made to date on their stolen goods, Brady, Dalhover, and another thief who had temporarily joined the gang robbed the Kay Jewelry Store in downtown Lima, Ohio, on March 19, 1936, scoring some $6,900 in jewelry. However, it was one of their more challenging hoists, in large part because of their inclusion of the new guy—if indeed there was a new guy; an FBI report made the following year simply identified Brady, Dalhover, Shaffer, as Geiseking as being the four involved—and that they had "held several customers and employees at bay with pistols" while they robbed the store.[13]

The gangsters drove their newest stolen car and parked near the store, located at 129 North Main Street. According to one police source, which did not mention a new man but rather included just Brady, Dalhover, and Shaffer, one of the store's proprietors, Bernard Brender, was showing a tray of engagement rings to a young man when the gang entered, announced that it was a heist and ordered them, "Up with your mitts!"[14]

According to police and the FBI, while the others in the store complied with the gang's orders, in the course of the robbery, one of the store owners, Bender it seems, jumped on Brady's back, and the two fought viciously. Then, according to the FBI source, the new gang member started shooting, seemingly at the store owner. Brady and the owner both responded by ducking or falling behind the counter. Brady then put his head back up above the counter, and the new guy fired at him. Brady ducked again, then raised his head once more, and was shot at once more. He yelled, "Stop that crazy fool!" apparently to Dalhover. By this time a crowd had gathered, but Brady was finally able to get up, and the gang managed to escape. But, they never took the new guy on a hoist with them again.[15] Either way, the gang made off with more loot, although perhaps less than they had wanted.

Soon after this, on March 21, 1936, the gang held up a grocery store. This one would have fatal consequences. They first robbed one small store in Ohio, but obtained little money, so they went on to the second one, in another town. There were perhaps thirty-five people in the store, Mohler's Grocery in Piqua, Ohio, when the gang arrived. Brady entered the front door, and Dalhover the back door.[16]

As Dalhover would later recount the story:

> As I entered the rear door, I estimated there were about thirty-five customers crowed in the store, and as I was dodging my way through the crowd, I heard a shot fired. The customers immediately began to run to the front door and pushed me out with them. As soon as they had cleared the place, I went back in. Brady was taking money out of the cash drawer. I asked Brady what the shot was about and he said, "some damn fool jumped me and I shot him and shoved him down the cellar stairs." We got the money, went out the back door, and got in our car, but because of the fact there was a great crowd gathered, we had to turn our car around in the middle of the street and then drive out of town. A car followed us for some distance, and I shot three times at it and stopped.[17]

Brady had killed Edward Lindsay, a twenty-three-year-old clerk. He had come up from the basement, seen the commotion, asked what was going on, and Brady shot him, supposedly before the young man even knew what was going on.[18]

Al Brady had kept in touch with his married paramour from New Orleans, and after the gang's latest heist Brady received a telegraph from her. It read: CANNOT LIVE WITHOUT YOU. AM LEAVING MY HUSBAND. WILL ARIVE ON GREYHOUND BUS IN CHICAGO ON MARCH 30. I LOVE YOU."[19]

Brady and Dalhover rushed to meet Margaret in Chicago, and Brady spent the afternoon with her. Then Brady purportedly told her that he had to go to Indianapolis on government business, but promised to call her every day, and then drove her to her mother's home. Brady next called on either Jack Becker—or possibly Robert Becker as both men, brothers, would become involved in the case—asking Becker if he knew a man who could serve as the gang's getaway driver as the one driving now "drives like an old woman." Becker recommended Jimmy Venetucci, also known as "Dago Jack" Ryan. Brady asked Becker to send the new guy to meet him in Indianapolis.[20]

The gang went on to Indianapolis and Brady telephoned Margaret to ask her to join him there. She immediately left to join him, and the two checked into the Graylyn Hotel as Mr. and Mrs. James Gentry.[21]

Dalhover soon came to visit the couple, and purportedly "sighed as he watched the couple eating breakfast in bed. 'Gee, you've certainly got the life,'" he then said to Brady, to which Brady responded, "Get yourself a woman too." At that suggestion, Dalhover's face supposedly brightened, and he said, "That's an idea." According to the story, Dalhover then asked Margaret if one of her friends whom he had met in New Orleans might be willing to have a fling with him, and she responded that the young woman, Marie "Babe" Myers, had asked her the same thing about Dalhover. Dalhover asked for Margaret to have her fly to Indianapolis, as he was in a rush, and Marie arrived later that day, and the two booked a room as a married couple.[22]

While these cozy domestic arrangements were going on, Brady met with "Dago Jack" Ryan or Venetucci, whom Becker had located and brought to Indianapolis. Brady looked the man over carefully, asked him if he was a good "caser" as well as a fast driver, and Dago Jack said that he was both. The gang then went with him to look over a possible job robbing a Sol Partner's jewelry shop in Dayton, Ohio, on April 2, 1937. They sent Dago Jack in to case the store, while they waited nearby. Dago then supposedly came out and told them that the place was ripe for a heist, that there was no guard and no burglar alarm, and that there were plenty of watches and chains in the store. He also supposedly told the gang that they should not be dealing with Becker, that Becker was an amateur fence, and that he knew a "'high class fence,'" a man who could get them better prices for their loot. They planned the robbery, and Brady told Dago they would let him know when they needed him. Then, according to the account given later, Brady called Dago, and Dago answered the telephone himself but lied, and said Dago was not there. He asked if the caller's initials were A. B., then said that Dago had had to go off on some other business. Brady was angry when he ended the call, and decided that they would pull the job themselves, then find Dago and set up a meeting with the fence he had mentioned.[23]

As it turned out, however, Dago, after Brady's telephone call, immediately went to his own gang of thugs, all of them known to local authorities, a few of them currently fugitives from the law. Dago told them that the Brady Gang was just a bunch of hick "apple-knockers" who could easily be separated from whatever loot they might bring in to be fenced in upcoming months. One of the gangsters was an arsonist, and wanted to kill Brady and his crew after taking their loot. Dago, however, said that they could simply be told to go home.[24]

On April 4, 1936, the proprietor of the Greenville, Ohio, store robbed in March, Roy Wieland, as well as two of his employees, were shown photographs of Alfred Brady and James Dalhover. All three men identified Brady and Dalhover as having been the robbers of their jewelry store. Dalhover, Wieland stated, had been the one to enter his store before the holdup to look over rings for his supposed girlfriend. The third member of the trio was still not identified, and probably would not be in terms of photographs as no one had had a close look at him.[25]

Not knowing about the identifications from Ohio, nor how Dago planned to double-cross them, the gang of four—Brady, Dalhover, Shaffer, and Geiseking—united briefly, and on April 9, 1936, drove a Studebaker—according to one source, although others declared it a Pontiac—stolen by Brady in Indianapolis to the Dayton, Ohio, jewelry store. Before they left, Brady had supposedly mapped out various escape routes, and given orders to each of the men. He purportedly told Geiseking to stand guard at the door after they entered and not let anyone else in. Then, too, he supposedly said to Dalhover, "Jim . . . the basement's for you. I don't want to have someone pop up while we're cleanin' the place out like that kid I plugged at Piqua."[26]

In Dayton, they robbed the Sol Partner jewelry store fairly quickly, although there were several customers in the store when they first arrived and they had to wait until the place thinned out to rob the store. When the right opportunity came, Shaffer had stayed outside with the car, and the others lined up the store clerks and a repairman. They raided the store of its valuables and hauled their loot—about $25,000–$27,000 in jewelry according to FBI sources although at the time the local press reported the theft to have been close to $75,000 plus cash, and the FBI in 1936 identified it as being $5,000—away in pillowcases or sacks, about eight of them, which took Brady three trips to load in the car and which he went through on the gang's two-hour return trip to Indianapolis. Dalhover would later say that from the price tags he thought the value of the items was about $68,000, and another source estimated it at $53,000.[27]

Regardless of the precise value of the loot, area newspapers carried the story, including witness testimonies, some in great detail. The *Dayton Journal* of Friday, April 10, 1936, ran a front page article on the heist, subtitled: DRAGNET BY POLICE OF TWO STATES LAID TO BRING IN GUNMEN; Descriptions of Robbers Broadcast After Escape in Tan Car. WITNESSES TELL STORY, Owner and Store Employees, Reporter and Customers are Menaced." The article then proceeded to tell the story of the robbery as told by witnesses as well as other details of the chase and so forth. Right off, the story stated that police were looking for *five* men who had robbed the Sol Partner jewelry store located at 20 North Ludlow Street the previous day, during the afternoon of April 9. The paper stated that police in both Ohio and Indiana had sent out descriptions of the bandits over police networks in the two states within one hour of the holdup. The robbers had sped away north of the store. The paper stated, "The quintet of robbers who fled with diamonds, gold and platinum settings, and watches, valued at about $75,000, and $2,000 in cash, are known to be driving a new Pontiac sedan, light tan in color." A woman had informed local Police Captain F. G. Krug of the make of the car, telling him her story of the robbery and escape. (A later article stated that other witness had given the make of the car as being a Pontiac.[28])

The female witness stated that she had been sitting in her car across from the gangster's vehicle and had seen "the men carry white bags from the store to a car double-parked on the street." She stated that there were definitely five men involved, and that the getaway car was a Pontiac. She did not understand what she had seen until she returned home and learned of the robbery, and had then contacted the police with her information.[29]

Other witnesses also reported what they saw and heard. More important to the paper, it would seem, was that one of the witnesses was one of its own reporters. To the left of the article including the woman's testimony as well as that of some other people, was a shorter article titled: "Informal Invitation to Robbery Costs Reporter His Breakfast." The article carried the subtitle: "Writer's Curiosity Prompts Him to

Look In, and the Party's On." The article was a first-person account written in by Max Hettinger. He wrote, "As a reporter, it has been my ambition to 'be around' when a holdup is staged but I can confess quite candidly now, that ambition has been completely satiated." He wrote that he had been informally invited to the holdup at the Partner jewelry store, "yet the only thing they robbed me of was my breakfast."[30]

Hettinger had been on the way to eat breakfast when he noticed two men carrying large white bags. "They came from the front door of the store and seemed wholly unconcerned," he wrote. However, the sight aroused his curiosity, he looked into the store through the front display window, and then, well, it was too late.[31]

The reporter heard someone say, "Hey Buddy," he stated, and, "I didn't like the sound of that voice. And it was then I knew that it was a holdup." Hettinger continued, "I turned. A short, well-dressed fellow stood by the door. One hand pointed to it. The other rested on a gun, which reposed in a shoulder holster. [A] very fascinating gun it was, too. It looked new—efficient—deadly."[32]

Hettinger started to put his hands up in the air, but the gunman said, "Keep your hands down," so the reporter put his hands down. The man then ordered him, "Get inside and keep still." Hettinger did so. The robbers then told him to walk to the back of the store, which he did also. He faced the robbers for the first minute or so. Two of the men had their backs to him, and were busy rifling through the display case. He said that another man was standing at the end of a display case, standing guard. A gun was visible, "an automatic, as efficient and deadly as the one I saw outside." The robbers then made everyone face the back of the store, Hettinger apparently feared for his life at that point, but the robbers told them not to make a move toward the front of the store, and soon thereafter the robbers left.[33]

Witnesses were able to supply the license plate number to local police: 893 CT, and police sent this out with their broadcasts to be on the alert. Cincinnati police quickly wired that the plates had recently been stolen, as had plate number 400 MM from the same location at the same time, in Miamitown of Hamilton County. Dayton detectives, meanwhile, combed all city hotels and lodging houses, searching for the men or any information that might help lead the police to the men. The Bertillon [Fingerprinting] Department was busy comparing prints from the Partner's heist to those taken at robberies in Columbus, Piqua,

Greenville, and Lima in recent weeks. In all of these jobs, the paper reported via information gleaned from the police, "the robbers worked quietly and smoothly and accomplished their robberies without undue confusion or conflict with police."[34] Clearly, authorities would soon be able to ascertain that it was the Brady Gang that committed the Dayton robbery, if indeed they were not already fairly certain of that fact. And, as another article would assert, the gang was becoming generally more professional, or simply more determined.

The proprietor of the Dayton store also had something to say about the robbery. He was in the store along with two employees, a postal deliverer, a female customer, and, eventually, the newspaper reporter. Partner told police that he had opened the display case to retrieve a ring he had been holding for the man who had identified himself as Jones a half-hour earlier, and, "When I turned to hand him the ring, the man pulled his gun [out] and said, 'This is a holdup.'"

A third man or employee, a watchmaker, was summoned from his work area upstairs by one of the gang members. The watchmaker, Stanley Matson, later stated that he had been cleaning a four-carat diamond when ordered downstairs, and dropped it into a pan of water on his bench.[35] That was one gem the gang did not steal.

Witnesses reported that four gang members emptied four glass display cases, as well as a large safe. Only recently, thousands of dollars' worth of diamonds had been locked in the safe, according to store employees.[36]

In a separate article printed the next day, with the header "Actions Show Jewel Bandits Professionals," the newspaper discussed how professional the gang appeared. Rumors that the federal government would enter the chase for the robbers were announced as being false, as the robbers on the 9th had been "too smart to detain or threaten a mail carrier who entered during the holdup." However, "had the bandits robbed or threatened the mailman, the case would have been referred to the department of justice." The local mailman, Lawrence C. Schlemann had entered the store "while the bandits were looting the cases and trays." According to the newspaper, when the mailman walked into the store, the robbers "dropped the muzzles of their pistols and stared hard at him without speaking. Realizing they might shoot if he made a dash for the door, Schlemann voluntarily joined the employees and customers who had been herded in a corner."[37]

The update also informed residents of Dayton and beyond that besides the postal carrier and reporter Max Hettinger having entered during the course of the robbery, three other people entered the store during the heist, two of them local and one from Tippecanoe City. "None of the customers were molested," the *Dayton Journal* reported, "but the bandits searched the employees, obtaining about $200 (versus the $2,000 reported earlier) from them and from the register."[38]

According to the *Dayton Journal* in its updates, the robbery had started at 2:30 p.m., and police had learned of the heist about twenty minutes later. The thieves stole all the valuable pieces from the display cases and the unlocked vault at the rear of the store, but had "scorned the cheap pieces and bulky pieces." (They also declined to take any of the pieces located in the repair department.) This selectiveness "confirmed belief of the police [that] the gunmen are professionals and jewel experts." Moreover authorities had stated that the robbers would probably not have any trouble disposing of the stolen goods in Cleveland, Cincinnati, or Detroit, receiving perhaps 20 percent of the wholesale value of the jewelry. One of the robbers had been seen to pick up a bag of jewelry tools as he left, and thus might well intend to remove gems from their settings. Police suspected that the gang was the same one that had staged robberies in Columbus, Piqua, Lima, and Greenville in recent weeks.[39]

Adding to the idea that the gems might be sold sans settings, perhaps, was that one of the robbers forced an employee to take him to an old safe upstairs. The employee said that the man had told him, "I know that there are a lot of unset diamonds here and I'm going to get them." The robber then jerked open drawers and boxes from the safe, but did not acquire any additional diamonds.[40]

Perhaps scores of people had passed by on the sidewalk while the robbery was in progress, but so smoothly did the gangsters act that nothing seemed critically wrong. And those few who did look inside for too long were forced into the store.[41]

Moreover, according to one witness, "The bandits drove around the block several times waiting for a parking space near the store. Finally they parked their car in the first space south of an alley, almost directly in front of the establishment. This insured that no other car would be parked in front of them, blocking their space."[42]

In another aspect that the Brady Gang would become known for, the crooks who robbed the Dayton store dressed well. According to the *Dayton Journal*, the men were "well dressed in light raincoats and topcoats." The men were described as being "of slight build and about 30 years old, with the exception of one who appeared to be not more than 19 or 20." The men "worked smoothly and spoke few words, indicating they had rehearsed the holdup. At all times the victims were covered by at least two of the gunmen."[43]

Sol Partner reopened his jewelry store the day after the heist. In spite of the various figures floating around, he said that he would not know the exact value of the items taken until he had time to make a full inventory. Some of the loss would be covered by insurance, and he had had "emergency shipments" sent on Thursday night, following the robbery.[44]

The Brady Gang would have disposed of their loot from the April 9 heist—as they had the gains from their previous jewelry heist—at greatly discounted prices, hence, perhaps, the discrepancies in the estimated value of the goods. However, they ran into at least one major obstacle in getting rid of the jewelry from the latest job.

Before they made the final arrangements to fence the jewelry, when the gang had reached Chicago in the early hours of April 10, they booked into the New Lawrence Hotel on Lawrence Avenue on the north side of the city. They informed the night clerk that they were businessmen from Indianapolis and, in the case of Brady and Dalhover, using assumed names, said that their wives would be joining them later in the morning. Margaret and Marie showed up shortly after daybreak, and according to Chicago police captain John Egan, Brady gave Margaret a valuable wedding ring from the Dayton heist and told her to throw the one her husband had given her out the window. He also gave her a string of pearls and a diamond-studded wristwatch from the stolen jewels, and supposedly told her that nothing was too good for her and that he would "deck her out with more rocks than the Queen of Sheba owned." Later in the day the men went to see Dago, who had contacted them and apologized for being out previously when Brady had tried to reach him.[45]

According to the FBI in a later source, the Brady Gang had been offered $22,000 (or closer to $10,000 according to another source) for the newest stolen jewelry by a group of fencers, plus, it seems, some other stolen jewelry, for a total price of more than that amount. They agreed to bring the jewelry to an apartment. Brady and Dalhover rode there with Dago and a supposed middleman. When they arrived at the apartment, a group of Chicago crooks, eight of them, the men Dago had set up, rushed out of another room and snatched the jewelry, laughing at the Brady Gang, accusing them of being just a bunch of punks. One of the rival gangsters held Brady at gunpoint (he had reached for his own gun as the men burst in) while they examined the loot, Brady supposedly cursing them all the while and threatening, "I'll cut some-one's heart out for this." The larger gang eventually told the "hayseeds" to get up and leave, and to keep going if they did not want to be shot full of holes.[46]

It may be that the men ultimately did not kill Brady and Dalhover when they robbed them because earlier in the day the two had come to meet with Dago and a couple of other men with Margaret and Marie. The Chicago gang had planned to steal the jewels then, at the initial meeting, and possibly kill Brady and Dalhover if need be. Venetucci—speaking in Italian to the other gang members—had been involved in the decision to hold off the double-cross. And, even after the change of venue, the women did know about the meeting with Dago. The larger gang let Brady and Dalhover leave the apartment, Brady again swearing that he would get even with the "dirty rats." The Chicago gangsters just laughed again, but soon learned from the underworld that the Brady men were cold-blooded murderers, not just a few "punks," and purport-edly agreed to bring the jewelry back. However, events transpired such that they did not return the goods. It also seems that Jack and Robert Becker had already disposed of some of the loot, or would soon do so.[47]

By spring 1936, Al Brady was mocking John Dillinger and his gang, which some contemporaries thought Brady sought to emulate. Both men were from rural Indiana, and the cities and towns of their crimes would overlap. Both had spent time early on in prisons or reformatories where older boys or young men showed them the ropes of hard crime. Brady purportedly said he would make Dillinger "look like a piker" (others attribute the statement to Shaffer) and also called him a "cream-puff" bandit, and later a "lollipop thief." The Brady Gang, in return, would sometimes be mocked as "diminutive" gangsters and "Midget Crooks"—as they were all between five feet, five inches and five feet, six inches in height, as well as slender, and *Time* referred to Brady,

Dalhover, and Schaffer in 1937 as "three undersized young men."[48] It may have been their small size that made the other crooks believe that it would be safe to cross them. But, Brady and his men had already shown their willingness to kill if need be, or simply kill to make things more convenient for them.

In later April 1936, the Brady Gang made another major mistake. Apparently after some discussion earlier, they held up a jewelry store and took their stolen booty across state lines. They did so in the Desoto sedan they had recently stolen from the government employee. Their latest crime would bring the federal government into the search for the increasingly notorious Brady Gang.

NOTES

1. General historical sources and United States Census materials.

2. "Memorandum to the Director," 25 May 1937, E. A. Tamm; "The Brady Gang," *FBI History: Famous Cases*, Federal Bureau of Investigation, 2014 posting; and *Greenville Daily Advocate*, 5 March 1936, and subsequent days for most thorough press coverage, along with brief AP article from Greenville, Ohio, as printed in the *Toledo Blade* and the *Alliance [Ohio] Review*, 5 March 1936, the news item Hoover seemingly referred to as a copy of it was in the FBI files; and National Stolen Property Act, FBI Report, 4 April 1936.

3. Ibid. Also see Special Agent in Charge (name illegible) to Special Agent in Charge, Cincinnati, letter of 7 March 1936, on the money stolen as being $350; Captain John Egan, Chicago Police Department, "The Second Dillinger," on the high estimate of $25,000 value of the jewelry and $500 cash and such and List of Stolen Goods compiled by R. O. Wieland, Jewelers, on file at the National Archives.

4. List of Stolen Goods compiled by R. O. Wieland, Jewelers, on file at the National Archives; FBI copy.

5. Ibid. And see John Edgar Hoover to Special Agent in Charge, Cincinnati, letter of 17 March 1936; AP article from Greenville, Ohio, as printed in the *Toledo Blade* and the *Alliance [Ohio] Review*, 5 March 1936; and Special Agent in Charge (name illegible) to Special Agent in Charge, Cincinnati, letter of 7 March 1936.

6. National Stolen Property Act, FBI Report, 4 April 1936.

7. *Greenville Daily Advocate*, 5 March 1936.

8. Ibid.

9. *Greenville Daily Advocate*, 6 March 1936. General information on the Pinkerton Agency from author's previous works.

10. *Greenville Daily Advocate*, 7 March 1936.

11. Egan and Hunt, "The Second Dillinger" and FBI letter, Agent in Charge, E. J. Connelley, to Special Agent in Charge (no name given), Chicago, 11 May 1936. Egan's work states that it was Jack Becker in question here, but the FBI would ultimately investigate both Jack and Robert Becker, as would the local authorities.

12. Egan and Hunt, "The Second Dillinger."

13. "Memorandum to Mr. Tamm," 12 October 1936, from E. M. Soucy, FBI; "Memorandum to the Director," 25 May 1937, FBI; and "The Brady Gang," *FBI History: Famous Cases*, FBI.

14. Egan and Hunt, "The Second Dillinger."

15. "The Brady Gang," *FBI History: Famous Cases*, FBI. Also see Egan and Hunt, "The Second Dillinger."

16. Ibid. Location taken from Captain John Egan's "The Second Dillinger" 1937 account. Another source gives the date as April 22, 1936.

17. Testimony of Dalhover, as quoted by the FBI in "The Brady Gang," *FBI History: Famous Cases*, FBI.

18. Ibid. And see related documents.

19. Egan and Hunt, "The Second Dillinger."

20. Ibid. And see FBI letter, Agent in Charge, E. J. Connelley, to Special Agent in Charge (no name given), Chicago, 11 May 1936. Egan's work suggests that it was Jack Becker in question here, but the FBI would ultimately investigate both Beckers, as would the local authorities.

21. Egan and Hunt, "The Second Dillinger."

22. Egan and Hunt, "The Second Dillinger."

23. Ibid. And see related FBI and later press records.

24. Egan and Hunt, "The Second Dillinger."

25. National Stolen Property Report, FBI Report of 4 April 1936.

26. "The Brady Gang," *FBI History: Famous Cases*, FBI. Supposed conversations taken from Egan and Hunt, "The Second Dillinger;" and see the *Dayton Journal*, Ohio, 10 April 1936, on make of car.

27. "The Brady Gang," *FBI History: Famous Cases*, FBI; supposed conversations taken from Egan and Hunt, "The Second Dillinger"; and "Memorandum to Mr. Tamm," 12 October 1936, from E. M. Soucy, FBI, on the $5,000 evaluation.

28. *Dayton Journal*, Ohio, 10 and 11 April 1936.

29. *Dayton Journal*, Ohio, 10 April 1936.

30. Ibid.

31. Ibid.

32. Ibid.

33. Ibid.

34. Ibid.

35. *Dayton Journal*, Ohio, 10 April 1936.

36. Ibid.

37. *Dayton Journal*, Ohio, 11 April 1936. Date not on paper located, but internal evidence suggests it was printed on the 11th.

38. Ibid.

39. Ibid.

40. Ibid.

41. Ibid.

42. Ibid.

43. Ibid.

44. Ibid.

45. Egan and Hunt, "The Second Dillinger."

46. "The Brady Gang," *FBI History: Famous Cases*, FBI; *NYT*, from Chicago Press, 12 October 1937, printed October 13, 1937, on the total price and the eight armed men; and Egan and Hunt, "The Second Dillinger," for other details and price estimates. Also see "Memorandum to Mr. Tamm," 12 October 1936, from E. M. Soucy, FBI, on Venetucci's role.

47. "The Brady Gang," *FBI History: Famous Cases*, FBI; *NYT*, from Chicago Press, 12 October 1937; and Egan and Hunt, "The Second Dillinger," on the meeting earlier the same day.

48. *NYT*, from Chicago Press, 12 October 1937, printed October 13, 1937, on the idea that Brady sought to emulate Dillinger, as well as articles from across the nation from 12 October 1936 to November 1938; and "Tough Customers," *Time*, 25 October 1937.

5

A CRIME REPEATED, A NEW MURDER COMMITTED, AND A WIDER OPENING MADE FOR THE FBI

On April 17, 1936, Al Brady, Clarence Lee Shaffer, and James Dalhover, along with Charles Geiseking, returned to the scene of one of their earlier crimes: the Kay Jewelry Store in Lima, Ohio. They had discussed hitting the store again, with Brady deciding that they should give the owner time to restock. Shaffer stayed at the wheel of the getaway car, while the other three went into the store. Pulling out their guns, they entered the store, Brady purportedly yelling out, "We're giving you an encore, folks!" The gangsters then held up the employees and patrons.[1]

Meanwhile, a police car came upon the scene, not knowing what was transpiring, and one of the officers got out of their vehicle and went into the five and dime store next to the jewelry store. Brady came out of Kay's with pillowcases or sacks of jewelry, spotted the police car—according to another version, Shaffer had already spotted the police and gave a warning whistle to his friends—went to the Desoto, put the loot in the backseat, then surprised the officer in the car with his revolver aimed at him. The gangsters disarmed the policeman. (One version had Geiseking holding up the first policeman, with Brady cursing him for a fool who had his back to the other police officer.) Dalhover came over and took the first officer's gun from him. At this point, the second officer exited the dime store, surprised the gangsters, and opened fire on Brady and Dalhover. They returned fire. Geiseking also returned fire, shooting through the window of the jewelry store. He came running out of the jewelry store, and was shot in the leg by the still-armed, second officer. The officer went back in the five and ten to reload his gun, and while Geiseking was helped into the car—probably by Dalhover, who took over the driving—Brady ran back to the jewelry store for the rest of the loot, which he had left by the door. In total, five sacks were filled with the stolen jewelry and other items. Brady rushed back out, and the gang sped off to the south. Shaffer it seems stood on one of the car's running boards and fired at the police with an automatic rifle.[2]

The two officers, patrolmen from the Lima Police Department, pursued Brady and his gang through the city. The policemen—Jesse Ford who had stayed with the car, and Edward C. Swaney, who had gone into the five and ten—crashed during the pursuit. Swaney was seriously wounded and spent months in the hospital for spinal injuries. Jesse Ford had crashed into a truck while trying to avoid a few pedestrians, one a woman with a baby. The police quickly radioed and telephoned out for blockades to be set up along nearby intersections, and squad cars set out in pursuit of the fleeing thugs. Two National Guard airplanes also searched the region by air.[3]

The gang crossed into Indiana, and made it into Indianapolis. They had stolen roughly $12,000 worth of jewelry. Then they had made a big slipup: they discarded the boxes the jewelry had been kept in near Geneva, Indiana. The boxes were found on the day of the robbery, which led authorities to presume that the three men had transported stolen property across state lines, thus committing a federal crime. This allowed the Federal Bureau of Investigation, which had been looking for just such an opportunity, to officially enter the case.[4] And the case was splitting wide open, by the hour, and although the FBI did not immediately appear on the scene, they had already been investigating holdups committed by the gang.

The gang soon realized that Geiseking needed medical treatment. They had a few of their gangster friends follow them to a residence, just in case they needed to desert their vehicle and make a fast getaway. They then secured aid for Geiseking from a doctor, E. E. Rose on Barth Avenue in Indianapolis at 5:00 p.m. at his home and office, telling him that a jealous husband had shot Geiseking. Brady stayed outside. Rose treated Geiseking's wound, but did not extract the bullet, which remained lodged in his leg. The bullet seems to have passed through both of his legs before lodging in one of them. The gang then took Charles to a hideout. Deciding that they had better make certain that the doctor did not tell anyone what had happened, they returned to the physician's residence later in the evening on April 27, 1936, without Geiseking. But, they were too late; the doctor had already reported the incident to the Indianapolis Police Department (IPD), to Chief Detective Simon, having looked out the window and noted one of the gang's license plate numbers as 403-303. Rose said that the car with the identified plate was a Buick, the other a Desoto with its license plates covered with mud.[5]

The Chief of Police and Detective Simon sent out radio messages to their squad cars, sending it in code so that the gang would not know what was happening should their car be equipped with a police radio or scanner. The gang did have a police scanner, but did not think the messages pertained to them. Rather, they thought Rose had decided to remain silent for the money, or, even if he did call the police, that there would be no danger until the next morning. However, they were wrong, and IPD officers were nearby when the Brady Gang returned that night. Geiseking, as the doctor had told them, needed further medical attention. His wounds were serious ones.[6]

One of the suspects, later identified as Al Brady, went into Rose's office after the gang—again bringing two cars—had scanned the area for any problems. Brady tried to convince him to go to treat Geiseking off the premises, to operate on him at their hideout. Rose had not seen Brady before, which perhaps led him to let the slight smiling young man into his office. Rose then argued with Brady about the idea, stalling for time by finally agreeing but saying that he had to pack up some "special tools" for the operation. His wife, overhearing the discussion, ran out the backdoor and to a nearby drugstore from where she contacted the police. A broadcast went out. Sargent Richard Rivers was nearby and able to pick up Mrs. Rose as she left the drugstore and get the story from her. Patrolmen Charles Sansone and Robert Chambers were with Rivers, who parked just a block away from the home. While Brady had gone into the Rose residence, Shaffer and Dalhover had hidden outside in the shadows, in the event that trouble ensued.[7] And ensue it did.

The police, after having laid their plans, arrived and gunfire immediately broke out. Forty-four-year-old Sargent Richard Rivers, who had served with the Indianapolis Police Department for thirteen years, lost his life in the battle, shot by Dalhover or Shaffer from outside the building, or from Brady firing out of one of the windows of the doctor's residence, at about 9:00 p.m. Rivers had headed to the front porch, and was shot at by all three men, even after he had fallen, but he still got off a few shots of his own. The police had already determined that the men Rose had described to them matched the descriptions of the men who had robbed the Lima jewelry store earlier. After some fumbling around looking for a way out, Brady either shot his way out or climbed out a window at the rear of the doctor's home and escaped capture. He was thought to have hidden under a loading dock at a nearby pickle factory.[8]

Police shot at the other gang members, then pursued the fleeing car, one supposedly saying to the other, "Don't miss. The rats got Dick." But they lost the gangsters when the chase speeds reached ninety miles per hour. They lost the gang's car about fifteen miles south of Indianapolis at Stones Crossing. Police initiated a statewide manhunt for the three men, describing Brady, who as far as they knew had fled on foot, and asked area hospitals to keep a watch out for him, as police believed he had been cut deeply by the window glass as he climbed out of the home.[9]

Broadcasts describing the gang and their escape vehicle were aired throughout the state via police radios and telephones. Lawmen everywhere were asked to be on the lookout for the men. Squad cars moved silently along the roadways and streets looking for signs of the gangsters. Dalhover and Shaffer, however, had suffered a flat tire in the chase and creeping along back streets doubled back to where the men had planned to meet had something gone wrong. Brady supposedly had a large cut, and realizing that he had probably left a blood-trail, decided that he had better make a move fast. He first made his way back to the doctor's house, but saw that police had the home and office surrounded. He then made his way to the *rendezvous* location he had chosen; a deserted school lot. There he purportedly snuck up on his partners in crime, who were busy changing the tire and who were almost convinced that "Poor Al" had been captured. He threw a stone against a nearby school wall, and when Dalhover turned to the sound, gun raised, Brady said, "It's only me," and laughed. Dalhover supposedly told Brady that he had nearly given him a heart attack, and that one day he would shoot him by mistake if he kept up those kinds of antics.[10]

The thugs, reunited, knew the roads nearby would all be "hot" and decided to flee the state, and head first to Kentucky where they knew people and had places to stay. Brady, however, said that no, they had to hole up in town. Supposedly, after they crept back to the area where they had stayed, Dalhover and Shaffer holed up in their rooms while Brady went out on another mission. Police later learned that the gang had escaped capture in part by burning vehicles in their wake and using shortwave radios in their cars to avoid the gathering police dragnets.[11]

The gang escaped, and, as noted, eventually set their cars on fire to conceal any evidence of their involvement of the shooting. Brady did this on his own, sneaking back to the doctor's neighborhood to set their abandoned car on fire, acting carefree and whistling away to seem like an innocent man out for a stroll, and then took the other vehicle to the outskirts of Indianapolis after finding an old acquaintance to drive him back into town. Brady supposedly burned the cars on the advice of a couple of alcohol smugglers, in order to destroy any fingerprints or other evidence in the cars. Brady had already decided that they could not make it to Kentucky, as all the roads would be watched. According to one police source, the day after the shootout Shaffer went out for some newspapers, and when Brady saw photographs of the burned out vehicles in the papers, he said, "I should have driven those cars into the river. Some guy's going to recognize them." The police were already asking questions about the vehicles.[12] However, it seems they were burnt badly enough to ruin any fingerprints or similar evidence.

Yet, a detective on the case soon found a gasoline attendant who recognized the burnt Buick, as he said he had often serviced it. He did not know the fellow's name who drove the car, but it was a young man who "went around with two or three other guys about his age. The last time he was in here was two or three days ago." When asked how tall the men were, the man responded by holding his hand down below his chin and saying, "A bunch of little shrimps." This all occurred within twelve hours of the three gang members killing Richard Rivers. The gas station attendant also remembered seeing the driver hanging around a Washington Street bar on numerous occasions. And the police then found someone willing to name the gang and its leader, he said because they had brought too much heat down on the local guys.[13]

While police were following up on their leads, the Brady Gang— heavily armed—went to meet with a fence in Chicago to dispose of the jewelry, supposedly valued at $12,000. They purportedly agreed to sell the jewelry for $850, but the deal did not go through—or, at least, the Brady Gang seemingly did not get their money. According to one FBI source, the gang did not finish the deal, but according to another Jack and Robert Becker did get a chance to dispose of at least some of the loot.[14]

The Federal Bureau and local police forces had moved quickly. Within days after the Lima robbery and the shootout at Dr. Rose's, the Chicago Police Department with the aid of the Indianapolis Police captured Al Brady, then age twenty-five, in a northern Chicago hotel and placed him under arrest. He was captured at the hotel with his "sweetheart" who, as the press described her, "Mrs. Margaret Barker Larson had met him in New Orleans and deserted her husband and baby to go with him." Brady was arrested on April 29, 1936. Margaret, identified also as Margaret Barry, was arrested also, but soon released. She was just twenty-one years old.[15]

Alfred Brady was almost immediately—on the day after his arrest—escorted back to Indianapolis by Indiana's Deputy Prosecutor James Watson, Indianapolis Police Chief Michael Morrisey, and four detectives. Brady confessed to the Lima, Ohio, jewelry heist, and stated that he was the man who was in Doctor Rose's office on the night Sergeant Richard Rivers was killed. Police soon opened a bank vault and found much of the stolen Ohio jewelry. According to the Indiana press, several of the "fences who had helped dispose of the gang's loot were also caught and promptly charged with larceny of receiving stolen property, some $50,000 of which was recovered."[16]

According to a later FBI report, it was Jimmie Vennetuci who had ratted out Alfred Brady and provided the information that had led to his capture. Vennetuci with Franz Soardini had "hijacked" the Brady Gang's "loot" from the robbery of the Sol Partner Jewelry Store on April 9, 1936. The Bureau surmised that Vennetuci turned on Brady "undoubtedly endeavoring to protect his own face." Vennetuci and Soardini would not be prosecuted and were released on June 10, 1936.[17] Al Brady might have previously sworn to kill the men behind the robbery of "his" stolen jewelry, but they got back at him first. No doubt, when he found out, if he did, Brady's rage would have increased exponentially, and he might well have aimed a gun at Vennetuci's "face" had he the opportunity to do so. At any rate, Brady would soon turn in the two

Beckers, who had been involved in fencing some goods from the Partner robbery as well jewelry from the R. O. Wieland and Kay Jewelry Store robberies, and who Brady may have believed were involved in the "hijacking" of his "loot."

On May 15, 1936, the Chicago Police Department captured Rheul James Dalhover. The Indianapolis Police Department had captured Clarence Lee Shaffer at his home in Indianapolis on May 11. Both men, like Brady, were held on the charge of murder of Indianapolis police officer Richard Rivers. The three thugs remained in jail until October 1936, Brady immediately and Shaffer eventually, being extradited to Indianapolis.[18]

When first incarcerated, Al Brady allegedly confessed—to someone, not necessarily to the police—to the murder of the store clerk in Piqua, Ohio. Moreover, an Indiana Reformatory inmate stated that he had knowledge that Brady and James Dalhover had killed Anderson, Indiana, Patrolman Frank Levy the previous November. This led the press to report in mid-May that authorities expected to have Levy's murder case "cleared up" in the near future.[19] Charles Geiseking remained at large.

On May 2, the United States District Attorney at Chicago authorized prosecution against Jack and Robert Becker in connection with the jewelry thefts. Robert was soon arrested, and some of the stolen loot recovered.[20]

The stolen goods recovered initially seem to have come—at least primarily—from the deposit vault opened on May 6, 1936, in Chicago. The jewelry and gems were estimated to be of $50,000 in value. Codes on the jewelry showed them to come from recent robberies in Lima and Dayton, Ohio. Chicago police stated that they were goods stolen by the gang headed by Al Brady who had since been taken to Indianapolis to "face prosecution for the death of Police Sergeant Richard Rivers." The vault had been rented under the name Isaac Beckman, known to be Robert Becker who had given federal agents and Chicago detectives information leading to the vault. His brother Jack, age twenty-four, remained at large, while Robert had been arrested just after Al Brady and Margaret Larson were apprehended, as was William Geftman, while the other gang and fencers involved were still at large. Both Geftman and Robert Becker admitted to "handling the jewelry, but denied knowing they were stolen," according Chicago Police Detective Sal Corsi.[21]

Then, on or about May 11, the FBI sent its Chicago agent the list of the jewelry stolen from R. O. Wieland in Greenville, Ohio, on March 4, 1936, so that the authorities there could try "to identify some of the merchandise recovered from Jack Becker and Robert Becker." The FBI headquarters was also, with the special agent in charge in Indianapolis, planning to "interrogate" one Elmer Borden in relation to the case.[22] However, Borden was quite likely Alfred James Brady, under one of his aliases.

Soon after the arrests of Brady, Dalhover, and Shaffer, Judge Frank P. Parker issued a search warrant for a safety deposit box at an Indianapolis bank, which was opened on May 18. Inside the box, Marion County Prosecutor Herbert M. Spencer and Indianapolis police detectives recovered a ring with one large diamond and four smaller ones, two uncut diamonds, three automobile certificates of title, some rent receipts, plus various other items. According to Police Lieutenant Roy Pope, the press reported, Brady had admitted to the location of the safe deposit box and to his having placed some of the items there on March 16, and that he had planned on "holding out" the items of value from his fellow gang members. Brady purportedly admitted to the murder of the salesclerk in Piqua, Ohio, and also stated that Dalhover was the "trigger man" in the Anderson murder of Frank Levy, although an Indiana Reformatory inmate had stated that Brady had told him that he and Dalhover had both murdered Frank Levy. In turn, Shaffe—the "gabby gunman" as the press nicknamed him—purportedly named Brady and Dalhover in the Anderson shooting. Shaffer stated that he was not at the shooting in Anderson, but, he "knew all about it."

Immediately after his arrest, Brady purportedly first made a confession, and then retracted it, stating "that he had killed Sergt. Richard Rivers in a pistol battle last Monday," according to Chicago Police Captain John Stege, as quoted in a local paper. The police captain stated that Brady had initially confessed "that he had fired the shots which killed Rivers, but later declared that he had fired no shots at all and had escaped while his three partners were engaging the policeman in a pistol battle." Moreover, Brady called the wounded gang member (Geiseking) Elmer Martin, and said Martin was hiding out in Indianapolis. He said his other two companions were Jimmy Williams and Lee Jackson, and they were hiding in Chicago with some of the gang's loot. At this point, not only Brady, but two women had also been arrested along with two other men; another woman was arrested the following day.²³ Dalhover, Geiseking, and Shaffer were still on the loose, with Brady seemingly deliberately giving them some time by using their fake names when talking to the authorities.

The police captain's name may also have been an error, as another AP report of the same day, seemingly one of a few hours previously, referred to him as Captain John Egan, who would soon help write a lengthy article about the gang. Egan was quoted in April 1936 as stating that the captured man—then being referred to as Al Bartun with a couple of false names listed, neither of them Brady—had told him, "Sure I killed him. . . . I killed him because I didn't want to go to the pen, that's why." His fences, along with his girlfriend and seemingly those of the other men were also under arrest at this point.²⁴

Dalhover was still being held in Chicago in mid-May, but Detective Captain William Russell of the Anderson Police Department and his detectives planned to go to Indianapolis to work with authorities there and to interview Dalhover once he arrived back in Indiana. Police Chief Joseph Carney had been the one to request of the federal agents that Dalhover be interrogated about Levy's murder.²⁵

Local authorities in various jurisdictions worked on tying the gang to several crimes while the three men were in prison. So, too, did the FBI continue to work on some of its cases, including, still, the R. O. Wieland jewelry store robbery of March 4, 1936. According to one internal letter of the Bureau's, the proprietor and employees of the Ohio store had been shown photographs of Clarence Shaffer and Charles Geiseking, but had not been able to identify either of them as having participated in the robbery.²⁶ This would not have been surprising, as the Bureau had already surmised that they would not be able to identify the driver of the getaway car.

According to the FBI, in a report of May 18, 1936, Brady had admitted to robbing both jewelry stores in question, and to stealing a gunmetal gray Buick sedan on January 14, 1936, at Anderson. Brady stated that he had gone with Dalhover and Geiseking to Greenville, Ohio, in this car, arrived there at about 5:00 p.m., and that once they arrived he had gone in and asked to see some diamond rings. He then told a clerk that he was going to go get his girlfriend so that she could look at the rings also and select one. Then he returned to the store with Dal-hover—the two men armed with revolvers—and had the employees lie on the floor while he and Dalhover put the goods into a sack. After they left the store, they rejoined Geiseking, who had been in the Buick parked nearby, and then they proceeded to Chicago. They sold the jewelry to Jack and Robert Becker for $400, according to Brady. (After this Brady confession, the two Beckers were charged under the National Stolen Property Act.[27])

Brady denied, the report stated, that "suspect Jackson was involved in instant robbery," meaning that one Lee Jackson, a current FBI sus-pect as a co-bandit, and already charged under the National Stolen Property Act, had not been involved in the holdup. Brady did say that Lee Jackson had joined himself and Dalhover in robbing the Sol Part-ner Jewelry Store in Dayton, Ohio, and that on two occasions they had robbed the Kay Jewelry Store in Lima, Ohio. The FBI had already determined that Jack and Robert Becker had purchased the stolen jew-elry in Chicago from the Wieland store, estimated to be worth approxi-mately $8,000, for $400. Lee Jackson was described as being about twenty-two or twenty-three years of age, five feet, seven inches tall, a white man with a light complexion and no known address, photograph, or fingerprints.[28]

"Lee Jackson" was actually Clarence Lee Shaffer, and the FBI docu-ment of May 18, 1936, seemingly prepared using materials acquired or requested on May 6, did not list Shaffer as a suspect, and Shaffer had not yet been apprehended by May 6 nor had Dalhover or Geiseking. Such confusion extends forward in time, as it seems that a fourth, or sometimes fifth, gang member was often mentioned in the press and various law reports, even when one of the primaries was not at the scene. In addition, various documents, including FBI ones, sometimes used one of the men's aliases when identifying them. Brady may have been trying to protect Shaffer by using a false name, and when the gang members were indicted for the killing of Rivers on May 19, the press still noted Lee Jackson as being an alias of Shaffer. Dalhover was still being retained by Chicago police, and Geiseking was still on the loose.[29]

Within the next few months, however, the FBI had been able to identify some pieces of jewelry as having been stolen from the Wieland Jewelry Store on March 4, and a few from the Kay Jewelry Store in Lima, Ohio, on March 15 and on March 17. By now, the FBI had a couple of specific case titles in use as the department had definitively linked the Brady Gang with the Wieland robbery and the Kay Jewelry Store robbery. One case was entitled, "Alfred Brady, with aliases; et al. Robbery of R. O. Wieland Jewelry Store, Greenville, Ohio. Nat'l Stolen Property Act," and the other, similarly, "Alfred Brady, with aliases; et al. Robbery of Kay Jewelry Store, Lima, Ohio. National Stolen Property Act; National Motor Vehicle Theft Act." [30]

By early October 1936, the Bureau had a clearer order of events than they had in May. All the primary suspects had been placed under arrest, as well as three other men: Jack Becker, George Whitley, and Chester Hart. Jack and Robert Becker had been charged with violating the National Stolen Property Act before the United States Commissioner on May 2, 1936. Jack Becker had entered a plea of guilty on May 21, 1936, to the charges against him in Chicago, Illinois (unspecified but seemingly for receiving stolen property), and was sentenced to one to ten years in jail. Robert Becker, meanwhile, was still "being sought by the Bureau in view of the authorization granted by the United States Attorney at Chicago." [31]

The other two men arrested, Chester Hart and George Whitley, were arrested on April 27 and May 1, respectively. Hart was charged with accessory to murder, and Whitley on similar charges. Chester Hart owned a garage, and his wife Katherine was also charged, along with Whitley, with being accessories after the fact. Hart's residence had allegedly been used as a hideout for the Brady Gang following one of the robberies that preceded the killing of Richard Rivers, and Whitley had apparently also given the gangsters shelter at one point. The local press noted the charges against them on the same day as it covered the indictments of Brady, Dalhover, Shaffer, and Geiseking by the Marion County Grand Jury on May 19, 1936, at Indianapolis for the murder of Richard Rivers, referring to the men as "the second Dillinger gang." William Barrett, Herman Chanjie, and Theodore Deeb were also "accused of receiving jewelry stolen in a Lima robbery in which one of the gunmen was wounded," according to the UP article of May 19. [32]

In an internal letter to the Director, J. Edgar Hoover, Special Agent in Charge, E. J. Connelley, noted that "the subjects in the Lima robbery are identical with those in this [the Greeneville case] in which Cincinnati is the origin. All subjects are presently charged with murder in the state court in Indianapolis, Indiana." The agent requested that "in order to correlate these cases properly, it is respectfully requested that the Indianapolis office be designated as origin in this case, the investigation having been completed in the Cincinnati district."[33] Of course, just because it appeared that Ohio had completed its investigation in the one specific case, this did not mean that other cases might not arise concerning Ohio, and arise they would.

J. Edgar Hoover did, however, authorize the request that Indianapolis be made the office of origin for the Brady cases. He instructed the requesting agent on October 22 to "make certain that the new office of origin has all serials in the case containing important data."[34]

Charles Geiseking, meanwhile, had been tracked to Henderson, Kentucky, and apprehended on September 12, 1936. After recovering from his wounds at least enough to function, he had held up a number of filling stations with a fellow criminal named Raymond Jones during the time he had remained at large.[35]

According to the *Greenville Daily Advocate*, which retained its interest in the gang after the jewelry heist in Greenville, Ohio, that March, and to *The Gleaner* of Henderson, Kentucky, Detective Clyde Adkins along with three patrolmen—Harry Boyle, Eugene Hall, and Fount Miller—arrested Geiseking while he was sitting in a parked car on Dixon Street. With him were two underage, teenage girls, who had been hitchhiking, plus another young criminal, Raymond Jones. Police sent the two girls back to their parents in Louisville, whereas Jones, age twenty-four, was arrested. Geiseking, identified first as being thirty-six and then as twenty-nine, was armed with a small revolver, but did not resist arrest.[36]

Facing extradition to Indiana, Geiseking initially fought the move, then decided to acquiesce. An Indiana officer accompanied him, and told reporters that Geiseking was wanted for robbing seven filling stations in recent weeks.[37]

Geiseking purportedly stated that if police could clear the other members of the Brady Gang by blaming him, then "I'll take them off your hands." However, he soon denied having had any part in the death of the Indianapolis police officer.[38]

The Brady Gang purportedly had committed some 150 robberies plus at least one murder between late 1935 through April 1936 when the FBI became involved after the gang crossed state boundaries during the commission of a crime. So, too, did the entire force of the

Pinkerton's National Detective Agency join with federal, state, and local police forces in 1936.[39]

By early October 1936, Brady had admitted to robbing the R. O. Wieland Jewelry Store, the Sol Partner Jewelry Store, and the Kay Jewelry Store, twice. He seemingly did not implicate Shaffer in any of the robberies. He did name Dalhover and Geiseking. On questioning, Shaffer had admitted to participating in the robberies of the Partner store and the Kay store. He also corroborated Brady's statement that Dalhover and Geiseking had been involved in those thefts. Brady, Geiseking, and Dalhover were implicated in all four jewelry heists, although Geiseking admitted to only "some" of them.[40]

Geiseking admitted to being part of the Greenville robbery, and said that he had used his portion of the haul, some $2,000, to visit England and France. He also told police that he had been involved in three gasoline station holdups in Richmond, two at Terre Haute, and one in Southport, Indiana. These gas station robberies were seemingly the ones he committed with Raymond Jones, who would be sentenced to ten to twenty-five years in the Indiana State Reformatory for the three Terre Haute gas station robberies.[41] As to whether Jones might have had other connections to the Brady Gang remains unknown, although an often unknown fourth or even fifth person—not necessarily the same person or persons—would appear to be working with the core of the gang from time to time.

Dalhover like Geiseking admitted only partial involvement in various Brady Gang crimes. Brady admitted stealing a Ford V-8 Coupe in Indianapolis "on or about December 30, and driving it to Chicago, Illinois, on or about April 28, 1936." He admitted having the loot from the latest robbery—the one which had cost a police officer his life—in the car, and, pressed further, stated that Dalhover and Shaffer had accompanied him on the drive. Dalhover admitted to being in the car and admitted that he had "heard" that Brady had stolen it. Shaffer admitted to being in the car, but there was no substantive evidence that he "knew" it was stolen. Geiseking was already severely wounded and did not accompany the men, so there were no further confessions on that score.[42]

All four men were initially held in Indianapolis to await trial for the murder of Sergeant Richard Rivers. Eventually, however, Brady, Dalhover, and Shaffer were transferred to the Hancock County Jail in

Greenfield, Indiana, on a change of venue agreement. Dalhover had requested the change of venue. Geiseking, having been found not to have been involved in the murder of Rivers, was first held at the Marion County Jail in Indianapolis and later transferred to Ohio, and eventually sentenced to ten to twenty-five years in the Ohio State Penitentiary for armed robbery, having been involved in the Lima heist amongst others. Brady admitted to the Ohio robberies and, at least inadvertently, to the murder of Rivers after his arrest in Chicago (but he stated that he was in the doctor's office and home, not outside where the killing shot was apparently fired). All three men, Brady, Dalhover, and Shaffer, however, would officially plead not guilty to Rivers's murder.[43] Either way, admitted or not at this point, the murder of Richard Rivers would not be their last. None of them were yet formally charged nor pled guilty to killing Frank Levy, although quite possibly they had, nor to murdering clerk Edward Lindsay during an earlier store robbery, and once again they probably had, and one of the gang members would later point the finger at Al Brady for the killing of the young man.

While the legal system worked to determine exactly which charges—in addition to River's murder—which of the gang members should be charged with, and where, the gang members worked to find a way out of their legal bind. They would find one. And it would not be pretty.

NOTES

1. "Memorandum to Mr. Tamm," 12 October 1936, from E. M. Soucy, FBI; "Memorandum to the Director," FBI, 25 May 1937; and related documents; "The Brady Gang," *FBI History: Famous Cases*, FBI; *NYT*, from Chicago Press, 12 October 1937; Egan and Hunt, "The Second Dillinger," on the warning by Shaffer and Brady's supposed words.

2. Ibid

3. Ibid.

4. "Memorandum to Mr. Tamm," 12 October 1936, from E. M. Soucy, FBI; "Memorandum to the Director," 25 May 1937; and related documents. General sources as listed below.

5. Ibid. Also see *NYT*, from Chicago Press, 12 October 1937, printed October 13, 1937, on the physician and his wife; Indianapolis Metropolitan Police Department website for general information; and *The Indianapolis Star*, 28 April–4 May 1936. Also see "The Brady Gang," *FBI History: Famous Cases*,

FBI; and see Egan and Hunt, "The Second Dillinger" on the plate numbers and car models, and the codes messages.

6. Ibid.

7. Ibid. The FBI reported that it was the doctor who alerted the authorities in its Memorandum of 12 October 1936.

8. *The Indianapolis Star*, 28 April–4 May 1936; and Egan and Hunt, "The Second Dillinger."

9. Ibid.

10. *The Indianapolis Star*, 28 April–4 May 1936; and see Egan and Hunt, "The Second Dillinger" on the supposed conversations and school meeting place. Egan may have taken some liberties with his wording, but he may also have been in a position to get direct quotes from the gang members a couple of months later.

11. Ibid.

12. Egan and Hunt, "The Second Dillinger."

13. Ibid.

14. "Memorandum to Mr. Tamm," 12 October 1936, from E. M. Soucy, FBI, and related documents; and "The Brady Gang," *FBI History: Famous Cases*, FBI. The more recent document stated that the gang did not get their money.

15. Ibid. Also see *NYT*, 13 October 1937, *Indianapolis Star*, 28 April–4 May 1936; *BDN* and Indianapolis Wire Service, Logansport, 18–19 July 1936, on the arrest of Margaret Barry or Larson.

16. *Indianapolis Star*, 28 April–4 May 1936; Indianapolis Metropolitan Police Department reports on Sergeant Richard Rivers. And see "The Brady Gang," *FBI History: Famous Cases*, FBI. Quote and information on the gang's fencers from *BDN* and Indianapolis Wire Service, Logansport, 18–19 July 1936.

17. "Memorandum to Mr. Tamm," 12 October 1936, from E. M. Soucy, FBI.

18. Ibid. And see other general press and legal sources.

19. *Daily Times Tribune*, 19 May 1936.

20. FBI letter, Agent in Charge, E. J. Connelley, to Special Agent in Charge (no name given), Chicago, 11 May 1936; and FBI letter, Agent in Charge, E. J. Connelley, to Special Agent in Charge (no name given), Indianapolis, Indiana, 4 May 1936; and "Memorandum to Mr. Tamm," 12 October 1936, from E. M. Soucy, FBI.

21. *Elwood [Indiana] Call Leader*, 7 May 1936.

22. FBI letter, Agent in Charge, E. J. Connelley, to Special Agent in Charge (no name given), Chicago, 11 May 1936; and FBI letter, Agent in Charge, E. J. Connelley, to Special Agent in Charge (no name given), Indianapolis, Indiana,

4 May 1936; and "Memorandum to Mr. Tamm," 12 October 1936, from E. M. Soucy, FBI. It is possible that the name Borden was an alias of one of the Beckers, but it was also an alias used by Brady.

23. Chicago AP article as printed in the *Rushville [Indiana] Republican*, 30 April 1936.

24. Ibid.

25. *Daily Times Tribune*, 19 May 1936; also see, *The Indianapolis Star*, 28 April–4 May 1936, and undated clipping, seemingly from the *Daily Times Tribune*, c. 1962.

26. FBI, National Stolen Property Act, Report of 6 August 1936.

27. FBI National Stolen Property Act, Report of 6 or 18 May 1936. (Headings unclear.) Also see "Memorandum to Mr. Tamm," 12 October 1936, from E. M. Soucy, FBI, on the Beckers being charged after Brady implicated them.

28. FBI National Stolen Property Act, Report of 6 or 18 May 1936.

29. See preceding and following sources for the use of the name Lee Jackson, and *Daily Times Tribune*, 19 May 1936, on the indictments of the Brady gang members.

30. FBI letter, heading indecipherable, filed on 10 October 1936.

31. "Memorandum to Mr. Tamm," 12 October 1936, from E. M. Soucy, FBI.

32. Ibid. The final sentence regarding the specifics of the two men providing shelter to the gang are illegible on the document. See the *Daily Times Tribune*, 19 May 1936, for the former charges against the two men and against Katherine Hart, as well as the jewelry fencers. The article appears to have been a UP one, but the first letter is blurred, and it might have been an AP article.

33. FBI letter, heading indecipherable, filed on 10 October 1936; and "Letter to the Director," 12 October 1936, from E. J. Connelley, Agent in Charge, letter originating in Cincinnati.

34. Letter, J. Edgar Hoover, Director, FBI, to Special Agent in Charge, 22 October 1936.

35. "Memorandum to Mr. Tamm," 12 October 1936, from E. M. Soucy, FBI; "The Brady Gang," *FBI History: Famous Cases*, FBI; *NYT*, 13 October 1937. Also see *The Indianapolis Star*, 28 April–4 May 1936.

36. *Greenville Daily Advocate*, 14 September 1936; and *The Gleaner* [of Henderson, Kentucky], 13 September 1936.

37. *The Gleaner*, 13 September 1936.

38. Ibid.

39. Indianapolis Metropolitan Police Department reports on Sergeant Richard Rivers; and "Officer Down Memorial Page," "ODMP Remembers Officer Richard Rivers," website.

40. "Memorandum to Mr. Tamm," 12 October 1936, from E. M. Soucy, FBI and related documents.

41. *Greenville Daily Advocate*, 15 September 1936.

42. "Memorandum to Mr. Tamm," 12 October 1936, from E. M. Soucy, FBI and related documents.

43. "Memorandum to Mr. Tamm," 12 October 1936, from E. M. Soucy, FBI; "The Brady Gang," *FBI History: Famous Cases*, FBI; *NYT*, from Chicago Press, 13 October 1937, on Brady's supposed murder confession and press for October 1937–November 1938, and legal records for Dalhover. See last two chapters.

6

BREAKOUT

The Gang Busts out of Jail, Flees the State, and Steps Up Its Criminal Rampage

The three thugs charged with the murder of Sergeant Richard Rivers of the Indianapolis Police Department—Alfred James Brady, Clarence Lee Shaffer Jr., and Rhuel James Dalhover—were transferred to the Hancock County Jail in September 1936; they were delivered by Indianapolis police officers. However, the Hancock County Jail and its sheriff could not long contain the principal members of the Brady Gang. On October 11, 1936, three weeks after they arrived, during the breakfast hour, when he was delivering their breakfasts, the three men assaulted the sheriff, Clarence Watson, clubbing him on the head with an iron bar until he was unconscious, stole his .38 caliber revolver, and escaped the jail in a car they stole from a Greenfield man who tried to aid the sheriff during the altercation, shooting at him in the process. They then, "dropped out of the news for about seven months" according to the Chicago press.[1]

The men had been able to attack the sheriff as he had allowed the gang to eat in the common room with the other prisoners. There was only the one sheriff working at the time, according to local writers Dorothy June Williams and Thomas E. Williams in their history of Hancock County. The sole law officer then at the jail, Watson, was paid just $75 a month. Watson would feed the prisoners by passing their food through an opening in a door into the common room. There had been no major problems with this arrangement in the past, it seems, but the Brady Gang was another matter. Al Brady had somehow torn off an iron bar from his cell window, according to FBI agents, and hid it in his cell. When the prisoners were released from their individual cells to go to the common room on the morning of the escape, Brady took the bar with him, hiding it under his shirt.[2]

Sheriff Watson passed the prisoners their food and a bit later opened the door to return a wastebasket to the room. Brady had been sitting out of the sheriff's direct view with his back facing the door. When Watson opened the door, Brady turned and lunged at the sheriff "with a growl." Watson was able to force Brady back, but when he tried to close the door, Shaffer and Dalhover entered the fray with their leader. "Brady," according to the local historians, "was determined to kill Watson with a blow from the iron bar and the sheriff was just as determined to take it away from him. The sheriff and the Brady Gang fought down that long hallway."[3] The goal of the gang beyond escape is not truly known, but Watson did later express his own determination to prevent the escape.

Brady and Watson continued to fight over control of the iron bar, which according to the *Greenfield Daily Reporter*, was four feet long and weighed fourteen pounds, down the long—fifty foot—hallway from the cell block. The sheriff was struck repeatedly in the head and face during the battle in the common room, but, after they forced the sheriff back, due to the cramped space, Brady could not wield the bar in the hallway sufficiently to kill the sheriff or totally disable him. Exiting the jail proper, the two struggled on the lawn of the sheriff's residence for control of the weapon.[4]

Meanwhile, the sheriff's sister, who helped out at the jail, ran to get a gun. The gun—a .38 caliber revolver—was kept in the sheriff's office. Dalhover saw the woman, Mrs. Edna Tinney, and followed her, then wrestled with her for control of the gun, which he ultimately won. By this time, Brady and Watson had rolled down a small hill to the sidewalk or roadway, where Watson was able to smash Brady's head on the pavement a few times. Then, Dalhover and Shaffer again came to Brady's rescue. As this was happening, Mr. and Mrs. Edgar Ridlen of Greenfield were driving by on their way to Cincinnati, and seeing that the sheriff was in trouble, Edgar Ridlen—owner of a local barbershop—stopped his car and rushed to assist Watson. Ridlen was able to sneak up on the gangsters and knock first Dalhover and then Shaffer to the ground. Then Dalhover, with the gun he had taken from Edna Tinney, told Ridlen to leave or he would be shot. Ridlen, however, went after Dalhover again, and Dalhover shot him. Fortunately, the bullet passed through Ridlen's coat and caused him no real injury.[5]

According to William and Williams, the mayhem continued, and Ridlen went after Dalhover again. Shaffer joined Dalhover in fighting with Ridlen. He pounced on Ridlen's back knocking him down. Brady then began demanding that Dalhover shoot the sheriff. At this point, Mrs. Lottie Ridlen got out of the car, tried to pull Shaffer off of her husband, and according to her niece she hit at least one of the gang members with her purse. She also pled with the gang members to just take their vehicle and leave. And so they did. Brady drove the car, and purportedly ordered Dalhover to shoot the Ridlens and the sheriff, but Dalhover did not shoot at them, or at least he did not further injure any of them with the gun.[6]

And the manhunt for the Brady Gang was on. Again. And again the local press exploded with coverage of the search, as did the media throughout the Midwest.

The *Greenfield Daily Reporter* covered the escape from the jail in depth. In their evening edition of October 12, the papers ran the headline "BRADY GANG BREAKS JAIL SUNDAY; Batter Sheriff Clarence Watson Over Head With Iron Bar in Early Morning Delivery—Steal Car and Escape." In slightly smaller type than that of the first clause, the leader continued: "EDGAR RIDLEN IN HERO PART, Went to Aid of Hard Pressed Officer in Battle in Front of Jail—Fights Gun-toting Bad Man—Comes Our Unscathed."[7]

The paper stated that Dalhover had shot at Ridlen more than once, the first time missing him completely. Dalhover also purportedly hit Ridlen once in the back and in one knee with the iron bar when he got him down in their struggle, having taken it from Brady, while the sheriff, bleeding profusely from his face and head and perhaps elsewhere, lay on the ground unconscious or nearly so. Moreover, before the gang decided to flee in the Ridlen's 1936 green Chevrolet sedan, the sheriff's twelve-year-old son, Phillip Watson, who had witnessed part of the struggle, had turned his dog Trix, a brindle pup, loose on the mobsters in an attempt to help his father. The dog supposedly bit Brady rather severely and at least nipped at the others.[8]

Sheriff Watson told the press that Ridlen had saved his life. "If he had not come to my aid I'm sure they would have killed me," he stated. In a rather surprising twist, another prisoner, Roy Mackey, held at the jail on a housebreaking charge, tried to come to the aid of the sheriff during the battle. Mrs. Watson had apparently come to see what was going on, and agreed to let Mackey out, and went to the office to get a shotgun kept there. By the time she found ammunition for it, however, the gangsters had fled in Ridlen's car. A local doctor examined Watson's injuries at the scene and determined that he did not have a fractured skull although he had numerous lesser injuries and was "dazed and groggy." Another physician later examined Ridlen, and determined also that his knee and his knuckles were bruised, and he had a sprained wrist. The local paper stated dourly, "He may not be able to follow his trade with any ease or comfort for a day or two."[9]

The *Greenfield Daily Reporter* commented, at the start of its coverage on the 12th, "Three more of Indiana's potential Dillingers were loose today again, to prey on society, as a result of [the] daring break from the Hancock County Jail at 7:45 a.m. Sunday morning." It concluded its article with the observation that the gang must have planned their escape for some time, choosing early Sunday morning as it was a time at which there were few cars on the road in front of the jail, and few pedestrians. The town did have a night officer, but he had just gone off duty, and the day shift had not yet reported for duty. The sheriff did have a deputy, but on Sunday mornings he came in a bit later than other days. "He arrived just a few minutes after the escape had been completed," according to the newspaper.[10]

In a separate article, the paper noted that Sheriff Clarence Watson had feared a jailbreak by the gang. Once he learned of the serious offenses presumed committed by the gang, he had said that he would request that they be transferred to the Pendleton Reformatory "for safe keeping." He had not been able to get the men transferred before they broke out of his jail. He had feared that "outside help" might break the trio free, but that had not proved necessary, as events had shown.[11]

Under Indiana law, or a loophole in the law, such transfers as Watson desired could only be requested by a sheriff directly to the Governor, and it was at the Governor's discretion that such a request be granted. A few years previously, two hardened criminals—at least one of them a supposed member of the old "Egan Rats Gang"—had been placed in the Hancock County Jail and a former sheriff had successfully had them transferred to the Pendleton institution. At the time of the Brady Gang's escape, one of them had been convicted and sentenced to life, which he was serving at the Michigan City prison. Michigan City and its prison would prove crucial later for one Brady Gang member. In the meantime, Herbert M. Spencer, prosecuting attorney for Marion County, who had secured the indictments against the Brady Gang members before the Marion County Grand Jury, and who would have overseen the prosecution of the three men, expressed his anger over the events in Greenfield.[12]

Prosecuting Attorney Spencer stated after the jailbreak that he planned to introduce a resolution in Indiana's General Assembly to make it mandatory to transfer inmates facing capital punishment, and to make death mandatory for persons convicted of murdering a peace officer on duty, and "giving the prosecuting attorney the right to ask transfer of prisoners awaiting trial to an adequate jail." Moreover, he stated that Sheriff Watson had been advised of the status of his escapees, and Spencer had understood that he would have immediately secured their transfer. Spencer did not explain the failure, and stated that it was not his place to answer for the sheriff as to why he had failed to secure the transfer and why the men had been able to escape; but Spencer did note that "none of the jails in the adjoining counties is adequate and our own Marion County Jail is woefully undermanned. Only by constant vigilance has a wholesale jailbreak been averted here." At one time, he noted, the sheriff there had had "twenty-two of the most vicious criminals with national underworld reputations in his custody. All except one—who had escaped—were now imprisoned at Michigan City—and the one escapee had led the sheriff "and his men to live up to their responsibility."[13]

No matter the issue of blame, as soon as word went out about the escape, not only did squad cars from the Marion County Sheriff's Department and Indianapolis Police Department officers arrive in Greenfield within forty-five minutes after the break, but also, the "wires from various news agencies were hot into Greenfield seeking the facts." "Within two hours, feature writers and photographers were here seeking additional details," the local paper reported, "and the noon TWA east, out of Indianapolis, carried pictures of the jail and the principals in the break."[14]

Not only the print media but also radio broadcasts carried the news. On the evening of the escape—after hearing the police broadcasts blaring every five minutes or so in an attempt by law enforcement agencies to throw a dragnet over the state, covering bridges and important roads especially—Greenfield's radio stations carried major coverage of the event. Two local stations made the escape their leading news, and others in the state did the same. [15]

The local newspaper also carried a few photographs relevant to the escape the day after it occurred. A strip of photographs published by the *Greenfield Daily Reporter* included one of Sheriff Watson. He was photographed with his head heavily bandaged and listening to his radio at the jailhouse "listening to police reports of the manhunt." The accompanying caption noted that Watson had received at least six severe scalp wounds "during the battle" with the gangsters. [16]

A photograph of Brady was printed next to that of Watson in his bandaged head and a light colored shirt. Brady was attired in a suit, his face shown in a three-quarter view, his thin lips in their typical straight line, his dark hair cut short, and his one visible ear prominent. He was noted as having told police that he "aspired to be a second Dillinger." [17]

The next photograph in the series, placed just to the right of Brady, was that of Edgar Ridlen, who had come to Watson's aid and had his coat pierced by a bullet. He was photographed in a three-piece suit standing with his arm around his wife, a slender woman with glasses and wearing a long-sleeved flowered dress, her hair seemingly in a wavy bob. The photograph was taken in front of a house, the porch pillars visible behind the couple. [18]

The last photograph in the series was that of the "Old Hancock County Jail," from which the Brady Gang had escaped and which rather eerily resembled Maine's Penobscot County Courthouse and Jail close to where the gang would eventually encounter an inescapable force. The two-plus-story masonry jail in Greenfield was long in its stretch from front to back, like the Penobscot County facility in New England. Both facilities were built to be multipurpose, with the lockup sections of each located at the rear of the building. Several boys and youth were standing in front of the Hancock jail in the published photograph, perhaps having gathered in excitement after the escape. [19]

The press continued to follow the search. A United Press article from Indianapolis noted on October 12, "The hunt for Al Brady and two members of his self-styled 'Second Dillinger Gang,' was concentrated on Marion County today after two persons reported seeing the fugitives." According to the report, a taxi driver and a "merchant policeman" reported to the Indiana State Police, to Captain Matt Leach, that they had seen three men whom they tentatively identified as the three Brady Gang escapees.[20]

Other possible sightings occurred. The United Press in Indianapolis on the 13th stated in an article with the lead "Federals Tap Gangland for Brady Outlaws" that it was believed that the gang had replaced the Chevrolet sedan they had stolen during their escape for a black Ford sedan, one police thought had been parked for some time for just such a necessity, the gang having already decided to escape. The press quoted Captain Leach as stating that the Brady Gang was "ruthless and desperate—even more dangerous than the Dillinger Gang" that had previously "terrified the Midwest for months." Indeed, the manhunt that was on for Brady and his cohorts was the largest and most concentrated the region had seen since the hunt had been on for Dillinger after his "two vicious attacks on civilians." Federal forces had joined the search, and were tapping the Midwest "gangland" for leads. According to Leach, the Brady Gang was not as cunning as the Dillinger Gang had been, and its members "were more likely to attempt to 'shoot their way out of difficulty than to think their way out'" as Dillinger and his men had often had.[21]

Authorities believed that the gang was headed toward Chicago, as a citizen of Hoppeston, Illinois, had reported that three men in a car matching Brady's had tried to force him off the road near State Roads 25 and 43 north of Lafayette, and then shot at him when he refused to do so. Later, a woman was "cuffed and shoved to the floor when she refused to give money to an intruder into her farm home near Archersville in Tippecanoe County," thus the focus of the search there soon after the escape. Two airplanes were used as part of the search team on October 12.[22]

However, authorities did not gain any clear evidence from the Tippecanoe County search by nightfall of the 12th, and police switched part of their focus to other areas. The State Police decided to search various haunts of the gang in Indianapolis and other cities to try to turn up new leads. Thus far, authorities had not located the car the gang had stolen to make their escape.[23]

On October 13, police investigated a robbery, seemingly in Indianapolis, of the previous night. Ted Nicholas, manager of the Lyric Theater, had been held up by a "handkerchief-masked bandit" at gunpoint and robbed of $6,000. Nicholas had been in the theater's office counting the receipts of the weekend, a weekend that had been quite lucrative as Ted Lewis and his band had attracted full capacity crowds. The bandit had taken only bills from the safe, however, which he had forced Nicholas to open. Police were attempting to discover if the masked man had been a member of the Brady Gang.[24]

Also, in Tulsa, Oklahoma, at about the same time, three young men matching the descriptions of Brady, Dalhover, and Shaffer were arrested. They were later released when it was determined that they were indeed Oklahomans.

By the day following the Indianapolis reports, the press in Detroit—on October 14—announced in bold headlines, "OFFICERS CONVINCED THE FUGITIVES ARE HIDDEN NEAR." Reports had come in that the gang had been spotted in Toledo, Ohio, headed toward Detroit. Authorities had broadcasted the report that the gangsters were believed to be driving toward Michigan in a coupe with Illinois license plates. The press noted that Indiana State Police Captain Leach warned people about all three men, especially Dalhover who had purportedly shot three times at Ridlen when he tried to prevent the escape—although only a few paragraphs earlier the paper quoted Sheriff Watson as saying that he did not think that Dalhover had wanted to kill him during the fight at the jail, as he had had every opportunity of doing so and had not taken the opportunity. Charles Geiseking, the press noted, was still in prison in the Marion County jail, having been apprehended in Kentucky on September 12. While searching various locations, authorities were also checking garages and other places the gang might have hidden the car they had stolen in Greenfield, and conjectured that the gang might have "holed up" somewhere, as the Ridlen car had not been seen.[25] Reports seemed contradictory.

Then, the search seemed to point back to Ohio, after men who resembled the three convicts were seen by seven different witnesses near Toledo on Tuesday, October 13, and this was followed by a sighting of an automobile carrying four men, with three of them matching the three known gang members' descriptions, near Celina, Ohio. In addition, three men had been spotted eating in a restaurant, while a fourth waited for them, also in Celina, leading to the conjecture that the gang had added a new fourth member. Authorities warned that the gang might be adding one or more new members and be preparing to make a raid to secure guns and ammunitions, much as the Dillinger Gang had earlier raided jails in Warsaw and Peru to secure munitions. Or, they might be planning another rash of robberies like those they had committed before their arrests and imprisonment for the shooting of Richard Rivers. However, reports of the fugitives were starting to decline.[26]

The *Shelbyville Democrat* on October 15 reported that its city police were "taking no chances" as during the previous night reports had come in that "The Brady Gang has invaded Shelbyville." Dalhover specifically had been "seen," but a thorough search of the area had failed to lead to the crook or further information. Yet, "one entrance to the police station in the city hall is kept locked at all times and all arms and ammunitions have been safely stored away." The headquarters had two entrances. Moreover, echoing reports from other localities, the paper stated that police throughout the state were taking similar precautions "to foil any attempt of the three gunmen to obtain arms and ammunition." Again, like others, the paper referred to the Dillinger and his men having raided a northern Indiana police station for weapons "during their sensational careers."[27]

The press in Indianapolis carried additional news on October 15, reiterating measures taken to secure munitions in the city as elsewhere, and stated that Brady and Dalhover had been two of four men identified by a farmer near Champaign, Illinois, on October 14. The farmer, George Struebing, stated that the car he had seen had held four men, and that it bore Illinois license plates. A machine gun and extra plates from Ohio and Indiana were in the car. In addition, the gang had supposedly been spotted moving "across northern Ohio from Celina toward the Indiana State Line."[28]

Yet, while police in the Midwest continued to seek the gang, and took due precautions to protect munitions and citizens, a possible sighting of the gang came in from Linden, New Jersey. A United Press article from Linden stated on October 15, "An automobile with Indiana plates and fitting the description of the escape-car of three men who overpowered the sheriff and escaped from the Hancock County jail at

Greenfield, Indiana, last Sunday, was reported to have been seen on Route 25 near here today."[29]

According to the press, a police teletype had described the automobile, and police in the northern part of New Jersey were asked to keep a lookout for the escapees. Just ten minutes after the sighting of the possible escape car near Linden, local officers surrounded the car and took three men into custody. However, after officers carrying "riot guns" escorted the startled men to the jail, the men had identified themselves, and both parties soon joined in laughter at police headquarters. The men were not gangsters, but rather dairymen. Police released the men, and promised not to embarrass them further by releasing their names to the public.[30]

The following day, October 16, the Indianapolis press acknowledged that the trail was getting cold and that authorities were waiting for another type of break in the case. The headline for the Indianapolis article stated: AWAIT BREAK BY BRADY GANG; First Foray of the Disappearing Bandits Is Expected to Reveal Their Location." There would indeed be a "foray of the bandits" in the near future, but it would not reveal their whereabouts in terms of where they were hiding out. As the paper noted, the trail was growing cold, and while sheriffs and municipal authorities sought to guard their munitions and banks had been advised to take extra security measures, Captain Matt Leach of the Indiana State Police believed the fugitives to be hiding in central Indiana.[31] But, he was wrong.

That same day, October 16, the United Press in Hammond, Indiana, noted that a night watchman for a petroleum plant near Hammond had reported to police that day that three men—one of them resembling Al Brady—had stopped near the roadside and asked him for directions "into Chicago and Indiana Harbor." The watchman reported that the men were traveling in a Plymouth coupe, with no license plates.[32]

Police had taken numerous reports of possible sightings, but in spite of their initial assessment that it was "only a matter of hours before a definite trace of the fugitives would be found,"[33] they were wrong. And being wrong for State Police Captain Matt Leach must have been especially frustrating. Captain Leach had been involved with more than one Illinois gang. In what would be an ironic coincidence—were it not that he was a high-ranking officer in the state law enforcement agency responsible for apprehending, or trying to, both sets of gangsters—Matt

Leach had been heavily involved in pursuing John Dillinger and his gang during their reign and after Dillinger's escape from jail, only to find later that Dillinger had moved over to Chicago, Illinois.

Matt Leach had come to the United States from Serbia at the age of thirteen in 1907. His family settled first in Pennsylvania, then moved to Gary, Indiana, where his father secured a job in a steel mill. Young Matt worked in a steel mill for a time, according to historian Bryan Burrough, joined the army in 1915, and later returned to Gary and became a patrolman. Leach eventually rose to the position of heading the Gary PD's vice department. In 1932, he became Indiana's first captain of the recently established Indiana State Police. He was second in command of the entire force, which in 1933 had just forty-one employees, including office staff. The force, like the Bureau of Investigation, were still evolving its procedures, technology, and so forth, when Leach became involved with Dillinger.[34]

According to Irving Leibowitz, who became a journalist with the Indianapolis *Times* in the 1940s and an historian of his adopted state, Captain Matt Leach, charged with solving the Dillinger holdups, became especially frustrated during the search for Dillinger when the public—clamoring for results—started questioning the effectiveness of the Indiana State Police Department in general, and of Leach in particular. As soon as Leach and his men would respond to a robbery or other Dillinger threat in one community, news of a new crime by Dillinger would arise in another town or city. Leach was miserable over the unfolding events, and the Indiana Statehouse was exerting political pressure on him.[35]

Then, Jack Cejnar, bureau manager for the International News Service in Indianapolis, played a trick on Leach. Cejnar had positioned himself in an enviable—for journalists—position during the Depression Era crime wave. He learned from the state insurance commissioner that American Surety insured perhaps 98 percent of the banks in the state, and that every bank was required to contact the company headquarters in Indianapolis about any robbery immediately—even before contacting the police. Cejnar then made an arrangement whereby for an instant tip on any holdup, he would guarantee a professional news report on the robbery within fifteen minutes, so that the insurance company could immediately initiate its own investigation into the crime before the trail turned cold. Moreover, the State Police Superintendent, Al Freeney, in lieu of an organized police radio system at the time, gave sheriffs the right to blockade all roads after a bank robbery and to commandeer all telephone lines. Cejnar was able to be contacted and make his phone calls before the sheriffs completed their actions. Thus, before the larger Associated Press, United Press, and various local and other newspapers were alerted to the latest stickup, all telephone lines were already busy, but Cejnar already knew of the crime. A couple of concerns came out of Cejnar's great scoops on other reporters and agencies: suspicion that many of the holdups were inside jobs with more thefts attributed to Dillinger than he actually carried out, and that Cejnar might be in cahoots with Dillinger.[36]

Then, at the height of the search for Dillinger, according to Leibowitz, Cejnar played a joke on Matt Leach. He bought a book at a secondhand store in Detroit for ten cents and sent it anonymously to Captain Leach. The title of the book was *How to Be a Detective*. Leach was enraged to such a degree that Cejnar was afraid to tell him that it was just a joke. Then the United Press sent all its newspapers in the nation a story that speculated that Dillinger had sent Leach the book as a sort of do-it-yourself detective manual. Leach was thoroughly frustrated, as he had continued to pursue questions about Dillinger, even questioning the Bureau of Investigation about having charges brought against the two women involved in Dillinger's last night out at the movies, who, as it turned out, were not charged—although Anna Sage did eventually leave the United States.[37] Then, after Dillinger was finally taken down, and Leach had irked the new FBI with his continued questions, along came Al Brady and his gang with their robberies and other crimes, and then their prison escape. Leach was back in the hot seat. And, while reports of possible sightings came in seemingly from all over the place, the Brady Gang was clearly on the lam.

NOTES

1. "Memorandum to the Director" from E. A. Tamm, 25 May 1937, and related FBI records; Indianapolis Wire Service, Logansport, 18–19 July 1936; "The Brady Gang," *FBI History: Famous Cases*, FBI; *Greenfield Daily Reporter*, 12 October 1936; Indianapolis Metropolitan Police Department reports on Sergeant Richard Rivers; and see *NYT*, 13 October 1937, for quote and some

details of the escape, as well as the *Indianapolis Star*, 12 October 1936, on the beating and attempted shooting.

2. Dorothy June Williams and Thomas E. Williams, *A History of Hancock County, Indiana, in the Twentieth Century* (Greenfield, IN: Coiny Press, 1995). The document is hand-typed and available at the Hancock County Library, Indiana. Also see "Memorandum to the Director," from E. A. Tamm, 25 May 1937, and related FBI records and the *Greenfield Daily Reporter*, 12–16 October 1936.

3. Williams and Williams, *A History of Hancock County, Indiana, in the Twentieth Century*.

4. *Greenfield Daily Reporter*, 12 October 1936, and Williams and Williams, *A History of Hancock County, Indiana, in the Twentieth Century*.

5. Williams and Williams, *A History of Hancock County, Indiana, in the Twentieth Century*; *Greenfield Daily Reporter*, 12 October 1936; and "Memorandum to the Director" from E. A. Tamm, 25 May 1937.

6. Williams and Williams, *A History of Hancock County, Indiana, in the Twentieth Century*; undated letter from Joyce Miller, niece of Mr. and Mrs. Ridlen, on Lottie's first name and the family legacy of her having hit the gang with her purse as well as her other actions, as well as Edgar having been hit by a bullet.

7. *Greenfield Daily Reporter*, Evening Edition, 12 October 1936. The coverage was probably also in their regular edition that day, as various reports appeared in both the daily and evening editions that week.

8. Ibid.

9. Ibid.

10. Ibid.

11. Ibid.

12. Ibid.

13. Ibid.

14. Ibid.

15. Ibid.

16. Undated clipping, probably from the *Greenfield Daily Reporter*, 12 October 1936.

17. Ibid.

18. Ibid.

19. Ibid.

20. UP article from Indianapolis as printed in the *Greenfield Daily Reporter*, 12 October 1936.

21. UP article from Indianapolis as printed in the *Greenfield Daily Reporter*, Evening Edition, 13 October 1936.

22. Ibid.

23. Ibid.

24. UP article from Indianapolis as printed in the *Greenfield Daily Reporter*, Evening Edition, 13 October 1936.

25. UP article from Detroit, Michigan, as printed in the *Greenfield Daily Reporter*, Evening Edition, 14 October 1936.

26. Ibid.

27. *Shelbyville Democrat*, 15 October 1937. Also see UP article from Indianapolis, printed in the *Greenfield Daily Reporter*, Evening Edition, 15 October 1936.

28. UP article from Indianapolis, as printed in the *Greenfield Daily Reporter*, Evening Edition, 15 October 1936.

29. UP article from Linden, New Jersey, as printed in the *Greenfield Daily Reporter*, Evening Edition, 15 October 1936.

30. Ibid.

31. UP article from Indianapolis, Indiana, as printed in the *Greenfield Daily Reporter*, Evening Edition, 16 October 1936.

32. Ibid.

33. *Greenfield Daily Reporter*, 15 October 1936.

34. Burrough, *Public Enemies: America's Greatest Crime Wave and the Birth of the FBI, 1933–1934.*

35. Irving Leibowitz, *My Indiana*.

36. Ibid.

37. Ibid. And see Burrough, *Public Enemies: America's Greatest Crime Wave and the Birth of the FBI, 1933–1934,* on Leach's continued questioning of the FBI.

7

THE FULL FORCE OF THE FEDERAL GOVERNMENT SEEKS THE GANG, WHILE THE GANG SEEKS YET MORE LUCRE

While the members of the Brady Gang had been incarcerated in Greenfield, Indiana, the Federal Bureau of Investigation had investigated previous criminal activities on the part of the gang. The FBI sought evidence of additional federal crimes for which the men might be prosecuted. On October 13, 1937, their case prepared, the FBI filed a complaint against Brady, Dalhover, and Shaffer before the United States Commissioner in Cleveland, Ohio. The three desperadoes were charged with the interstate transportation of stolen property (jewelry valued in excess of $5,000) from Lima, Ohio, to Chicago, Illinois, on April 27, 1936. The charge reflected the fact that transporting the stolen property across state lines made it a case within the federal jurisdiction, and the FBI thereafter pursued the Brady Gang to the very end of its existence. However, although the gang had already been apprehended, it had not long remained in custody, and the FBI would not have an easy job in seeing the men apprehended again, be they federal fugitives now or not.

After their escape in Indiana—authorities eventually learned, while roadblocks were set up throughout the region—the Brady Gang of Three traveled back to Ohio. They broke into a house in Gallipolis, a small city along the Ohio River in the southeastern part of the state, and stole blankets and clothing. They then moved on to Wheeling, West Virginia. They purportedly debated robbing a jewelry store there, but decided that they were "too hot" to make the attempt and risk the exposure, so they moved on, this time to Baltimore, Maryland. Their eastward progression was undertaken while police from several states were looking for them on charges ranging from robbery to murder. In addition, the FBI had formed a special squad to search for the Brady Gang, now for charges under both the National Stolen Property Act and the National Motor Vehicle Theft Act. The FBI would later add bank robbery to the list of federal charges.[1]

As described by the FBI in early 1937, "These men have been armed with submachine guns, revolvers, shot guns, and high-powered rifles during the robberies committed by them, and are desperate characters who have not hesitated to shoot their way out of impending difficulty."[2]

Posters of the gang featuring their mug shots—front and side shots—were sent out. The aliases the men were known to go by were included. For Al Brady, the aliases of J. A. Barton, James Barton, John A. Barton, Earl Gentry, James Reid (a name which appeared as the primary one on one "information wanted" sheet for Brady), Joe Reid, Al Borden, Elmer Borden, and James A. Reed were listed, as was a birth date of October 25, 1910, an age of 26, and a birthplace of "Indiana," no town indicated. Rhuel James Dalhover was identified as having aliases of James Williams, James Miller, Jack King, Ted Stewart, Albert Goins, and James Dalhover. His birth date was indicated as being August 24, 1906, his age as 30, and his birthplace as Madison, Indiana. Clarence Lee Shaffer Jr. was identified as having the aliases of Lee Jackson, Clarence Lee Shaffer, and Al C. Layton. His birthplace was noted as Indianapolis, Indiana, and his age as 20. The $1,500 reward was noted, and police stations and prosecuting officers posted the flyers or wanted posters. Various wanted sheets were produced over the course of about one year.[3]

The wanted notice sent out by John Edgar Hoover, Director of the Federal Bureau of Investigation, in June 1937, specified that $500 would be paid for information pertaining to each of the men, as of June 15, 1937. The rewards had been issued by Homer Cummings, Attorney General of the United States. The notice stated, "The Brady Gang, famed throughout the country as one of the most notorious in the nation, are recorded by the Federal Bureau of Investigation accordingly!" Hoover supplied any distinguishing characteristics of the men, including height, weight, hair and eye color, and complexion. Information could be "communicated in person, or by telephone, or by telegraph collect to the undersigned, or to the nearest office" of the FBI. The undersigned was J. Edgar Hoover, although he used his full first name. Officials and employees of the FBI were not eligible for the award monies. Fingerprints of the three felons were circulated along with their photographs and descriptions.[4] Before the above posters went out, various other bulletins had been circulated and various forces marshaled in the search.

The search continued, as did the Brady Gang's crime spree. The press in Logansport, Indiana, located in north-central Indiana, printed a column in mid-July 1937—possibly originally published somewhat earlier—that informed readers not only of some of the worst deeds of the gang, but also what authorities wanted to see happen to the fugitive men. Their header ran: "Police Hope to Oblige Brady With Exact Replica of John Dillinger's Death." The subtitle read, "Indiana Gangster Who Seeks to Duplicate Dillinger's Career in Banditry Can Count on Cooperation of Police in Making the Ending the Same."[5] Dillinger's end, of course, was death.

According to the article, which went over the wire and was printed in numerous U.S. cities, Brady sought to emulate Dillinger in his career, and had stated in the past that—in a slight variation of other statements—that he would "make Dillinger look like a hick." The news article then noted the similarities of the two men: that both had been Indianan farm hands, both had ended up in the state reformatory while young for theft—Brady for automobile theft and Dillinger for breaking into a store. Brady had formed a gang in the pool halls of Indianapolis, and then, according to the article, started on his quest to emulate John Dillinger and his life in crime. Both gangsters eventually engaged in bank and jewelry store robberies. They both staged robberies in Lima, Ohio. After that, Dillinger had been "liberated from jail when his thugs cold-bloodedly killed Sheriff Jess Barbar." The Brady Gang had robbed a jewelry store there with one of his men (identified under the name Elmer Martin in the article—but clearly Charles Geiseking) shot in the leg, which led to the shootout at the doctor's home and to the Brady Gang's killing of Sergeant Richard Rivers. Then, both guilty of killing at least one lawmen, the thugs had both fled, and the Brady Gang now, "like Dillinger, . . . felt the desperation of the electric chair."[6]

By the time Brady was arrested in Chicago, the press stated, it appeared that the "three month attempt to emulate Dillinger was washed up." However, the Brady Gang staged an escape such as Dillinger's by clubbing Sheriff Clarence Watson in an unguarded moment into unconsciousness, then shooting at bystanders and stealing a bystander's car. Then, "despite the most energetic man hunt since Dillinger, the trio escaped."[7]

Time magazine covered the trio and quoted the captain of the Indiana State Police. The magazine quoted Captain Matt Leach as stating, "Because of their viciousness and the way they operate, the Brady mob is going to make Dillinger look like a neophyte." The FBI, in May 1937—in an interoffice memorandum to the Director J. Edgar Hoover—stated, "The statement that the exploits of this gang would rival those of John Dillinger is attributable to Brady."[8]

Meanwhile, as the manhunt continued, although the authorities as yet did not know it, nor would they for some time, Al Brady, Clarence Shaffer, and James Dalhover holed up in Baltimore, arriving there by mid-October. They considered their options, and decided to stay in Baltimore and to make their lives in their new home-city quiet, peaceful ones, and to confine any criminal activity to distant locations, thus lessening the chances of their being traced to Baltimore. But, they still needed money. They robbed several grocery stores in Maryland—in places fairly distant from Baltimore—to acquire money to finance yet more distant criminal heists. Brady sought to acquire a bar or nightclub soon after they arrived.[9]

The Brady Gang members took on new identities. Al Brady became Edward Maxwell. James Dalhover became Herbert Schwartz. Clarence Shaffer became George Riley. They ate in local restaurants or diners, and in October met eighteen-year-old Minnie Raimondo in a diner, where she was working as a waitress. Under his assumed name, Shaffer told her that he was a cabinetmaker from Bangor, Maine. Exactly why he chose Bangor is unknown, but the choice would have lasting repercussions for him and his cohorts in crime. Shaffer or Riley also told the young woman that his two friends, Brady and Dalhover, aka Maxwell and Schwartz, owned a furniture factory in Maine. He said that they earned a good income from the furniture business, but that they had to go to Maine every few weeks to keep an eye on their business.[10]

Shaffer started to date Minnie Raimondo. After a short time, she invited him to her family home for an Italian dinner. She also invited his two friends to come along. Minnie had an older sister, Mary, who was twenty years old. Dalhover and Mary hit it off, and they too began dating. They had a third sister, Josephine. The dark-haired, heavy-set curvy sisters bore a strong resemblance to one another. After only a few weeks, both couples discussed getting married. (Dalhover, however, was perhaps still married to his first wife, with whom he had two young children.[11])

First, however, the gangsters decided that they needed more money. They decided to rob a bank in Indiana, and started looking for a new car to use for the robbery.

In early to mid-November 1936, the three fugitives located a Buick sedan they decided would be right for their purposes and followed it and the man driving it to the outskirts of Baltimore. They held up the man, and made him and his female companion exit the car. They then stole the vehicle and stored it in a rented garage, much as they seemingly had done previously with another stolen automobile, until they had their plans set. They also purchased two long-range rifles and ammunition.[12] They were prepared for a police battle, should it come to that.

On November 22, 1936, Brady, Shaffer, and Dalhover retrieved the stolen Buick and drove to North Madison, Indiana. They drove around the area some, and having decided that they would rob the State Bank of North Madison, they stole a set of Indiana license plates to reduce their odds of being noticed and traced. On November 23, in the early afternoon, Brady and Dalhover entered the bank. They left Shaffer in the driver's seat of their stolen getaway car. They held up the bank at gunpoint, and secured about $1,630. They made a clean escape, and returned to Baltimore. However, after the heist, witnesses identified from photographs the two bank robbers as Alfred Brady and James Dalhover. Shaffer had been in the car, and apparently remained unseen.[13]

The North Madison bank was a Federal Deposit Insurance Corporation bank, the new designation and its protections being recent creations of the Roosevelt Administration. Robbing an FDIC bank was a federal offense, so the gang now had another strike against them.[14]

Back in Baltimore, the discussions of marriage resumed, and on November 28, the four decided that they would indeed go ahead with the marriages. Shaffer and Minnie, and Dalhover and Mary, had a double ceremony performed on November 30, 1936, in Elkton, Maryland. Al Brady and Josephine Raimondo, Minnie and Mary's sister, served as witnesses. Brady purportedly made advances to Josephine, but, although she may have spent some time with him, she apparently had no long-term interest in Brady.[15]

After the double wedding, Shaffer and Dalhover moved into the Raimondo house in Baltimore with their new wives and family. Soon thereafter, however, determining the house was too small for them all, the newlyweds rented a house together at 3632 Roberts Place in Baltimore. Dalhover and Shaffer built a workshop in the basement, and just about every day Brady would come over and the three men would disappear into the workshop. When the men were not in the shop, they kept it locked. Indeed, they probably locked the door when they were inside it, too, as it was later discovered that the gang was working on their guns, plus making magazines and extra shot clips.[16]

Of course, money is something the Brady Gang continued to want or need more of, so they decided to rob another bank. Leaving their new domestic arrangements, Dalhover and Shaffer with Brady drove to Marietta, Ohio, on December 15, 1936. They spent the night in a tourist camp, then drove on to Carthage, Indiana, the following day. They stole a set of new Indiana plates from a car in Richmond, Indiana, although extant FBI records state that the plates on the car they used were the same as those used in the North Madison heist. The day after they stole the new plates, December 17, 1936, they robbed the State Bank of Carthage, another FDIC bank, which thereby created yet another federal offense against the gang. The gang stole approximately $2,154 plus some valuable silverware. During the robbery the thugs forced the customers and employees to lie on the floor, face down, and "compelled the cashier to accompany one of the bandits into the vault under threat of death if he did not comply." This was a statement from the FBI, and the FBI was not amused.[17]

The latest heist, the Indiana press would report, ended the Brady Gang's first year of emulating Dillinger's gang. Although neither the press nor the FBI knew it at the time, the Brady Gang returned to Baltimore after the robbery, and continued their outwardly peaceful lives, Dalhover and Shaffer telling their wives when they went off on their various robberies that they were going to Maine to check on their business there. However, after the gang had left the scene of its most recent crime, once again witnesses identified two of the three robbers as being members of the Brady Gang.[18]

Then, with the new year came new crimes, the first known one being in Ohio. On February 26, 1937, the gang purportedly robbed the Citizens State Bank of Greenville, in Greenville, Ohio. However, according to one report there were four robbers, although this may have been an error. The men who robbed the bank that February day did so unmasked and carrying a machine gun. They stole $8,000 and a .30 caliber Krag rifle. After the robbery, witnesses identified Shaffer as being the driver of the getaway car, Brady as being the person who physically carried the loot out of the bank, and Dalhover was tentatively identified as being the robber who had carried the machine gun. The fourth person was not further mentioned in FBI case notes, but in a robbery under investigation in May 1937, the gang again seemingly had a fourth person working with them. The Greenville robbery does not appear in subsequent FBI postings, it may be that another group was involved, or that they simply made no progress in solving the case.[19]

Later in April 1937, the gang decided it was time to pull another heist. They retrieved the stolen Buick on April 26, and left Baltimore for Farmland, Indiana. They drove the roads as was their habit, then in the early afternoon of April 27, held up the Farmland branch of the Peoples Loan and Trust Company, headquartered in Winchester, Indiana. They robbed the FDIC Farmland bank of some of $2,600 or $1,427, and then headed back to Baltimore via Ohio. Contemporary case notes mentioned there being a fourth person involved in the robbery, and that both Brady and Dalhover had been identified as being inside the bank during the holdup with two unknown persons waiting outside in the car, an Oldsmobile sedan, with machine guns. The car had Indiana plates, number 340756. Once again, the gang seemingly had a fourth person with them. Perhaps, after losing Geiseking to the American justice system, the gang added a temporary fourth person to aid them, much as they had apparently done on at least one of their robberies previously.[20]

Before their latest robbery, the gang had gone in search of a few things: new license plates and a machine gun. They had driven to Chicago in early April to try to purchase a machine gun from a sporting goods store there, which they had heard might be able to get one for them. This did not transpire however, but on the way back to Baltimore, in Ohio, they had been able to steal new plates from a Cincinnati suburb. They had the new 1937 plates for the Farmland bank robbery, and soon thereafter stole two machine guns.[21]

They found one machine gun on their return trip from the Farmland bank robbery. As they passed through Ohio, in Moscow they stole a .30 caliber machine gun from an American Legion monument. They repaired the formerly displayed gun, determined that it worked and that they wanted another one, and about a week later they stole another .30 machine gun from the municipal American Legion monument in Felicity, Ohio. The two new machines guns now in hand, the mobsters went home to Baltimore.[22]

After the latest holdup, the Brady Gang decided they needed a new car, and to get rid of an older one: the Chevrolet they had earlier escaped jail in, in Greenfield, Indiana, and had driven to Baltimore. To this end, on May 11, 1937, they drove the Chevrolet to Bellefontaine, Ohio. The next day, May 12, they spotted two young women in a new model Ford sedan. The drove up alongside the young women, pulled out a gun, and stole their car. They then took both cars to Hamilton, Ohio, and burned the Chevy there. Trying to avoid any ties to their adopted home-city, before setting the Chevrolet on fire they removed a tire they had purchased in Baltimore from it.[23] With a newly stolen car at their disposal, it was only a matter of time before they decided to pull another bank job. When they did, it would result in tragedy.

NOTES

1. "The Brady Gang," *FBI History: Famous Cases*, FBI; and see Indianapolis Metropolitan Police Department reports on Sergeant Richard Rivers.

2. "Memorandum to the Director," FBI, 25 May 1937.

3. As reproduced in *BDN*, 14 October 1937, and as reproduced in the FBI file at the National Archives at College Park, Maryland.

4. Letter of Notice from John Edgar Hoover, c. June 15, 1937. Reprinted in *BDC*, 12 October 1937. Wanted "posters" also found with FBI materials and online sites.

5. Indiana Wire Service, Logansport, and *BDN*, 18–19 July 1937.

6. Ibid.

7. Ibid.

8. Quotes from *Time*, 7 June 1937, and from the FBI, "Memorandum to the Director," 25 May 1937, from E. A. Tamm.

9. "The Brady Gang," *FBI History: Famous Cases*, FBI.

10. "The Brady Gang," *FBI History: Famous Cases*, FBI; and Circuit of Appeals, Seventh Circuit, United States v. Dalhover, 96 F.2d 355 (7th cir. 1938), 16 April 1938. Rehearing Denied May 18, 1938.

11. Ibid. Also see *Baltimore Sun* and *Baltimore News-Post*, 9 August–20 October 1937.

12. "The Brady Gang," *FBI History: Famous Cases*, Federal Bureau of Investigation; and related FBI documents.

13. "Memorandum to the Director," 25 May 1937, from E. A. Tamm, FBI; and "The Brady Gang," FBI *History: Famous Cases*, FBI.

14. "Memorandum to the Director," 25 May 1937, from E. A. Tamm, FBI.

15. "The Brady Gang," *FBI History: Famous Cases*, FBI; and *Baltimore Sun* and *Baltimore News-Post*, 9 August–20 October 1937.

16. Ibid.

17. "Memorandum to the Director," 25 May 1937, from E. A. Tamm, FBI; and "The Brady Gang," *FBI History: Famous Cases*, FBI. And see Indiana Wire Service, Logansport, 18–19 July 1937.

18. Ibid.

19. "Memorandum to the Director," 25 May 1937, from E. A. Tamm, FBI.

20. Ibid. Also see "The Brady Gang," *FBI History: Famous Cases*, FBI

21. Ibid.

22. Ibid.

23. "The Brady Gang," *FBI History: Famous Cases*, FBI 2014 posted website, has the car being taken from two young women, while the "Memorandum for the Director" 25 May 1937, from E. A. Tamm, FBI, stated that the car was stolen at gunpoint from a man. Perhaps he owned the car and friends or relatives were in it at the time of theft. And see Indiana Wire Service, Logansport, 18–19 July 1937, on the car description.

8

OFFICERS DOWN

A Fatal Decision and Another Fatal Shooting

By May 1937, the Brady Gang's money was running low. Still hiding out in Baltimore, the gang continued to look west to steal their way through life. They decided to rob another bank, perhaps two. The three men left Baltimore on May 23, 1937, and headed first to Illinois. They drove the newly stolen Ford, it seems, the getaway car later being described as a "maroon-colored sedan," and planned to rob a bank in Sheldon, Illinois. However, once they arrived at their destination they discovered that the bank had gone out of business—as many did during the Great Depression.[1]

The men then drove on to Goodland, Indiana, and "ran the roads" there for a time, scoping out their next hit and the area. They decided to rob the Goodland Stateland Bank, but first returned to Illinois and stayed in a tourist camp there for a day or two.[2]

Returning to Goodland in northwestern Indiana, in Newton County, about ten miles from Brady's native town of Kentland, on May 25, 1937, they robbed their newest target of about $2,688. The bank was insured by the Federal Deposit Insurance Corporation, as were many at this time, including the most recent targets of the Brady Gang. Clarence Lee Shaffer stayed behind in the car, at the wheel, while the other two entered the bank. Alfred James Brady and Rhuel James Dalhover reportedly held a female clerk and the bank director, Lyle Constable, at gunpoint for fifteen minutes while they looted the bank. The thieves had to wait fifteen minutes for a time lock to open the vault. The wait did not appear to concern them. Dalhover even took the time to send what was thought to be a greeting to an acquaintance, telling bank director Constable to "Say hello to Winns for me," in his hometown of Madison, where Constable had also grown up. Another report had a more formal exchange or statement: "If you see a state detective named Winn, give him my regards." According to the article, both James Dalhover and State Police Detective Donald Winn were from Madison.[3]

The heist itself seemed to have gone "well enough" for the gang—no one was killed and they got out of town safely, even taking a green, steel, filing case or cabinet with them. They drove east and north from Goodland. But, about fifteen miles outside of Goodland, on State Road 16 about two-and-one-half miles west of Royal Center, they saw a state police car about a half-mile in front of them. Closing the distance, at about one-quarter of a mile away, they decided to turn back. They switched directions in the road and headed back toward Goodland. The police car, responding to a call for help in the chase, spotted the car, and after pursuing the vehicle for some time, shots being exchanged during the pursuit, lost sight of the gang. The gang turned in toward a rural church at the first crossroads they came to. They hid their car behind the church, Caley's Church, and the three men exited the vehicle. Brady took one of the machine guns with him, and the other two grabbed rifles, Dalhover taking a thirty-forty Krag rifle and passing Shaffer a thirty-o-six rifle. They awaited the troopers.[4]

A few moments later, the Indiana State Police car drove up to the intersection—known as Caley's Crossing. State trooper Paul V. Minneman was driving the vehicle. He opened his car door and leaned out slightly, first looking for a certain landmark, and then to trying to determine from tire tracks which way the gang's car had gone. The officers did not know the bandits had hidden behind the church. The Brady Gang opened fire and fatally wounded Minneman, who fell out of the car after being shot. (According to one source, Minneman—age thirty-three and on the job for just over one-and-one-half years—was shot more than twenty times.) The vehicle continued forward driverless until it struck the church.[5]

The Brady Gang also seriously wounded Deputy Sheriff Elmer Craig of Cass County, Indiana, who staggered out of the police vehicle, while the car was still moving forward, "his shotgun clattering from his hands as three bullets found him," reported the Indiana press. According to subsequent legal records, Craig had dropped a shotgun he had been holding, fell, then got back up and ran to a fencerow at the northeasterly corner of the church. He fell again, and Al Brady came over to him, and at gunpoint took away the officer's revolver. Craig heard other gunfire erupt as he lay on the ground, he would later report. According to one report, he also heard one of the gangster's say, "Well, we got one of them. What about the other?" Conjecture was that they thought Craig had died when he passed out. Unknown to the gangsters, a farmer witnessed much of the event, and would later testify that the shooting when the police arrived on the scene was, it seems, so extensive that one "could not distinguish any number of shots at all."[6]

After the initial shooting of both officers, Brady had returned to the gang's car, thrown his machine gun into the sedan, picked up a rifle, and then went around the church while Dalhover and Shaffer had backed their vehicle into the roadway and drove to where Minneman had fallen. Dalhover exited the car, took Minneman's gun from its holster, and Brady then came back from where Craig lay wounded, picked up Craig's shotgun where he had dropped it, then removed Minneman's belt and holster from his body. Dalhover stole a first aid kit from the state vehicle, thinking that it contained shells. The three gangsters then fled back to Baltimore.[7]

Minneman and Craig were taken to a hospital at Logansport, Indiana, Minneman in critical condition. In particular, he had a severe hemorrhage from a chest wound. He was given numerous blood transfusions but to no avail. Doctors performed emergency surgery, and discovered that the lower portion of his lung had been shot away and that his bowels had been perforated in two places. While he lay in his hospital bed, Minneman stated of the gang, "They sure threw the lead into me. Of course, we [are] officers, we expect that, but never did I think they would shoot me after I was down and kick me." Minneman died two days after the ambush, seemingly with at least six bullets still lodged in his body. It was just before Minneman died that the Indiana press published its article about Brady trying to emulate Dillinger.[8]

As stated, purportedly one of the gangsters, after the thugs had stolen the officers' weapons, went over to Craig, stood above the wounded smart and asked, "Should I finish this guy, too?" The answer was, likely from Brady, "No, come on. Let's get out of here!" The mobsters did, however, take the time to take the policeman's revolver and the car's medical kit. They also stole the deputy sheriff's gun out of his hand. They then decided to remove the seemingly dead state trooper's holster and belt, and the handcuffs from his back pocket. Freshly supplied with more munitions, they drove back to Baltimore.[9] The press heard no more of the gang until August 7, 1937, when the gang had its next shootout with police in Baltimore.

The Indiana press, however, vociferously damned the Brady Gang while Minneman lay on his deathbed. In May 1937, while the FBI was making internal reports regarding the case, the *Kokomo Tribune*, of Kokomo, Indiana, wrote that the trail had gone "COLD" in bold headlines, while the "OFFICER SHOT BY GANGSTERS BATTLES DEATH." Some three hundred "Special Deputies" with state police (over 130 of them) from three states were guarding the roads, vowing to "get [the] killers," the headlines proclaimed. "G-men joined local officers in the search for a bandit gang whose leader termed the notorious John Dillinger 'a piker,'" while "State Policeman Paul Minneman hovered precariously between life and death," according to the paper. Both officers and volunteers were searching the roads, using automobiles, airplanes, and radios the day after the Goodland Bank robbery. The "G-men entered the search on the basis of a Cleveland, O. warrant charging Brady, the gang leader, with interstate transportation of stolen property." Of course, the FBI had already been involved in the case, even if its involvement changed over time. State police from Indiana, Ohio, and Illinois sought the gang, and Indiana's State Police Captain Matt Leach, meanwhile, had sworn, "We'll get that gang if we have to follow them to the end of the earth." The newspaper printed his statement under the subtitle of "Leach Vows Vengeance." Every county sheriff's office in Indiana was "on the alert," according to Leach, and, in one region, members of the American Legion had joined the search.[10] Everyone in the search had been instructed to be armed. The Brady Gang was a dangerous gang.

Officer Craig was expected to recover although he remained hospitalized. In mid-1937, Indiana State Police continued to scour the state for any sign of the gang, using methods developed during the hunt for Dillinger. According to the press in July 1937, the police were determined "to oblige Al Brady in his efforts to parallel John Dillinger's career. They want to make certain that even the endings are the same."

Accompanying the July article were photographs of Al Brady and his consort Margaret. Al Brady was photographed in suit and tie, with his head slightly downward and his eyes looking directly at the camera. His thin lips were stern, his distinctive ears protruding somewhat more than normal from his skull. Margaret was captured on film wearing a small hat perched jauntily on her head, seemingly wearing a coat, and looking to one side with a frown on her face. The photographs may have been taken on the day of their arrest months earlier, and they would reappear in later press coverage.[11]

One regional paper, published on the evening of the same day as the robbery, had stated in an Associated Press article that both Matt Leach of the State Police and Sheriff Harry Hufty of Newton County, where the robbery occurred, were already convinced that the robbery was the work of the Brady Gang. The Associated Press identified the getaway car as having been a maroon Ford sedan with Indiana license plates 340-756, "The same used in the holdup of the Far[m]land State Bank on April 27, in which Alfred Brady and his aid, James Dalhover, were identified."[12]

The Federal Bureau of Investigation of course continued to work the Brady Gang cases as did state and local police. By late May 1937, bank employees had identified Al Brady as being the leader of the thugs who had robbed the Goodland State Bank. The other two thieves had not yet been identified, although authorities clearly believed that James Dalhover and Clarence Shaffer were involved.[13]

On May 25, 1937, an internal memo of the FBI directed to J. Edgar Hoover made the official position of law enforcement clear. According to the memorandum, "A net of police officers and Bureau Agents has been drawn around Central Indiana in an effort to apprehend this gang. It is believed that subsequent investigation will in all probability disclose that this gang has participated in other bank robberies in the middle west." The document had included the bank robberies in Goodland, North Madison, and Carthage, Indiana, as well as that in Farmland, Indiana.[14] Other robberies were clearly suspected to have been carried out by the gang.

Moreover, the Bureau had clearly determined that the Brady Gang simply had to be eliminated from the byways of America. According to the same May memorandum discussing the bank robberies, Brady had been the one to state that his gang's exploits would rival those of Dillinger. The Special Agent noted too, "These men have been armed with submachine guns, revolvers, shot guns, and high powered rifles during the robberies committed by them, and are desperate characters who have not hesitated to shoot their way out of impending difficulty."[15]

Just after the FBI May communication, the coroner's inquest into the death of Paul Minneman commenced on June 1, 1937. Held at Logansport, Indiana, the evening edition of the *Pharos Tribune* announced that the inquest, held by Dr. M. B. Stewart, Cass County coroner, "Parade[d A] Score of Witnesses at Minneman's Inquest: Two Identify Brady Gang." The two witnesses who identified were the Goodland bank director, Lyle Constable, and assistant cashier, Mrs. Leona L. Hamilton. They both related the events at the Goodland bank on the day of the robbery, and both identified Brady and Dalhover as being the bank robbers. Leona Hamilton added that it was to her that Dalhover had made the greeting to a third party, stating that he "requested" of her, "If you ever see Officer Winn of the state police give him my regards. I know him."[16]

"Prosecutor Norman Kiesling of Cass County, Sergeant Charles W. Biltz, Patrolman Loren Ayers, and Detective Wayne Timmons of the Indiana State Police," all "assisted" the local coroner "in questioning witnesses." A doctor at St. Joseph's hospital, where Minneman died following the shootout, and the doctor who had performed the autopsy both testified, relating their findings and the results of "x-ray pictures" and the postmortem.[17]

Charles Hicks, the rural witness to the shootings, testified also. An affidavit taken from Elmer Craig, wounded in the shootout with the gang, was likewise presented to the inquest as part of the testimony of record.[18]

Paul Minneman had been buried the day before the inquest. Members of the police from Indiana, Ohio, Michigan, and Illinois joined family and friends at the service. More than a hundred law enforcement officers assembled, along with hundreds of other people at a local church. Deputy Craig was still hospitalized. "Paul Minneman is in his grave, but is not forgotten," the local paper stated. "Nor will the serious crime that cost his life be forgotten by his fellow state policemen, for today they will take up the trail which they vow will end in the early elimination of the Brady Gang of murderers."[19] And so another call for vengeance went out.

On June 15, 1937, the Attorney General of the United States, Homer Cummings, issued a reward for information about the gang's whereabouts. An award of $1,500 would be given to anyone supplying information that led to the apprehension of the three fugitives. Information leading to the capture of any one of the three gangsters would be rewarded with $500.[20]

NOTES

1. "The Brady Gang," *FBI History: Famous Cases*, FBI; "Memorandum for the Director," 25 May 1937, from E. A. Tamm.

2. Ibid.

3. Circuit of Appeals, Seventh Circuit, *United States v. Dalhover*, 96 F.2d 355 (7th cir. 1938), 16 April 1938. Rehearing Denied 18 May 1938; "The Brady Gang," *FBI History: Famous Cases*. FBI, and press. First quote from *Kokomo [Indiana] Tribune*, 26 May 1937, second from *The Tipton [Indiana] Daily Tribune*, Evening Edition, 23 May 1937, and see *Pharos Tribune* [Logansport, Indiana], 25 May 1937, for more in-depth, coverage and statements.

4. Circuit of Appeals, Seventh Circuit, *United States v. Dalhover*, 96 F.2d 355 (7th cir. 1938), 16 April 1938. Rehearing Denied 18 May 1938; *Pharos Tribune* [Logansport, Indiana], 25 May 1937; "ODMP Remembers Trooper Paul Vincent Minneman," Officer Down Memorial Page, website, on the trooper being shot over twenty times; and see *NYT*, 13 October 1937, and other press from that week.

5. Ibid.

6. Ibid.

7. Circuit of Appeals, Seventh Circuit, *United States v. Dalhover*, 18 May 1938.

8. Quote from Circuit of Appeals, Seventh Circuit, *United States v. Dalhover*, 18 May 1938; also see Indiana Wire Service, Logansport.

9. "The Brady Gang," *FBI History: Famous Cases*, Federal Bureau of Investigation; *NYT*, from Chicago Press, 12 October 1937, printed October 13, 1937; Indiana Wire Service, Logansport, and *BDN*, 18–19 July 1937.

10. *Kokomo [Indiana] Tribune*, 26 May 1937.

11. Indiana Wire Service, Logansport, and *BDN*, 18–19 July 1937.

12. AP article as printed in *The Tipton [Indiana] Daily Tribune*, Evening Edition, 23 May 1937.

13. "Memorandum for the Director," 25 May 1937, from E. A. Tamm, FBI.

14. Ibid.

15. Ibid.

16. *Pharos Tribune* [Logansport, Indiana], 1 June 1937.

17. Ibid.

18. Ibid.

19. Ibid.

20. "The Brady Gang," *FBI History: Famous Cases* Federal Bureau of Investigation.

9

AND THE GANG SHOOTS ON

Another Shootout with Police, and the East Coast Sounds the Alert

Yet, in spite of all the force being brought to bear against them, perhaps feeling ever confident about their prospects, the Brady Gang purchased a few pleasure items in Baltimore. They bought a motorcycle and began visiting local taverns and roller skating rinks. Brady in particular discovered that he liked skating, and he had a pair of roller skates made specifically for him that he carried with him all the time. He had also decided that he liked taverns, and had purportedly purchased one and operated it for about a month. The gang also bought a motorboat and a motor made for a Packard automobile. They put the automobile motor in the boat, fixed the boat up in other ways, and used it for fishing trips and just for fun.[1]

Still, the gang purportedly could not get enough weapons to meet their appetites. According to one source, they once considered holding up a police department in Ohio, which they had heard had several machine guns. They only gave up the idea after actually driving to the town, and checking out the location and deciding the robbery would be too risky. Another time they supposedly talked about raiding an exhibit of guns at the FBI center in Washington, DC—although even if they had made the heist, the guns had been rendered unusable before being placed in the exhibit.[2]

But, once again they decided it was time to rob a bank. To that end, they loaded up their stolen Ford and a 1931 Buick which Brady had actually purchased, and drove to the outskirts of Baltimore to switch some clothing and weapons from the Buick to the Ford. However, a couple of officers from the Baltimore Police Department watched what the men were doing, and, becoming suspicious, approached the men to question them. The gang members then jumped into their two cars and tried to speed away. The Buick, however, was a 1931 model, not as fast as the new vehicles, and could not outrun the police. As the police started to overtake it, Brady and his cohorts opened fire, and a running, or driving, gunfight ensued. The gang disabled the squad car, and Brady and his men escaped after abandoning the Buick. The police found a .30 caliber rifle in the old car, and soon determined that the men who had engaged in gunfire with the police were members of the Brady Gang. The police found the revolver removed from Deputy Sheriff Elmer Craig of Cass County, Indiana, at Caley's Church, as well as Craig's shotgun and other munitions.[3]

The press once again exploded with coverage of the most recent events, this time bringing Baltimore into the spotlight. "POLICE, 3 MEN IN GUNFIGHT HERE" was the top headline in the *Baltimore News-Post* evening edition of Saturday, August 7, 1937. The paper reported that three men traveling in two cars "fought running machine-gun battle with the crew of a [police] radio car, finally escaping after scores of shots were fired, with one of their machines disabled and one man believed wounded." The men had been traveling along Hillen Road during the chase.[4]

"A passing truck was riddled with bullets" according to the paper, and during the battle "automatic pistols, police revolvers, and subma-chine guns were used." Police had run out of ammunition, but contin-ued to give pursuit until shots fired at their car's motor eventually "shot [their car] dead under them." According to the report, the two patrol-men, Joseph Herget and Fred Fleischmann, were traveling "leisurely" along the road, just preparing to turn around, "when they noticed a Ford coupe and a Buick sedan pull into a side road." The officers thought that the cars "looked suspicious," so they pulled over to investi-gate, and "were about 100 feet from the machines when three men jumped out with pistols and sub-machine guns, known as 'Tommy guns,' and started firing at the police car."[5]

The police drew their revolvers and returned fire, at which point the three men jumped back into their cars and started racing toward the county line. The cars exchanged fire, with one of the suspects using a machine gun. The pursued men turned onto another road, and the police continued to give chase, guns firing "intermittently." The man whose truck was "riddled with bullets" was featured on the front page, pointing in a photograph to the bullet holes in the cab of his truck, and empathizing, "They didn't get me because I'm short." He was about five feet tall, and he thought that the gunmen had taken deliberate aim at him. A number of bullets had struck the cab right over his head.[6]

Firing on the innocent bypasser aside, the gang continued to try to flee, until the Buick swerved off, a tire seemingly struck by police fire. The Ford stopped for the driver of the Buick, and he "staggered" toward the other car, got into it, and the men then continued their flight, "traveling south on the wrong side of the boulevard, still firing at police." It was at this juncture that "suddenly, a shot killed the motor of the police car." Initially, police jumped out and then used a truck as cover while they shot at the men. The police then commandeered a car to try to continue their pursuit, but to no avail, and the as yet unknown men got away.

According to police, shots from the men had shattered a headlight on their squad car, another bullet passed through the radiator, and others barely missed their heads. After they commandeered the car of the passing motorist, they continued to give chase, and the bandits fired through the glass of that car's windshield. Then, as one of the officers described it, "As we had no more ammunition, the driver of the commandeered car and ourselves jumped into the woods. The men then got into their car [they had gotten out temporarily to fire and perhaps rearrange themselves and their position] and drove southward. We saw no more of them." Both officers had had their hands cut by flying glass. According to another local newspaper, the *Baltimore Sun*, in the battle between the fugitives and the two patrolmen in "radio car No. 27," the pursued men had fired more than a hundred rounds from at least one pistol and a "pump gun." Both cars driven by the gunmen bore Maryland plates.[7]

The alarm had been raised, however, and reinforcements arrived and began to examine the abandoned Buick. Police had taken the license numbers of both vehicles, and soon found that the plates on the

Buick were registered as belonging with a Plymouth sedan. The plates on the escaped vehicle, which police identified as probably being a Ford coupe, had been issued to a Buick, to a man named Edward Maxwell.[8]

It took a few days, but eventually authorities determined just who was involved in the August 7 shootout in Baltimore. And, finding out their identities proved to be a rather circuitous route. But, the gang's cover was largely blown at this point, and the authorities soon discovered the marriages of Dalhover and Shaffer as well as where the three men had resided since their prison escape. By the time they did so, however, the men had fled once more.[9] They left the women behind, as well as many of their belongings, getting out of town as fast as possible.

Within a day of the shootout, police located the room Edward Maxwell had been living in. After the shootout, authorities traced the fugitives' abandoned car, and discovered that it had been purchased by one Edward Maxwell, the same person to whom the plates on the escaped car had been issued. They then found "Maxwell's" habitat. He had been living in a rented room on Beaumont Avenue in Govans, and an empty pistol box, police believed, linked him to the shootout, as did Maxwell's ownership of the Buick abandoned during the chase. On close examination, it turned out that the box had the same identification number as did a pistol found in the empty car. Not only was that pistol found in the car, but also two others and a shotgun.[10]

The owner of the house told the press that Maxwell had lived in the home since November, and had stayed there until that Saturday morning. He had given her to understand that he was a machinist, and clothing found in his room, police disclosed, did indicate that the man who had worn them worked around machinery. Police told the press that they had some leads, but that an arrest was not imminent. One of the leads, the *Baltimore Sun* reported on August 8, was believed to be the name of a woman who had recently been spending time with Maxwell. Police had purportedly removed some mail and a coat from the boarding house, as well as other evidence, which likely led them to her.[11]

Within two days of the shootout, the Baltimore Police Department (BPD) found Maxwell's boat. It was docked at a nearby shipyard. No doubt, the fact that its previous owner had also sold the abandoned car to Maxwell led police to the man, who in turn led them to the shipyard.

The men had purchased the boat there about a month earlier, and had visited the shipyard almost daily, according to the shipyard's director. The men had brought two young women with them on several occasions, and had said that they would like to buy another boat for sale at the yard, if the owner would come down on his asking price, $10,000. The press quoted the director or "executive" as stating of the men, "They always seemed to have plenty of money. They paid for everything right away, and always pulled out big rolls of money." The men had paid $250 for the boat they had purchased, and when asked what they would do with the large cruiser should they buy it, one of them had answered "Haul bananas."[12]

The men had put their boat in drydock the day before the shootout for recaulking. The boat was a v-bottom cruiser, and the men had modified it by replacing its engine with one from an automobile.[13]

Police also—likely both discoveries happened the same day—located a young woman who had spent some time with Maxwell after meeting him at an amusement park. They had gone out riding in the young man's automobile several times, and the "girl" said that "he had always been a perfect gentleman." The woman was a local Sunday-school teacher. She was shocked to find out that the man she knew as Eddie Maxwell had been in the shootout. He had told her that he was an auto mechanic and machinist—which of course, he really had been at some junctures in his life, and in a sense still was. The woman was believed not to have known anything about Maxwell's criminal activities, and indeed it was still early in the local investigation and police did not yet know the extent of that background. Police quickly cleared the teacher from any suspicion, kept her name out of the press, and purportedly gained new leads from her.[14]

The BPD did not yet know the true identities of the men they sought. The bulletins they put out on August 9 asked for people to be on the lookout for Edward Maxwell, Herb Schwartz, and one "Mickey"—the last described simply as being about seventeen years old. Only Edward Maxwell had anything like a complete description and that perhaps because of the young Sunday-school teacher who had identified him, and the people he rented from, and his having purchased the abandoned car.[15]

Police (and seemingly regular citizens) were warned to "use caution in apprehending these men, as they are heavily armed." Local authorities believed the trio to be "'big time' operators," of the underworld, having, as they had, assembled a large cache of weapons and ammunition as used in the shootout. It was posited that they might have been planning a large-scale robbery or holdup in the Baltimore area. Key to the future of the search, the local police had sent a fingerprint retrieved from the shaving box in Maxwell's room off to the "G-men" in Washington, and were circulating descriptions of the fugitives to nearby states and larger cities in the region. The FBI, moreover, were being asked not only to help with the fingerprint, but also to work with the BPD "in ferreting out the identities and whereabouts of the three men."[16]

The men were said to be posing as nightclub entertainers. Maxwell had posed as a tap dancer and roller skater. The men had been known to frequent amusement centers and entertaining at a hotel on North Broadway.[17]

The next few days revealed more clues, and by August 12 the men had been identified. The men had caused the women they left behind trouble, or, at least three of them had encountered trouble, even before police knew with certainty that they were dealing with the Brady Gang. The sisters Shaffer and Dalhover had married, Minnie and Mary Raimondo and sister—Josephine Economides—were taken into custody in Baltimore. The Associated Press reported on August 11 that Baltimore police had located the sisters and were holding them in custody due to "fears for their safety." Federal agents were questioning the three sisters. According to a local paper on August 12, their brother was also in custody and being questioned.[18] Yet until sometime late in the night of August 10 or in the early hours of August 11, the true identities of the fugitives were not known.

According to various accounts, a local detective lieutenant had been tracking the Brady Gang for over two months along with agents of the Federal Narcotic Bureau, without actually knowing the identity of the men. Detective Lieutenant Thomas P. O'Donnell had been trailing Edward Maxwell and had spoken to him by the entrance of a small "banking corporation," a few weeks before the shootout. The events were not reported in an especially clear manner, but it seems that local suspicion had arisen that the flashy Maxwell might be "a diamond smuggler or big-time dope runner." When the detective had spoken with Maxwell after following him into a small building, Maxwell asked him what he wanted, and the detective replied that he was searching for a vacant apartment. Local officers did not arrest the man then, as they hoped to catch his companions also, and thought waiting would be the best choice.[19]

Brady, as Maxwell, had given rise to suspicions by his actions in Baltimore. He had ordered some lavish clothing from local shops, including a rather elaborate belt with an inside compartment and zipper, part of which had to be sent from Rochester, New York. The detective had then consulted his captain, and the department had secured Federal support to trail Brady, but this came just a bit too late. A manufacturing jeweler had seen a posted picture of Brady a few weeks before in the local Federal Building containing the local Postal Service. He, a silversmith, had just made Maxwell a buckle, and it seemed to be for a fancy belt. He recognized the man the local authorities and the federal narcotics had been watching. He contacted the detective, who said, "I then went to the Federal Building, got one of the flyers, and took it to Captain Cooney, and reported that the silversmith had positively identified the picture of Brady as Maxwell, leader of the mob." Two hours later, the wives of Dalhover and Shaffer had identified Brady from the circular and the detective circular and from an "official detective circular."[20]

According to the *Baltimore Sun*, the women identified the two men they had eloped with to Elkton as Dalhover and Shaffer, and Edward Maxwell as Brady. They expressed surprise that the three men they had known under fake names were wanted for murder and robbery. Josephine Economides stated for the three of them, "They treated us swell, and were damned good guys."[21]

Discovering the assumed and then the true identities of the fugitives, police also were able to search locations the men had frequented. At a store where Dalhover and his brother-in-law had worked, police recovered slain Indiana State Police Officer Paul V. Minneman's belt. Gun parts as well as ammunition, gas bombs, and facemasks were also discovered at the store in burlap bags. The brother-in-law stated that he had known Brady as Eddie Maxwell and that the other two thugs he also knew through his sisters, under their assumed names, and that his sisters had taken some articles of theirs to his grandmother's house. The metal file cabinet stolen from the Goodland Bank was found at Shaffer's home, as was the first aid kit taken from Minneman's and Craig's cruiser.[22] If there had been doubts about Maxwell/Brady, those doubts were now over. As were those about the identities of his two cohorts.

According to the press in Baltimore, "Following a tip [that] the [men] had [had] a package delivered to a building in the business district here, police late Wednesday found a small arsenal of grenades and machine gun ammunition." This would seem to pertain to the store—or another location the gang used in Baltimore—not the family house on Roberts Place, and the "tip" may have actually been the testimony of one of the Raimondo siblings. Police had also found "the belt and holster of an Indiana State Trooper murdered last May by bank robbers," although they had not yet been identified as such. However, eventually these last two pieces of evidence would prove crucial to the fate of one of the gang members.[23]

Police had only realized late on August 10 or early on the 11th, that the Brady Gang had been using Baltimore as a hideout. The police began questioning the sisters married to Dalhover and Shaffer first, and then "the brides together with their sister . . . were ordered locked up Wednesday by Police Captain John A. Cooney and FBI agents began questioning them." The women stated of the gangsters that they thought the three men were machinists, and that the three were often away for three to four days at a time, but offered the women no explanations, or so it seemed at the time. Police also stated that the dates when the men were away from Baltimore corresponded with the dates of various crimes in Indiana for which the Brady Gang was wanted. Other states were not mentioned in the article, but were no doubt under consideration by police and FBI agents.[24]

By late on August 12, police also discovered what the press termed "a secret gun shop" in the basement of the house where Dalhover and Shaffer had lived with their two young brides, who upon their marriages, as far as they knew it, had become Ms. Minnie Riley and Mrs. Mary Schwartz. Their sister also apparently lived with them in their house on Roberts Place. The agents of the law "raided the home" after, it seems, warning people nearby that they had to leave quietly, that the house on Roberts Place was going to be raided. A child there at the time still remembered the incident in 2015. And he had later made law enforcement his career. In addition to the police warning, he recalled having gone up to one of the fugitives one day and having said, "My daddy wants to know what you are doing over there to make our lights flicker." His family would soon learn the answer to that question.[25]

As well as equipment used to convert rifles to submachine guns, and other evidence that the men had been making machine-gun clips at the home, police found a secret compartment under the front seat in the car the men had abandoned after their shootout with police. Within the compartment they discovered a "home-made machine gun, apparently the product of the machine shop," the press reported.[26]

Soon thereafter, on August 14, by which time the gang members' true identities had been discovered, police found silverware stolen by the Brady Gang. Around one hundred pieces of fine silverware was found in the house at Roberts Place, and it had been the silverware the men and their women were using on a daily basis for their meals. Police traced the silverware to one of the gang's bank holdups in Indiana, most likely the one in Carthage. The fine silverware—forks, spoons, general "knives" and butter-knives, and other ware—was "considerably out of keeping with the general furnishings" of the house, according to the local press. Police apparently discovered it or found it worth consideration, upon their second search of the premises. The police matched the silverware to a list of items stolen out of one of the robberies the men had committed while living in Baltimore.[27]

And, while they continued to investigate the gang, the Baltimore police commissioner also decided to rush putting in a new radio system that the force had been contemplating for some time. Among other things, the new system would place police two-way radios in all police vehicles, and the broadcasting range of the system would be broadened. Such improvements, the police thought, might have helped officers Herget and Fleischman in their pursuit of the Brady Gang earlier that month. It might have allowed them to call for aid in chasing and hopefully catching the Midwestern thugs. Local police were likewise given lessons on operating "riot guns"—which had greater penetration capabilities than other similar sized guns—for similar reasons. The police department already had one hundred of the guns in its arsenal, in storage, and would begin using them as well as beefing up other police arms and technology. Moreover, the two officers involved in the chase and shootout were to receive a commendation for their work in flushing out the gang.[28]

On August 11, as the *Baltimore News-Post* announced in bold headlines "LINK GUN GANG TO SLAYING HERE," the fugitives had been tentatively identified. That day, two Indiana State Police Detectives, Meredith Stewart and William Spannouth, came to Baltimore to help with the investigation. At the time, Indiana wanted the gang for "two murders, several shootings, and at least eight bank robberies." The local press stated that in the Midwest the gang was known as "the new Dillinger mob," giving the gang a slightly different moniker, and, now identified the three fugitives, as identified by BPD Detective Captain John A. Cooney as: "Alfred Brady, twenty-six, leader of the gang; Clarence Lee Shaffer, twenty-one but looking younger than his age, and James Dalhover, thirty." Another description included their heights and weights. Brady was five feet, seven inches tall, Dalhover was five feet, four-and-one-half inches, and Shaffer five feet, five inches. Shaffer weighed the least at 124 pounds. Brady was reported to weigh 160 pounds and had gray eyes, light brown hair, and a ruddy complexion. Dalhover weighed 134 pounds and had blue eyes and light brown hair. Shaffer had brown hair and gray eyes, plus a small scar on the back of his right hand.[29]

As the *Baltimore Sun* described the gang quite succinctly, "The Brady Gang, according to police records, specialized in bank and jewelry store holdups. Prison escapes and murder embellish the record." The *Sun* reiterated earlier police statements that Brady had confessed to the murder of the Indianapolis police sergeant while incarcerated, and then retracted his confession, and that he had admitted a number of trips in Ohio to rob jewelry stores. Moreover, the paper uncovered another heist: according to police sources, fingerprints retrieved from the scene of an Indianapolis theater held up the day after the trio escaped from a nearby jail in October 1936, linked the $6,000 robbery to the Brady Gang.[30]

Local readers might well have been concerned when they read that Indiana detectives had stated that the men were being sought for the murders of Richard Rivers and Paul Minneman, and that after shooting Minneman and his partner Elmer Craig, that the gangsters had stood over Craig while he played dead, and discussed whether they should make certain the lawmen were indeed dead and had then shot four more times into the prostrate Craig's body and some twelve or fourteen more times into Minneman. Lest readers have any doubts of the gang's innocence, the news reported that Minneman had lived long enough to identify his killers, naming Brady specifically as his killer, and Craig's testimony was also that the Brady Gang members were the murderers. Local authorities had turned over to the Indiana detectives a medicine kit found at Roberts Place—believed to be the metal one taken from Minneman's state police car—as well as a pearl-handled pistol found in the abandoned automobile after the August 7 shootout.[31]

One local paper also said, "At least one murder and half a dozen holdups and robberies in the Baltimore-Washington area were ascribed today [Wednesday, August 11] to the 'Brady Gang' of bandits, believed to have been the trio who staged a running gun duel with police on Loch Raven boulevard on Saturday."[32]

The evidence seemingly tying the gang with the local killing were news clippings related to the murder found in the house shared by two of the gang members and their wives. Police also recovered a note pad bearing the name of a printing company, whose president had been held up for his $650 payroll the previous week. Both the taxi driver and the merchant were named Goldstein, but were not related. So, too, were police investigating the possibility that the murderous trio was involved in the kidnapping and robbery of a local clothing merchant, Bernard Cohen, who had been carjacked by two men and had robbed of $700. Several other robberies were being investigated to determine if the Brady Gang might be responsible; especially ones in nearby Washington, where it was believed the fugitives had made frequent forays during the time they lived in Baltimore. In following days, police attempted to connect a gun found in the gang's hideout on Roberts Place, wrapped in flannel and concealed in a cedar chest, to the death of Charles Goldstein, who had been shot dead about two weeks previously, his body found next to his taxicab. "Two empty shells were still in its chamber," one source stated.[33] However, it does not seem that the gang was ultimately deemed responsible for the killing, or for any others in the Baltimore area.

With the identities of the men now believed known, local Magistrate Hugh H. Jones had, that same day, August 11, issued warrants for the arrest of Brady, Shaffer, and Dalhover, charging them with assault and attempted murder for the shootings at Patrolmen Joseph Herget and Fred Fleischmann.[34] The list of charges against the gang was only growing.

The authorities investigated every aspect that they could about the criminals' lives in Baltimore, including the types of things the men liked to do, their habits, and so forth, and another massive manhunt began, this one spearheaded by the Federal Bureau of Investigation. They discovered Brady's fondness for roller skating and compiled a list of every roller skating rink in the nation; FBI agents established contacts with their owners. Identification Orders or "wanted posters," previously widely distributed, were now sent out to every police department in the nation. In addition, the identification posters were sent out to every bank, filling station, and other businesses the FBI deemed possible sites for the gang to visit.[35]

Meanwhile the Raimondo sisters—Mrs. Mary [Dalhover] Schwartz, Miner [Shaffer] Riley, and Josephine Economides—and their brother Anthony remained in legal limbo for some time. Their younger brother, age thirteen, had also been questioned following raids conducted by twelve law enforcement agents at the Roberts Place residence. The sisters and their older brother were interviewed by local police and federal agents, their brother being the last of them brought into the case. Initially, police hinted that they were being held for their own protection, and, initially, the women had been technically at liberty until the men's true identities were known. The FBI agents conducted most of the interviewing once the case had unfolded, and according to the press had been demanding on the siblings, but the agents soon decided that they would not expect federal charges to be brought against the siblings. Josephine, moreover, stated that she been married, but that her husband had died about a year previously. She broke into tears while being questioned, was referred to as "miss" in some records, and she was docketed as "unmarried." With the assistance of Mrs. Riley, police had made raids not just on the home the sisters had shared, but also two other residences, not including, it seems, the place where Brady had lived nor where Anthony Raimondo lived.[36]

The sisters stated that they had been on the gangsters' boat with the men, fishing, as had their little brother on occasion, and authorities now expressed concern that the craft had enough power to outrun local law enforcement boats, and that the gang might have been planning to use the boat as a getaway vehicle should the need arise. At about the same time, on August 12, the police found a motorcycle owned by Brady at yet another Baltimore location used by the gang, equipped with saddlebags and "leather slings that apparently have been especially designed to hold firearms." That, too, might have been used to escape police or other law enforcement officers.[37]

On August 12, after close questioning of family members, the four siblings were arraigned before Baltimore Magistrate John A. Janetzke Jr. in the Eastern Police Court, on conspiracy charges. Only Anthony Raimondo (also known as Anthony Raymond) made a statement, and he simply said, "I only done it to protect the family." Raimondo had admitted that he had met with the gang numerous times and that the gang had asked him more than once about "large payrolls in the city." The gangsters had also asked him to procure machine guns for them, offering him $250 for each gun that he might be able to steal from the nearby One Hundred and Fourth Medical Regiment Armory. He insisted that he had not even responded to the machine-gun proposition. He also stated that the gangsters had asked him to check on the movements of a local pawnbroker reputed to carry large sums of money with him.[38]

In addition to Anthony Raimondo's statements, one of the sisters purportedly had taken four hundred quarters—stolen from an Indiana bank—and converted them into paper money at a Baltimore bank. The admissions of the brother, the alleged participation of at least one sister in essentially laundering stolen money, plus the discovery of the machine shop in the shared home at Roberts Place, the numerous absences of the gang while robberies and worse were being carried out by the gang in the Midwest with just the flimsy work excuses provided to— and they asserted believed by—the women,[39] all led to the authorities deciding that the family must have known something was not quite right with the men they had taken into the family. This, plus the belief that the quartet of siblings, or at least some of them, might have knowingly participated in illegal activities to some degree, led to the obstruction of justice charges.

The specific charges against the four siblings were that the women and their brother had "hidden ammunition and guns belonging to the gangsters." The magistrate ordered a $5,000 bail each "for action of the grand jury." Their mother visited the four briefly. The papers described her as an elderly Italian woman who spoke little English, and stated that, "all four children burst into tears and it was five minutes before officers were able to quiet them."[40]

On August 16, 1937, the three sisters and their brother "were presented . . . by the Grand Jury on charges of conspiracy to move and conceal bombs, grenades, machine guns, and other weapons and ammunition" owned by the Brady Gang. The weapons and ammunition had been seized in the various searches. Bail was fixed at $5,000 each, while authorities proceeded to draw indictments for them.[41]

The Indiana State Police officers decided to leave Maryland. They would leave for a few days, over the ensuing weekend, and not return unless something further developed in the Baltimore area. They were certain that the Brady Gang had fled the area. But, Officer Steward added, "There is always the possibility they may double back, but if they do the splendid Baltimore police force can handle them." The Indiana State Police, however, was not giving up on the pursuit. "It is the biggest case we have," the officer stated. "If it takes one man or fifty and the trail reaches to the far reaches of the continent or foreign continents, we are determined to get these killers."[42] The Indiana State Police would indeed not give up, nor would the FBI, and now the Maryland police were also involved in pursuing a case against the Brady Gang.

NOTES

1. "The Brady Gang," *FBI History: Famous Cases*, FBI; *Baltimore News-Post*, 15 October 1937.
2. "The Brady Gang," *FBI History: Famous Cases*, FBI.
3. Circuit of Appeals, Seventh Circuit, *United States v. Dalhover*, 18 May 1938; and "The Brady Gang," *FBI History: Famous Cases*, FBI.
4. Circuit of Appeals, Seventh Circuit, *United States v. Dalhover*, 18 May 1938.
5. *Baltimore News-Post*, 7 August 1937.
6. Ibid.
7. *Baltimore News-Post*, 7 August 1937; and *Baltimore Sun*, 7 and 8 October 1937.
8. *Baltimore News-Post*, 7 August 1937.
9. Circuit of Appeals, Seventh Circuit, *United States v. Dalhover*, 18 May 1938; and "The Brady Gang," *FBI History: Famous Cases*, FBI.
10. *Baltimore News-Post*, 9 August 1937; *Baltimore Sun*, 8 and 9 August 1937.

11. *Baltimore Sun,* 8 and 9 August 1937.

12. *Baltimore News-Post*, 9 August 1937.

13. Ibid.

14. Ibid.

15. Ibid.

16. Ibid.

17. Ibid.

18. *World Herald*, Omaha, AP article from Baltimore, MD, 11 August 1937, and *Baltimore News-Post,* 12 August 1937.

19. *Baltimore News-Post*, 12 August 1937; *Baltimore Sun*, 13 August 1937.

20. *Baltimore News-Post*, 12 August 1937.

21. *Baltimore Sun,* 11 August 1937.

22. Circuit of Appeals, Seventh Circuit, *United States v. Dalhover*, 18 May 1938; and "The Brady Gang," *FBI History: Famous Cases*, FBI.

23. *World Herald*, Omaha, AP article from Baltimore, MD, 11 August 1937.

24. Ibid.

25. *Baltimore News-Post,* 12 August 1937; and discussion with the police officer/child's nephew, March 2015. The decorated retired officer was still alive in 2015, but his health had recently taken a turn for the worse.

26. *Baltimore News-Post,* 12 August 1937.

27. *Baltimore News-Post,* 14 August 1937.

28. *Baltimore News-Post*, 13 and 14 August 1937; and *Baltimore Sun*, 14 August 1937.

29. *Baltimore News-Post*, 11 August 1937.

30. *Baltimore Sun,* 11 August 1937. Spellings of Detective Spannouth's name vary in different sources.

31. *Baltimore News-Post,* 11 August 1937.

32. Ibid.

33. *Baltimore News-Post,* 11 August 1937; details on gun and quote from *Baltimore Sun,* 14 August 1937.

34. *Baltimore News-Post,* 11 August 1937.

35. "The Brady Gang," *FBI History: Famous Cases*, FBI.

36. *Baltimore Sun,* 9 and 12 August 1937.

37. *Baltimore Sun*, 14 August 1937.

38. *Baltimore Sun*, 14 August 1937.

39. Ibid. And see previous editions of both the *Sun* and the *News-Post*.

40. *Baltimore Sun*, 14 August 1937.

41. *Baltimore News-Post,* 16 August 1937.

42. Quotes from *Baltimore Sun,* 14 August 1937.

10

ON THE ROAD AGAIN

Fleeing Maryland, the "Braga Squad" Heads North

Almost two months before the Baltimore shootout of August 7, on June 15, 1937, the Attorney General of the United States had issued a reward for information about the Brady Gang's whereabouts. An award of $1,500 would be given to anyone supplying information that led to the apprehension of the three fugitives, as stated previously, and information leading to the capture of any one of the three would be rewarded with $500. Now, with the latest chain of events, the Brady Gang had yet another state and another police force looking for them and—adding to what at least three states and the FBI had against them—the gangsters now had assault and attempted murder charges in Maryland standing.[1]

But the fugitives were not standing; they were fleeing. Brady and his gang were on the run. Following the shootout on the outskirts of Baltimore on August 7, the men had returned to their homes and packed up their clothes and ammunition and perhaps other supplies. They left the Ford used in the shootout in a garage, and placed their stuff in a Buick they had stolen sometime previously in Baltimore. They then fled the city—without their wives or girlfriends.[2]

Reports of possible sightings and stolen vehicles again appeared in the press. They were purportedly seen in Frederick; indeed two of them were reported as having been shot at by police before fleeing into the woods, after crashing their car into a stone wall. The men had bought gasoline at a local gas station without paying for it. Police were alerted to the car when a policeman on a motorcycle saw the car being driven too fast and recklessly, and started giving pursuit. By that time, the theft of gasoline had been telephoned into the police station. This all happened at about 2:00 a.m. By the time police thought they had the pair surrounded, it was about 5:00 a.m. Police believed that the two men were Brady and Dalhover. Police continued the search into the day, discovered that the plates on the car did not belong with that vehicle, and eventually posited that the men had secured a ride with another person into Baltimore. The stolen car in which the unknown men had been traveling was identified as belonging to a man who lived at Curtis Bay. Another man reported his car stolen about six hours after the Baltimore gun battle, and stated that he thought that when he rushed out of the tavern where he had stopped, that he saw one of the gangster's—Shaffer—at the wheel of his car. This avenue of pursuit led nowhere, but on August 17, the AP stated that three men who had fled authorities in Vincennes and then Lawrenceville, Illinois, were Brady, Shaffer, and Dalhover.[3]

As far as is known, however, from Maryland the gang drove north to Buffalo, New York, on August 8, and stayed in a rooming house in the city for about a week. They then headed south, to Nashville, Tennessee. They stayed there for probably just one night, in a tourist camp, then headed northwest to Milwaukee, Wisconsin. Low on money, they drove around for a bit looking for a bank to rob. On August 23, 1937, they held up the Peoples Exchange Bank of Thorp, Wisconsin. They robbed the bank of close to $7,000 and obtained another revolver.[4]

The bandits were eventually identified as members of the Brady Gang, and they had followed a procedure similar to those they had employed elsewhere. According to the *Milwaukee Journal*, "Two of the gang entered the bank and forced employees and three customers to lie on the floor while they rifled the vault of $7,000 in cash." A male cashier had identified pictures of Brady, Dalhover, and Shaffer from photographs as being the robbers of August 23. Unless Shaffer (or Dalhover, but it was more often Shaffer who had stayed behind in the car in the bigger heists) came into the bank at some point, it is uncertain how he was identified. The gang usually left someone in the getaway car so that they could make a quick escape.[5]

Thorp was a fairly small city in 1937. Police later reported that the robbery at Thorp on August 23 was the state's largest bank robbery of the year. They also stated that the gang must have thought Wisconsin Banks "easy pickings," yet apparently did not ascribe any other robberies to the gang.[6]

The gang stayed overnight in Wisconsin after robbing the Thorp bank. They then drove back to Buffalo, New York, where they stayed until September 3. They next moved on to Bridgeport, Connecticut.[7] In Bridgeport, the gunmen seemed to settle in for the long-run, perhaps choosing the city as it was known as a munitions manufacturing center, and it had housed several gangsters and thugs in the 1920s and 1930s.

The gang purchased an older model—1927—Studebaker in Connecticut, perhaps in order to acquire Connecticut plates as well as to make available another possible escape vehicle. Brady parked at least one of their cars in a local parking lot in Bridgeport, on John Street, paying storage for the space. The gang at some point seems to have switched the plates on the Studebaker, and to have kept a car parked on Congress Street while they stayed at their first rooming house in the city. At about the same time as the gang was purchasing the 1927 sedan and securing lodging, police representatives from Indiana, Ohio, Kentucky, and Michigan met to discuss establishing an interstate roadblock to try and catch the fugitives.[8]

Also while in Connecticut, the gang rented an apartment or suite of rooms, for at least a time, in more than one boarding house. Brady and Dalhover stayed at one of these locations separately at some point, the three perhaps splitting up their residences to avoid detection, just around the corner from the police headquarters in Bridgeport. They stayed in Bridgeport from early September 1937 until the second week of October 1937. Initially, according to the wife of a hotel manager in Bridgeport, Mrs. Florence McLeod, three men matching the descriptions of Brady, Dalhover, and Shaffer had come to her hotel with two women and requested three rooms—two doubles and one single. Because the group had little or no luggage, the request was at first denied, but then arrangements were made for the women to stay at the hotel, and the men went to rent rooms at a boarding house or two. They seem to have stayed in one rooming house for about a week then moved on to another one, and then to a third. The identity of the two women is unsubstantiated.[9]

However the identity of one woman who did spend time with the gangsters while they were in Connecticut is known. Brady found a young woman to socialize with while in Bridgeport. He spent time with twenty-year-old Alicia Frawley, whom he met while the gang was living in the city.[10]

Alicia Frawley was a young blond-haired woman who had a police record before she met up with the gang. Like the fugitives, she also had an alias: Alicia Hill. She had spent time at the State Farm for Women in East Lynne the year before the gang fled north, purportedly being picked up by authorities on the request of a female parole officer. Frawley had been doing some work for a photographer and "canvassing the East Side." Frawley, once released, secured work as a stenographer, a job she continued to hold while she passed time with the men, especially Al Brady.[11]

Brady met Frawley on Main Street in Bridgeport in early September, apparently while she was in the company of a male friend who already knew Brady. Brady introduced himself as Ed Mason. After the two met, Brady spent it seems at least some portion of most days with her. He introduced Dalhover to her as Charles Harris, and Shaffer as Frank Harris, the two posing as brothers. The three men said they were oil salesmen.[12]

Alicia Frawley lent Brady a typewriter that he took back to his rooming house. Later conjectures were that the men had used the typewriter to falsify automobile registrations and perhaps other documents. The men apparently liked to read detective magazines and the like, and even purportedly had an article about their own exploits.[13]

As in Baltimore, the gangsters established a lifestyle in Bridgeport in which they made female friends and frequented a number of nightclubs, bowling alleys, restaurants, and movie theaters. They bowled at a couple of different alleys, and ate at the major downtown eateries. They went to see movies on most days, Alicia Frawley often accompanying them. Alicia's mother met the three gangsters, and later said that they were "perfect gentlemen," and that she had harbored no suspicions about them. The trio and Alicia also had at least one other woman with them on some of their outings, an auburn-haired woman Brady had seemingly met with at some point. Alicia went out to eat with the gang numerous times, as well as to the movies and bowling.[14]

The thugs sometimes went out of town, and on one occasion brought their landlady, seemingly the one where they had first secured lodging, a silk pillowcase from New Hampshire. The pillowcase featured the image of "The Old Man of the Mountain" from the White Mountains. The men had told her that they were salesmen, in the hardware business (ironically, perhaps, the men sometimes called guns "hardware"), and told her that they had previously had business in the West. They said that they were on a vacation, and wanted to rent lodgings for a month, requesting a suite but settled on the two rooms she had available. They paid her $40 in advance. If they found the city agreeable, they might decide to stay longer. They had saved up their money for the past four years, they said, and were looking for a place to live in the East. Brady was known to the woman, a widow, as Edward Macy, and Dalhover and Shaffer as brothers Fred and Charles Harris. The proprietor of the Washington Avenue boarding house found the men to be quite agreeable, said that they had never given her any trouble, nor had they drank as far as she knew, and they were well-dressed, well-spoken, and polite with her. She also stated that the men went horseback riding fairly often. She stated the following month, "I never had more quiet or gentlemanly men in the house." Yet, she and the "gentlemen" would soon have a "misunderstanding" that would cause the men to move to another location. However, for about three weeks she rented the men a couple of rooms. [15]

Then, the widow decided to take a close look at the rooms she had rented. Shaffer apparently saw the way she was looking over their quarters and told her that she seemed like a "'suspicious' landlady," and, perhaps uncomfortable with the situation, she informed the gangsters—which they were, be they "gentlemanly" or not—that she would not hesitate to contact the police if she "became suspicious of their activities." Then, one night she heard pounding or knocking coming from the gang's quarters at about midnight. She went to their rooms and gave them a close look over. Only Brady and Dalhover were there. They said that they had not heard anything, and Dalhover added: "It seems to me that you are very suspicious. We dislike living where anyone would think ill of us." She replied that if she were suspicious of them, she would not try to deal with three men on her own, but rather she would contact the police about the situation. The next day, she came in to clean their rooms and discovered that they had moved out and taken everything with them except a hat. A few days later, Shaffer came back, took his hat, and left his key with her. "He said that he was very sorry to leave and wished me the best of health," she stated in October 1937.[16]

The owner of the Washington Avenue rooming house where the men stayed for about three weeks would also state in October that there had never been any inappropriate behavior in her house by the men. She stated more than once words to the effect that "they were well dressed and had a fine command of the English, never drank or gave me any trouble."[17]

But the men had continued to give trouble to the women and the family they had left behind in Baltimore. On August 17, Judge Eugene O'Dunne lowered the bail of all four Raimondo family members from $5,000 to $500 each for the sisters married to Dalhover and Shaffer; to $250 for the third sister, Josephine; and to $1,500 for their brother Anthony. The judge stated that Anthony was "dumb" for running afoul of the law once more after having spent some seventy-seven days in jail previously for a lottery violation. He should have known better than to get involved with gangsters after his previous troubles. Anthony Raimondo, however, asserted that he had no knowledge of who his brothers-in-law truly were. The two women who married into the gang asserted that their husbands had told them little about their work, just that they had to go to Bangor, Maine, every month to collect money from investments there. The judge decided that they were simply frightened when they found out that their husbands were gangsters, but also stated that the gang members might have "a half-dozen wives" in various locations. The men had just been using the Raimondo sisters, he stated, "for convenience."[18]

Josephine Economides raised her bail money first, on the same day it was lowered, and she was released, but not before the judge stated that she, too, was "'simple and dumb' in not telling police the truth about some gangster equipment she is alleged to have moved." If any further evidence against the four were to come to light, the judge stated, the various parties' bail could be increased, or new charges could be brought against them.[19]

It was not until October 6, 1937, that the four members of the Raimondo family were freed of legal charges: Minnie, Mary, Josephine and Anthony. The first two, the sisters who had married Shaffer and

Dalhover, continued to use the names they had taken at the time of their marriages.[20] Within a week, it would be much less of an issue for them, or at least her marriage would be for one of the sisters.

On October 6, Judge Eugene O'Dunne freed the four siblings from the charges, to be effective after Anthony Raimondo paid court costs of $52.10. The judge did not find the quartet innocent—they had been arrested on charges of obstructing justice after the Brady Gang's shoot-out with Baltimore police, and were not found not-guilty. The judge instead considered them "nominally" or "technically" guilty, although he freed them from further punishments, and told Anthony Raimondo's attorney that he at least should have known better as he had been involved in "a minor lottery racket" previously.[21] By now, however, the gang had found other women with whom to consort, other men to give them aid, and other crimes to plan.

Just before the Raimondos were freed of charges, it appeared that the gang had headed West once more, and had killed again. All three of the core members of the gang were considered suspects in the murder of patrolman George Conn near Freeport, Ohio. Conn was murdered on September 27, and his "bullet-pierced body" was found in a roadside ditch the next morning. He had been shot more than twenty times. The tactics used, the superintendent of the Ohio Highway Patrol would state after their initial investigation, matched those of the Brady Gang.[22] Investigations were continuing, and would continue for some time. Dalhover would purportedly say that he, Shaffer, and Brady had indeed killed the Ohio officer. The gang was still on the loose, and America was uncertain as to where they might turn up yet, or what mayhem they might yet cause.

One of the last news reports of the gang before they decided to move on yet again appeared on Monday, October 4, 1937. The *Rushville [Indiana] Republication* carried an article, originating in Indianapolis, with the headline: "G-Men Rate Brady Gunmen Tops, But Women May Snare Them Yet." The article stated, "From Indiana, home of John Dillinger, has sprung the gang that G-men label the most vicious now operating." After mentioning that "according to underworld gossip" the three men on the lam had "boasted frequently" that they would "'out-Dillinger' Dillinger," the article stated that the gang had actually "gone a long way towards making good" on that boast. In early October 1937, Midwestern police held charges against them specifically for three killings (Lindsey, Rivers, and Minneman), plus several bank robberies and holdups (including Carthage, Farmland, North Madison, Anderson, and Goodland in Indiana, according to later coverage, and Greenville, Lancaster, and Weston in Ohio). The reward for $500 each remained on their heads, the reward offered by the federal government.[23]

The article then proceeded to make a number of comparisons. It stated that:

> Like Dillinger, they broke out of jail after one whirl at outlawry. Like Dillinger and his henchmen, they started then on a series of bank robberies. Like the Dillinger gang, they have the G-men on their trail. Director J. Edgar Hoover ha[s] set after them a picked squad of federal agents, as usual in such cases. His men have a code word for the gang—"the braga squad." Most importantly of all, possibly, the gang has its known weakness. Like Dillinger, its members are overtly fond of women.[24]

The article then called the men "two farm boys and a big city youth who went wrong." It noted that all three men "are small. Police call them the 'half-pint killers.'" All, the article asserted, were the products of broken homes. All were young. But, while "both Brady and Dalhover are morose, . . . Shaffer is boastful and talkative. To him is credited a crack about 'making Dillinger look like a piker.'"[25]

In a perhaps surprising twist, the article quoted one of Brady's "first sweethearts." She had stated, "He's too sweet to hurt anyone." Apparently he had grown up to be someone other than the young man she had once known. The article "credited" Brady with being, the "gang organizer."[26]

Women, be they mothers who were absent or dead, or consorts both legal and illegal, had figured predominantly in the lives of the men thus far. The paper noted that Shaffer had blamed Margaret Larsen for the gang's being arrested in 1936, as she had wanted to spend a night in a Chicago hotel with Brady instead of having the men—possibly with her—move on. The Brady Gang had escaped yet again in Baltimore. What were the chances of the law catching them again, the article posited. Its answer: "Officers predict the capture eventually will be made through a tip from some castoff sweetheart."[27]

The article ended with a telling quote. It quoted Shaffer as having said, seemingly after his arrest the previous year, "Do I know what's coming to me? Sure, the electric chair . . . What's the difference? I had a good time while it lasted."[28] He was mistaken about some things, but right about a few others.

However, the gang was still living in Bridgeport and seemingly enjoying their time there when the *Rushville Republican* article appeared. After they had left the Washington Avenue home, at least some of the men took rooms on Cottage Street for a few days, then the gang moved to Barnum Avenue in Bridgeport, yet another rooming house. Brady took Alicia Frawley's typewriter there, and the gangsters would stay there during the duration of their time in Connecticut. Later on, expensive clothing, riding habits, and maps with a few banks and various cities starred were also purportedly found in the rooms. Moreover, the men had acquired a small printing press, which Brady used to make business cards, ones for the Skelly Oil Co. Besides oil company representatives, the men also posed as hardware salesmen, mechanics, and longshoremen during their time in Connecticut.[29]

Moreover, the gang seemed to be branching out a bit. It appeared that they were gathering up information on New England roadways and possible crime or hideout locations (they would soon be under suspicion for robbing a Providence, Rhode Island, bank and for planning to rob a Hartford, Connecticut, bank[30]). Brady may have taken his gang and other people to various locations during their time in Bridgeport, but one place that Brady seems to have taken only Alicia, in terms of women, during this time period was to the local airport. Al Brady apparently decided that cars, boats, and motorcycles might not be enough to ensure his future security and safety; airplanes should be added to the list.

Brady started making regular visits to the Bridgeport Airport, often accompanied by Frawley. He took a number of flights, possibly casing the region in general. Two members of the Bridgeport Flying Service piloted Brady on most if not all of his trips out of the airport, and knew him as Edwin Mason. Brady made five flights with the two pilots over Bridgeport proper and the surrounding country, as well as one trip that went as far as New York City. Brady had first approached the manager of the airport to enquire about arranging flying lessons, as well as approaching another person at the airport about flight lessons, before signing up for the chartered flights.[31]

However, not only did Brady show a keen interest in taking flying lessons and flying over the region, he also asked numerous questions about the cost, seating capacity, and flight range of a Ryan monoplane with a cabin. He informed the two pilots that he was a salesperson for the Skelly Oil Co. of Baltimore, and that he was mapping the region for the company. He also said that he had a learner's permit for flying, but that he had left it in Baltimore. The pilots took him on the five flights, spread from September 9 to October 7, but would not let him take the controls.[32]

Frawley is the only woman definitively known to have visited the airport with Brady. However, a brunette was also reportedly seen in Brady's company at the airport. This woman may have been Frawley, also, for although she was generally identified as a blonde, photographs of Frawley suggest that her hair fell at the dark end of the blonde spectrum. On this one occasion, the blonde- or brunette-haired woman seen by one of the pilots was waiting for Brady when he returned from his flight. She was supposedly "pouting" about something, and to soothe her Brady had her taken up for a short flight. One of the pilots also spent an evening socializing with Brady, and found him to be "a hell of a fellow."[33] Either way, Brady had established a new social life in Bridgeport, Dalhover and Shaffer appear to have done so to a lesser extent, and the three thugs were seemingly scoping out new possibilities. At least two women were identified with the gang during their time in the city.

Yet, while the Brady Gang was planning its future and seemingly enjoying its present, the law continued to look for the three fugitives. And, with the law and the press at their heels, the gang decided to visit a place to which they claimed to have had business connections: Bangor, Maine. In large part they were in search of more guns—in particular, they wanted to secure a few new Thompson submachine guns, also known as "Tommy Guns," still a favorite weapon among 1930s gangsters and lawmen alike. They thought they knew an easy place to get the guns. They were wrong. They might have wised up to their situation along the way and changed their minds, but they did not. They may have planned to make additional outings with Bridgeport as their home base much as they had done for the past month or so, and had done in Baltimore previously for close to a year, but they did not.

NOTES

1. "The Brady Gang," *FBI History: Famous Cases*, FBI; *Baltimore News-Post,* 11 August 1937.

2. General sources as previously cited.

3. *Baltimore News-Post,* 11 August 1937; *Baltimore Sun,* 12 and 18 August 1937.

4. "The Brady Gang," *FBI History: Famous Cases*, FBI.

5. *Milwaukee Journal*, 6 October 1937.

6. Ibid. And see statement by Thorp history project.

7. "The Brady Gang," *FBI History: Famous Cases*, FBI.

8. *Bridgeport Times Star*, 14 October 1937, on the car and plates and parking; *Bangor Daily News* (*BDN*), 14 October 1937, on the parking also; and *Baltimore Sun*, 14 August 1937, on the planned roadblock.

9. *BDN*, 14 October 1937, on the hotel and living arrangements and *Bridgeport Times Star*, 13–18 October 1937.

10. *[Bridgeport] City Herald*, 17 October 1937; and *Bridgeport Post*, 14–15 October 1937.

11. Ibid.

12. *[Bridgeport] City Herald*, 17 October 1937. Also see *Bridgeport Post*, 14 October 1937.

13. *[Bridgeport] City Herald*, 17 October 1937. Also see *Bridgeport Post*, 15 October 1937.

14. Ibid. Also see *Bridgeport Times Star*, Evening Edition, 15 October 1937.

15. *Bridgeport Post*, 14 October 1937.

16. Ibid.

17. Ibid. And see *Bangor Daily Commercial (BDC)*, 14 October 1937.

18. *Baltimore Sun,* 14 August and 13 October 1937.

19. Ibid.

20. *Baltimore Sun,* 7 October 1937.

21. Ibid.

22. AP release from Columbus, Ohio, 12 October 1937. This may have been a reprint.

23. *Rushville [Indiana] Republication*, 4 October 1936.

24. Ibid.

25. Ibid.

26. Ibid.

27. Ibid.

28. Ibid.

29. *Bridgeport Post*, 14 October 1937 and *Bridgeport Times Star*, 14 October 1937.

30. *Bridgeport Times Star*, 14 October 1937.

31. *Bridgeport Times Star*, 14 October 1937.

32. Ibid.

33. Ibid. Also see this and other Bridgeport papers for 15–18 October 1937.

11

THE BEGINNING OF THE END

The Small City That Will Do in the Brady Gang

When Alfred Brady decided to take his gang to Bangor, Maine, he was taking it to another city dealing with the effects of the Great Depression. Although two of the three men then part of the gang voted to go—Brady and Shaffer voted to go, Dalhover voted no, but went with the others as he had been outvoted—-Bangor would prove the ruin of all three.

Bangor—in spite of some recent positive business developments—had entered the Great Depression already feeling the strains of a few years of economic difficulties, in terms of government and service expenses. However, Bangor, in spite of some issues in city government, still had plenty of honest, hardworking, and generous people. And the city was doing its best to counteract the nation's economic downfall, and, amongst other things, was in the process of modernizing its police force, although the Brady Gang could not have known that without doing some serious research. Moreover, other departments of the city government, perhaps a surprising number of them, would also ultimately have some part in the Brady story.

Numerous individuals and organizations aided the community and the poor and helped the city through various problems. Bangorites contributed funds and left bequests that aided the city in everything from establishing school programs to building war memorials and parks to bringing more culture to the city. While some such groups disbanded within a few years, others lasted for several decades or longer. They remained active during the late 1920s and through the Great Depression.

In terms of Bangor's population demographics, total population was about 28,000 in the early 1930s and close to 30,000 by the close of the decade, fluctuating a bit from year to year. Native-born Americans made up the majority of Bangor's population, yet there were 3,700 foreign-born people living in the city as the decade opened.[1]

Because of its location on the Penobscot River—the river being fully navigable for ocean-going vehicles as far as Bangor—and its long-standing railroad service, the city had long had a large number of transient people moving through its harbors, stations, and now traveling along its streets and roadways in the 1930s. It also had received immigrants and emigrants from all the country and the world over the decades. The Brady Gang might have passed by largely unnoticed, had they not acted to bring attention to themselves.[2]

In terms of culture and recreation—which the Brady Gang seemed quite fond of when they were not planning robberies, upgrading their arsenal, and shooting their way out of trouble—the city had a long-established opera house where plays and musical performances were held regularly; a large fair, the Bangor Fair, held each year; as well as numerous music festivals and public concerts. Many events like these took place outside, as did other forms of entertainment and recreation. In addition to improving venues for outside events, Bangorites by the early twentieth century clearly realized some of the other benefits of having green spaces—open public spaces—within their community. Some citizens sought to create more public places and city parks and to improve existing ones. The Brady Gang would ultimately find this to their disadvantage.

The City of Bangor had started to develop parks for public use during the late nineteenth century and devoted even more attention to them in the early twentieth century. Public works projects would only add to the parks and recreational sites during the Great Depression. Perhaps Bangor's first true attempt to establish a place that set aside and developed scenic qualities in the city landscape—and one that would be part of Brady's history, too—however, was that of the private Mount Hope Cemetery, founded in 1834. It was originally incorporated as the Bangor Horticultural Society and included fifty acres of land, and being the second such garden cemetery in the nation—one designed to provide beauty for the living as well as burial space for the dead—the cemetery corporation continued to plant ornamental trees, create waterways, and design environmentally cohesive architectural details later in the nineteenth century and in the twentieth.[3]

However, although Mount Hope continued to attract visitors to walk, rest, and enjoy its flora and fauna, especially its geese and other waterfowl, into the twenty-first century, in 1937 the adjacent city section of the cemetery—established in the mid-1800s from land originally part of the private Mount Hope—was much less inviting. The city government had placed most of its attention on parks established specifically for the living up until the late 1930s, and allowed some of its burial spots to decline.[4]

By early 1930, Bangor had constructed playgrounds in various parks, as well as building a city skating rink and a swimming pool. With numerous events hosted in its parks, the city appropriated funding for band concerts and a special fund for Fourth of July concerts, and celebrated its centennial as a city in 1934. As the economy started to improve again in the mid-1930s, the federal government helped the city undertake further development of its parks and green spaces.[5] Brady might have enjoyed the skating, the access to a large river, and other aspects of the city's environment and culture had he decided to choose Bangor as a living place, but he did not.

During the first full year of the Great Depression, 1930, while the young members of the Brady Gang were just getting underway with their more serious criminal lives, the Bangor city government struggled on as best it could, not knowing how long the severe economic downturn would last or the ultimate depths it would reach. The mayor noted in January that the financial situation of the city was not good, but it had not been good for some time.[6]

In 1931, financial strains were worse in Bangor, and the current mayor expressed dissatisfaction with the cost and efficiency of the Bangor Police Department—which a few years later would encounter the Brady Gang—and with the Bangor Fire Department. Throughout the history of the city, most—if not all—previous mayors had commented favorably on the work performed by the two departments, even during problematic times. Mayor Norman E. Whitney, however, saw substantial room for improvement. He wrote in January 1931 that the police department had cost the city about eighty thousand dollars the previous year, or about three dollars per capita. "This," he stated, "is a tremendous sum, and our citizens have a right to expect 100 percent efficiency of its police officers." Whitney stated that he believed "in law enforcement . . . tempered with justice and common sense." He made no suggestions on how to decrease costs for the police department or how to improve its efficiency.[7]

However, Bangor's police chief, politically appointed, believed that his force was doing a good and efficient job guarding the city. Police had made 1,355 arrests in 1930 and would make 1,594 in 1931. Arrests in 1930 included 40 for assault, 1 for manslaughter, 50 for larceny, 2 for maintaining a house for prostitution, and 1,040 for drunkenness.[8] Bangor continued to have its social issues, many of which rose during these years, and heavy drinking—in spite of Prohibition, instituted under the Eighteenth Amendment and repealed by the Twenty-First in 1933—remained among them. This would be true right up to 1937.[9] The one-time bootlegger James Dalhover, and probably Clarence Shaffer, too, might have tried running another still in Bangor.

Bangor police investigated and made arrests for other crimes and mishaps during the 1930s; they also provided valuable aid to the needy. Police transported hundreds of people to the Eastern Maine General Hospital in Bangor (which would see some action in the events of 1937 involving members of the Brady Gang), the State Hospital (for the insane), and to the city hospital and the city farm, both located at the Bangor Almshouse, established over one hundred years previously. All of these people were in need of one form of help or another. The city police also provided shelter for more than 5,000 people in 1931 alone, and this continued in following years. Homelessness was on the rise in America, as people took to the roads looking for work—most of them searching for honest work—and many found themselves in dire need of food and shelter, even those who stayed in their hometowns. No doubt many more people needed shelter than those who sought it from local police. In another indication of America's tough times, Bangor police responded to a number of suicides over these years. Other people were discovered dead without explanation. In 1931 the new police chief, Thomas I. Crowley, thanked his officers "for their loyalty and co-operation that contributed greatly in making my administration a success."[10] The mayor and other citizens might or might not doubt the efficiency of the department; the chief did not. The department would continue to improve its methods and communications in subsequent years, and subsequent events would prove that Crowley and his men could compete with the best of them when it came to criminal activity—be the offenders local or not.

Other issues confronting Bangor in the 1930s were disease and traffic in the Bangor Harbor. Disease was high; river traffic was not.

City health officials had long struggled to increase sanitation and health. Yet disease and contagion still impacted Bangor in the 1930s; and in 1937, when Al Brady and his gang arrived, over a hundred active cases of tuberculosis plagued Bangor. There was also a major concern about "infectious disease of a syphilitic nature." The city tried to track the sources of all contagious diseases to prevent further spread of contagion. Inoculations were provided during these years, and the city regularly tested food, milk, and water for contaminants.[11] Brady's predecessor in crime, Al Capone, had died of complications of syphilis.

Meanwhile, the once booming Penobscot River had seen a tremendous decrease in the number of ships coming into its harbor during the Great Depression, a problem that had started with World War I and then lessoned somewhat in the 1920s. Incoming ships had not, however, reached their prewar levels before the Great Depression hit, perhaps simply because transportation changes had had a large impact on the freight business. Trains, trucks, and other transportation had taken on some business, and improvements in ship design allowed fewer vessels to carry more freight. The harbor continued to see, in varying numbers, hundreds of steamers, regular schooners, and some motor schooners into the 1930s. It also had yachts, various U.S. Coast Guard boats, the odd U.S. destroyer, and a showboat or two. However, after 1930 the traffic had decreased from even the late 1920s.[12]

Then, although shipping activity on the Bangor waterfront continued to suffer, the year 1936 proved historic for the waterfront. The Bangor Harbor was open for navigation a record 293 days, as a "United States Russian type ice breaker, the *Kickapoo* . . . smashed a channel into Bangor on the night of March 14th through two feet of solid blue river ice," as the harbormaster described it. This seems to be the first time a U.S. icebreaker operated in the harbor, and the harbor remained open for the remainder of 1936.[13]

Bangorites saw another historic change on their waterfront that year. The Eastern Steamship Company, "the last of the big steamship lines

operating into Bangor," ceased operating its passenger and freight service between Bangor and Boston and sold its Bangor wharf property in
1936. Limited steamship passage to Boston continued for a time, and
the diminutive steamship the *Bon Ton III*, launched in 1921, continued
to ferry people across the Penobscot between Bangor and Brewer—just
across the river—for three cents until 1939.[14] The Brady Gang had lost
some travel options had they decided to try coming to Bangor via
steamship, but it still remained a possibility.

During 1937, when Brady came to town, the Bangor Harbor remained open until December 23—having never closed since the March
1936 ice breaking—and then ended the longest continual "season" in
Bangor's history. Harbor arrivals did increase during 1937, totaling 578
ships, not a high number for the port, but an improvement over the
previous few years. Foreign arrivals had been slowly increasing also,
and in 1937, 137 ships arrived from foreign ports. Tonnage reached
almost its highest levels since 1930, but the following year the harbor
would close for much of the winter, and tonnage decreased again. But
by then, the Brady Gang was gone.[15]

Overall the economy of Bangor suffered greatly during the early 1930s,
reaching its lowest point circa 1932. Perhaps surprisingly important for the
future of the Brady Gang, in 1932 Bangor adopted a city management
form of government, changing from a mayor-aldermen–common council
to a city manager form of government. The new government inherited
numerous problems from the old, but made significant progress before the
Brady Gang arrived in town.[16]

Under the new system, the chair of the city council served as "may-
or" for ceremonial purposes. The city reorganized some departments
and combined others. In an interesting twist, as a contemporary community study described it, "under the new City Charter, the City Council is officially [the] Overseers of the Poor," responsible for the almshouse and for all outside aid.[17] The Overseers of the Poor would have
an impact on Al Brady's future—or lack thereof.

In Bangor, authorities in the mid-1930s faced increasing demands
for aid even as its demands for other services increased, at the Bangor
Almshouse, and elsewhere.

The almshouse—established more than a century earlier—continued
to play an important role in Bangor as the 1930s progressed. The facility
farmed about twenty-five acres of property and kept livestock. It attended

to the medical needs of the impoverished and helped clothe them. In addition, the Bangor Charity Department helped provide rental payments, groceries, fuel and lighting, burial expenses, and aid to dependent children. It also buried the destitute.[18]

In addition to continuing its long-standing aid programs, Bangor citizens demonstrated a proactive approach to the Great Depression, helping avoid some of the troubles other New England cities faced. Bangor established a Municipal Odd Jobs Bureau and a Citizens' Unemployment Committee. The city's many private relief societies and organizations also aided the unemployed or underemployed, and the local YMCA, YWCA, and Salvation Army helped the city address its transient problem. Together these organizations—public and private—helped relieve the situation of the welfare department.[19] Other twentieth-century organizations such as Mothers' Aid, the Red Cross, the local auxiliary of the American Legion and the Veterans of Foreign Wars, and the Salvation Army likewise helped people eligible for their individual services.[20]

Still, conditions worsened in the mid-1930s. The city continued to receive less money from taxes at the same time as it received less funding from other sources. The assessed value of the city fell. The almshouse was now frequently referred to as the City Poor House and no longer accepted children under age sixteen except in emergencies. It admitted "no feeble minded, insane, or criminal inmates" as it had previously done. In previous decades, criminals and the insane had been housed side-by-side with the poor, although none as deadly as the Brady Gang members were ever purposely put there.[21]

By the time the city began to experience its greatest need, however, the national Civil Works Administration, or CWA, established by incoming U.S. President Franklin Delano Roosevelt, reached Bangor as it did other municipalities. The incoming president created the CWA as part of his New Deal program for America. In Bangor during late 1933, the CWA employed eight hundred people who worked on sewers and sidewalks, inspected and trimmed trees, built an athletic field, and began to gravel the new Bangor Airport, or Godfrey Field, opened by Edward R. Godfrey in the late 1920s.[22] At least one member of the Brady Gang would pass through the Bangor Airport—as would a number of lawmen. Brady—in view of his flying activities in Bridgeport—might have considered visiting the airport for flying lessons or other reasons, but would not have the opportunity to do so, at least, not as far as is known.

In another twist, the Bangor Public Welfare Department served as the application center for men and boys seeking work with FDR's Civilian Conservation Corps, the CCC, in some cases working with a review board in Augusta. The city was becoming more and more tied to other cities in the 1930s, beyond its history as a shipping and distribution center, and this would work to the detriment of the Brady Gang.[23]

Need for aid, however, continued right up until the time the fugitives arrived in the city. The almshouse on average housed seventy inmates—as people residing in any institution were still commonly called—at any given time in 1937, and served 88,000 meals—a significant number, but still far less than the more than 100,000 meals served in the previous years of the Depression. However, with more of the burden falling outside the facility, the number of grocery orders increased greatly, and the welfare department placed scores of new families on its roster. The city physician—who would also play a role in the Brady saga—continued to see patients outside and in the almshouse, and the city provided other services at various locations.[24]

The large number of transient men and women indicated that, in spite of all the relief provided by the federal government, the City of Bangor, and Bangor's private organizations, many people remained homeless during these years. The Brady Gang might have fit right into the local population in 1937, had they but tried.

During 1934, CWA projects, augmented by FDR's new Federal Emergency Relief Administration (or FERA), allowed the city to undertake additional work, including further improving and expanding city parks. The FERA also undertook widening the shoulders of the runways at the Bangor Airport in the mid-1930s. Yet certain parts of the downtown district still needed basic roadwork into the late 1930s, as some sections still held the old wooden-block pavement as a surface, which city engineers called "a constant source of trouble," as it was often slippery and dangerous.[25]

Federal money helped the city to undertake several projects in 1936 and for the rest of the decade that might not otherwise have been possible. Federal funding had already financed some improvements at the Bangor Airport, which, however, remained a small airport into the mid-1930s. Then, in January 1936, the City of Bangor held a large general public meeting in conjunction with the WPA and the United States Department of Commerce. As a result of that meeting, the three entities undertook a major project to "develop an up-to-date Municipal Airport" capable of serving "high speed planes." To that end, "the city obtained title to the runways, and also to a location for a Radio Beam Station." The city appropriated $30,000 to the airport project, and the federal government appropriated $68,000. By the close of the year, these two steps were close to completion.[26]

Both aspects of the project, radio towers and airport construction, were complete by late February 1937. The radio-beam station was put into operation under federal guidance in May and all lighting tests at the airport completed in July. Additional work continued. (The city had two private radio stations which the local government used sometimes to disseminate local news or information about its various programs: WABI and WLBZ. They too, would play a part in the events of October 1937, when the Brady Gang came to town.[27])

The abysmal economy during the Depression did not preclude the city's responsibility to provide basic ongoing services. The charity department topped the list in some ways, but, in terms of funding, police and fire services did so. The large number of people on the move—especially, it would seem, the large number of people coming into the city—called for a vigilant police department.

After the city reorganization of 1932, the Bangor Police Department and the Bangor Fire Department instituted new federal civil service standards, hiring all candidates based on rank in examinations and on character and physical preparedness, not on political or other considerations.[28] Some civic leaders had long been calling for a depoliticization of the police department; in 1932 this goal was finally achieved.

Reportedly with "greatly improved" effectiveness and morale after the reorganization, the BPD continued to battle primarily the same types of problems it had during earlier years, in particular public intoxication and traffic violations. The city revised its traffic ordinance, giving increased authority to the police department, including allowing it to establish traffic lanes in the main city streets. This proved successful, and the city later extended the use of traffic lanes to other streets. The BPD helped standardize traffic signs and markers in 1933 and established safety lanes in the busy downtown section. The BPD also replaced its now old, outdated and unsafe patrol wagon with a new combination ambulance and patrol car.[29]

All of these would have some bearing on events related to the Brady Gang when they arrived in Bangor.

Not just concerned with the safety of its own vehicles, the Bangor Police Department reported that it was "carrying on a determined war against speeders, reckless drunks and drunken drivers, in a firm, courteous, but impartial manner." Its 1934 report included photographs of the department's ambulance (metal bars in its windows clearly visible) and one of its "scout cars." The department had purchased two new automobiles earlier in the year for use in patrolling the residential and outlying portions of the city and purchased another vehicle in 1935. The department noted that it still needed a modern radio broadcast system and "a suitable jail."[30] It would not have one by 1937.

During the later 1930s, further evidence that Bangor was becoming increasingly tied to the broader world—in particular the federal government—became apparent in the functioning of the Bangor Police Department. The department continued its other duties, but also introduced various innovations, some tied to Washington, DC. The department in the mid-1930s essentially split into three departments: "Criminal, Traffic, and Safety" at roughly the same time as it came under the new civil service regulations and received a new signal board connected with recently purchased police signal boxes. Another innovation, one that was the first of its kind in the region, was the purchase of a "convertible prowl ambulance car."[31]

The department added the position of night inspector in 1937 and opened a Bureau of Identification and Fingerprinting that took roughly 344 sets of fingerprints and 337 "photographs of wrongdoers" during its first three months of operation. The following year the department added 1,562 sets of fingerprints to its records, along with 1,697 sets of photographs. The new bureau operated out of City Hall, as did an "Inspector's Office." The department also sent one of its sergeants to a three-month Federal Bureau of Investigation training school for "criminal detection" in Washington. The returning graduate then started a police school for other department members.[32] The newest developments in the BPD did not happen in a vacuum. They were directly related to the appearance of the Brady Gang in the city.

NOTES

1. "The Brady Gang," *FBI History: Famous Cases*, Federal Bureau of Investigation.

2. See Trudy Irene Scee, *City on the Penobscot*, for further information.

3. See Trudy Irene Scee, *Mount Hope Cemetery of Bangor, Maine: The Complete History* (Charleston, SC: The History Press, 2012), for more information on both the 1800s and 1900s.

4. See Scee, *City on the Penobscot*, for further information.

5. Ibid.

6. Ibid.

7. Ibid. And see Bangor Mayors Annual Report (MAR) of 1931.

8. Scee, *City on the Penobscot*; and city reports with MARs of 1930 and 1931.

9. Scee, *City on the Penobscot*; reports with MARs of 1930 and 1931.

10. Ibid. During these four years, a number of people, usually seven or eight per year, were simply "found dead" or had drowned. These may or may not have involved some suicides.

11. Scee, *City on the Penobscot*; reports with MARs of 1933–39.

12. Scee, *City on the Penobscot*; reports with MARs of 1925 and 1929.

13. Scee, *City on the Penobscot* reports with MARs of 1933-36.

14. Scee, *City on the Penobscot*; report with MAR of 1936; discussion with David C. Smith, September 2009, on ongoing steamship service; and *BDN*, June 28, 1984.

15. Scee, *City on the Penobscot*; MARs of 1937–1940.

16. Scee, *City on the Penobscot*; MAR of 1932; and Junior Welfare League, "Bangor: A Community Study."

17. Scee, *City on the Penobscot*; MAR of 1932.

18. Scee, *City on the Penobscot*; report with MAR of 1931.

19. Scee, *City on the Penobscot*; report with MAR of 1932.

20. Junior Welfare League, "Bangor: A Community Study"; and MARs of 1930–1935.

21. MAR of 1933; report with MAR of 1933; and Junior Welfare League, "Bangor: A Community Study," 122–23. See Scee, *City on the Penobscot*, for further information.

22. MAR of 1933. See Scee, *City on the Penobscot*, for further information.

23. Ibid.

24. Report with MAR of 1937, 16–18. See Scee, *City on the Penobscot*, for further information.

25. See Scee, *City on the Penobscot*, for further information, and reports with MARs of 1934 and 1935.

26. Scee, *City on the Penobscot*; MAR of 1936; and report, quotes from both.

27. Scee, *City on the Penobscot*; report with MAR of 1936.

28. Scee, *City on the Penobscot*; MAR of 1932.

29. Scee, *City on the Penobscot*; MAR of 1933; reports with MARs of 1932 and 1933.

30. Scee, *City on the Penobscot*; reports with MAR of 1934; MAR of 1935.

31. Scee, *City on the Penobscot*; report with MAR of 1937.

32. Scee, *City on the Penobscot*; report with MAR of 1937.

12

BLOOD IN THE STREETS
Maine Meets the Brady Gang and Wins

Into the angst of the Great Depression in Bangor, Maine, and bringing perhaps a whole new variety of crime to the city, one about which local radio and newspaper businesses eagerly reported and which various departments of the city had to address, stepped "Public Enemy Number One": Al Brady. The FBI sought Alfred, or "Al," Brady and his gang for an estimated 150 to 200 robberies by late 1937, for four murders (they had no doubt committed at least three of them), and a vicious jailbreak when they came to Bangor. Plus, they were wanted for questioning in various other assaults and incidents. Brady and his gang had stolen tens of thousands of dollars in jewels before they came to Bangor in autumn 1937. Brady—or Shaffer—had bragged that he would make the more infamous gangster John Dillinger "look like a piker." Bangor, Maine, however, proved Brady's undoing. His activities in Bangor also made him appear a fool, although some of his and the gang's actions were not necessarily out of sync with the time and place, especially their attempts to purchase firearms in Maine.

Nonetheless, Alfred James Brady, Rhuel James Dalhover, and Clarence Lee Shaffer Jr. walked into a trap laid by the Federal Bureau and other law enforcements agencies in downtown Bangor on October 12, 1937. The Brady Gang themselves had created the perfect opportunity for the trap. After realizing that they needed supplies, and hoping specifically to purchase some submachine guns, Thompson guns if they could get them, Brady and his men had traveled to Bangor on September 21, 1937, apparently thinking that they could buy munitions there without arousing suspicions.[1] They could pose as hunters, perhaps, and pull off their scheme without incident.

The gang purchased several rounds of ammunition at Dakin's Sporting Goods Store on September 21, plus two Colt .45 automatic guns, as well as other weaponry. Brady and his men returned to the downtown store two weeks later, on October 5, and bought a third Colt .45 automatic and some extra clips for their guns. The men aroused the suspicious of one of the store's clerks, Lewis Clark, who did not believe that they were hunters as they said they were—the men did not dress like hunters, nor talk like local men—and so he alerted the store's owner. Between making the purchases, the men apparently returned briefly to Connecticut. They also approached another store, Rice & Miller, located on Broad Street, about purchasing revolvers, also causing that store's clerk, C. E. Silsby, to become concerned about the men, but he sold them the guns as there was no legal reason to deny the purchase. Before stopping in Bangor, they had stopped in Augusta, at a hardware store, Hussey Hardware, and had been referred to Dakin's.[2]

Brady wanted to purchase machine guns from Dakin's also, but the store did not carry them. On their second visit to the store, Brady asked the store's owner, Everett "Shep" Hurd, to order the weapons and said he would return the following Monday or Tuesday—October 11 or 12—for the guns. Hurd contacted the local authorities. (He had also called earlier to report the men he thought were suspicious, speaking with the police deputy. Silsby had also contacted a police officer, but nothing was done.) Hurd also contacted the Maine State Police. At this point, having been skeptical earlier about the possibility of the men being members of the Brady Gang, now knowing the thugs had been traced to New England, the police chief contacted Bangor-based Sergeant F. R. Hall of the Maine State Police, who contacted the chief of the Maine State Police, Wilbur H. Twole of Augusta. Twole in turn contacted the FBI at its Boston Field Division, and a trap was set. An FBI agent came to the store with photographs of the gang members and spoke with Hurd, who indentified James Dalhover as having come into the store on September 21 and October 5. A clerk, possibly Clark also identified as James Seeley, likewise identified Dalhover.[3]

October 12 was Columbus Day, and the day before Dakin's received a call from a customer asking if the store would remain open during the holiday. The clerk replied that, yes, it would. The clerk thought he recognized the voice, and the store contacted the police about the call.[4]

The FBI came to the city en force in the form of its Special Squad, spoke with Bangor Police Chief Thomas I. Crowley about their plans, positioned cars and men around the sporting goods store and the immediate area, and waited. The agents had come to Bangor in small groups to avoid suspicion. Once they arrived, they mounted a machine gun in the second-story window of a store opposite Dakin's. Members of the Maine State Police and a couple of Indiana State Police also moved in (and were charged with guarding the entrances to Central Street and to blockade the roadway where the men might try to escape), as did thirty Bangor policemen. One FBI agent, Walter R. Walsh, a master marksman, took a place in the store as a clerk, and another hid in a rear section of the store along with a member of the Bangor Police Department. And along came the Brady Gang.[5]

The FBI agents, by autumn 1937 popularly known as "G-men," closed the streets surrounding Dakin's Sporting Goods as soon as Brady and his men appeared. Some agents posed as casual shoppers and the like. The gangsters' car carried Ohio license plates. The gangsters drove by the store twice, presumably to ascertain that the coast was clear. They parked the car, and while Brady waited in the back seat, Dalhover and Shaffer went to the store. Photographs taken minutes later would show the three men attired in neat dark suits. Brady and Shaffer waited outside the premises, each with two automatic pistols and a revolver at the ready. Dalhover carried two fully loaded revolvers into the store.[6]

The federal agents captured James Dalhover while he was in the store. As Agent Walsh would later state, after he helped apprehend Dalhover by holding two pistols at his back after Dalhover approached Hurd to ask if the Tommy-guns had arrived, he had asked Dalhover where his pals were. Dalhover had answered, "They're outside." In spite of the guns at his back, Dalhover did start a fight, which caught Shaffer's attention, if the moments previous to this had not. As would later be reported, part of Walsh's job that day had been to signal thirteen fellow G-men, plus the Bangor police and the Indiana and Maine State troopers as soon as one or more of the gang members entered the store. Walsh had moved to pull a cord that would send the signal via the window, and Dalhover realized that he had entered a trap, and fired a shot or shots, seemingly to warn his comrades. Variations exist in the details given of the events that day, and those preceding it. However, the major points are not in question.[7]

Shaffer had stayed outside on guard, and Al Brady waited in the car. Clarence Lee Shaffer soon appeared on Central Street and drew his weapon—and Alfred Brady supposedly did the same after saying, "Don't shoot, don't shoot, I'll get out," while exiting the gang's car. The two gangsters exchanged fire with the FBI agents. Shaffer, seemingly trying to help Dalhover escape from Dakin's, had fired into the store. Agent Walsh later stated that Shaffer had started toward the store, "and that's where the shooting started happening."[8]

Shaffer was still outside however, and other federal agents and presumably police members also opened fire. Federal agents fired from cars, windows in nearby stores, and along the street. The FBI, according to eyewitness accounts, shot Brady almost in half after he exited the Buick shooting. He died instantly. Shaffer survived for at least eight minutes after being riddled with bullets. Their blood ran together in the street, and a crowd soon appeared. The dead men were about fifteen feet apart, their bodies partially laying over the city's streetcar or trolley tracks. A black decoy car, parked near the store by lawmen, had had its windows shattered and was riddled with gunshot holes. The bodies were soon removed to the undertakers White and Hayes.[9]

Walsh had struck Dalhover with the butt of his gun after being shot in the shoulder, and Dalhover, his face streaming with blood, had run into the store's basement. He then tried to escape through a back door, but two Bangor policemen seized him. He then submitted to arrest.[10]

Dalhover was taken to the local police lockup at City Hall and grilled there by Federal agents for hours into the night and the early morning before he was finally allowed to sleep. The following morning, only a few hours later, he had his first meal in about twenty-four hours: a breakfast of bacon, eggs, and coffee at the jail. For lunch that day, he was given a few sandwiches and coffee, and grilling by the agents resumed.[11]

These are the basic facts of the case, but elaborations and conjectures abounded in the following days. The shootout between the FBI and the Brady Gang became sensationalized in the press with questions and suppositions about everything from what the men wore and ate to speculations as to their intentions in Maine and New England.

The *Bangor Daly News (BDN)* ran a huge leader of "G-MEN KILL BRADY AND PAL: One of America's Most Widely Hunted Desperado Trios Taken Alive as Guns Roar in Heart of Bangor's Business District—Federal Agent Wounded as Carefully Planned Plot Traps Notorious Gang," on October 13, 1937. The *BDN* described the air as being "electric" when Dalhover stepped into "the iron jaws of the trap," set by the FBI. Federal G-men had been stationed in the store, in cars parked along the street, in second-story windows across from Dakin's, and on the sidewalks posing as regular citizens. Hurd with three real clerks— Harold or Harry Ellingwood, Glen Furey, and Al LeBrun—were in the store as well, as was Bangor dentist Dr. Albert MacDougall, who was making a purchase. One witness stated that when he realized he had walked into a setup, Dalhover made a "mad effort to escape," while another witness standing only a foot or two away from the events said, "When Dalhover wouldn't answer [where his friends were], one of the G-men used his revolver as a club, sweeping it down over his nose and cheek." The agent then asked him, "Now will you talk?" Dalhover purportedly answered, "They're out front." Then, after the agents surrounded Brady and he "lied to the last" coming out of the gang's car shooting instead of peacefully, "Central Street became a madhouse— and, a moment later, a shambles." After the G-man, seemingly Walsh, "turned his machine gun upon Brady; and the man who was to make a piker of Dillinger met Dillinger's end. He lay grotesquely on his back— a human sieve, his flesh torn into bits." In case anyone needed further clarification, the paper stated that, "Again was written the truism—this time in blood—that crime does not pay." Brady "had sought to wear the soiled crown of the underworld," but instead, it seems, would soon just be part of the soil, although the paper did not point that out. [12]

Meanwhile, according to the account, "Shaffer, caught like a rat in a gigantic trap, backed into the middle of Central Street and continued to shoot—probably blindly, at the deadly machine gun above him." As would become an object of continued speculation, the newspaper reported that, "Perhaps Shaffer tried then to run toward the Norembega Mall [one of the city's small parks or green spaces, located nearby and partly built over Kenduskeag Stream]—the position of his body indicated it." However, "He hadn't a chance." The paper noted that G-men by that time "were converging from all sides. Lead continued to rain from the machine gun nest." Almost immediately, "The lieutenant of America's most notorious criminal gang fell across the tracks; his blood mingled with that of Brady. It spread in an ever widening, crimson lake. For a few minutes the street seemed full of it." Yet, no matter how still he seemed, by the afternoon of October 13 the press knew that, "Shaffer didn't die immediately. He was still breathing eight minutes later when Dr. Harry D. McNeil, head of the city's health department, examined him." Although Bangor had been developing its health department over the years, it is doubtful that its current head had thought to have such an experience in his work. Shaffer, the *BDN* stated, "at least lived until the flashing guns were stilled."[13]

Then, the *BDN* reported, "The ghastly drama ended as quickly as it began." Firemen quickly came to the scene, and washed away the blood with their hoses. Federal agent Frank Golden and the local police inspector John F. Hayes, had been stationed inside the store, the *BDN* noted, and "the two [taking custody of Dalhover], marched [him] through a rear door into the alley—thence across Central and Hammond Streets to City Hall." He would be questioned there and await arraignment. The police made Dalhover keep his hands up, with a gun jammed in each side of his body. "He was wiser than his chief had been; he didn't try to get away." The dead bodies of Brady and Shaffer went to a local funeral parlor. It was soon discovered that nearby windows had been broken, one "a big plate-glass window in the tailor shop of Barnet Landon on the second floor diagonally across from the Dakin store." Another bullet passed "through the window of the Singer Sewing Machine Company on the first floor. A fourth [bullet] struck an ornate advertising sign of Louis Kirstein & Sons, shattering it."[14]

The *BDN* was much more dramatic in its coverage of the events in Bangor than was the community's other local paper, the *Bangor Daily Commercial* (*BDC*). Whereas the *BDN* covered its papers with images of the aftermath of the shootout, and essentially all things and people deemed related to the case, the *BDC* printed only a few photographs, and devoted less print space to the case as well.

The *BDC* did eventually print a photograph of the G-men on Central Street, but did not print the fairly close-up shots of the dead gangsters on October 12 and 13 as did the *BDN*, although it did like the *Bangor Daily News* run a special edition on the 12th. Its lead on the extra edition of the 12th was: "Two Members Brady Gang Die Under G-Man Gunfire in Business Section Here Today." The subtitle read "Al Brady, Mob Leader, Killed; Third Man Held" with other subtitles following the first subtitle and a few articles printed along with the lead one. The article described the basic scene—without all the flourishes of the *BDN*'s first coverage—with G-men firing machine guns from an upper story across the street from Dakin's Sporting Goods, and with two of the gangsters being shot in the streets and Dalhover captured. It noted that members of the various law enforcement agencies had formed a "V" with the point of intersection being Dakin's, and noted that Al Brady had been, "according to witnesses, knocked into the air by the force of the harsh slugs and fell in the middle of the street, horribly shot. He received the brunt of the slugs around the waist and chest, and was dead when he hit the pavement." Shaffer had been killed "almost instantly," with bullet shots to the head, chest, and stomach. Walter Wash, FBI agent, had managed to stay on his feet after being shot in the shoulder, and was now at the Eastern Maine General Hospital. (The next day the paper commended Walsh again for staying his post, noting that he "is but five feet five inches tall and is a light weight," and that in addition to having been shot in the shoulder, he had been cut by flying glass.[15])

The FBI would also later report that one of its agents had been "hit" by one of Brady's bullets. In addition, the FBI would reveal after the fact that the gun taken from Brady's hand after the shootout was the same gun he had taken from Indiana State Policeman Paul Minneman. It was a ".38 caliber revolver from which four shots had just been fired," presumably by Brady in the seconds just before his death. In addition, Brady had a .32 and a .45 automatic revolver on his person at the time of his death. It had taken the agency 365 days to get Public Enemy No. 1, but with local help and that of a couple of state police departments, get him it had.[16] J. Edgar Hoover was a happy man that day.

The *BDC* made a point of stating that

> James Dalhover, the gangster who escaped for a few short minutes, was captured almost before the firing ceased by none other than what the gangsters frequently refer to as "small town cops." . . . But the "small town cops" who happened to know all the tricks in this instance were Inspectors Frank Golden and Jack Hayes of the Bangor Police Department.[17]

One thing that the *BDC* did have was staff members who saw the events as they unfolded. One, Fred Elias, reported in an article titled "*Commercial* Men on the Scene":

> I was coming to the *Commercial* to work, and I reached Buckley's corner. I saw two New York cars on the right, near the middle of the road, and practically obstructing traffic. I slowed a bit and noticed that there was only one big fellow in the car, just piling out with his right hand in his right pocket. He made a mad dash down Central Street.
>
> I pulled my car to the curb, and then the firing started. I thought at first automobile backfire, but as I continued I realized that it was gunfire. A fellow in gray came rushing back to the car. And the fire was continuing all the time. I left my car and two police officers— Bill Ferry and Ralph Smith—warned me back. Incidentally the work of these two was magnificent; they stood in the road holding back traffic and would-be spectators while bullets churned the air around them.
>
> I swung around the corner and sighted a big G-man in blue with a Tommy-gun pumping lead and two men were in the middle of the street, prone and apparently badly hurt. Then two men ran down an alley and pounced on a third man to carry him off.
>
> At this point I looked about a bit and sighted many more G-men armed and who had been throughout the fight coolly pouring lead. The crowd seemed like curious sheep pouring from all directions to the scene of the shooting, and seemingly all unconscious of the danger of flying death in the air. They seemed altogether fearless. The fine work of the local police in keeping back the throng probably saved some injury to the bystanders. [18]

The *Commercial* included a second first-person account of the shoot-out, one from another staff member, G. E. Huntley, one of the newspaper's printers. Huntley had been near the Hazzard Shoe Store when the gunfire erupted, and would witness part of the events from the same corner. He told his reporters:

> I thought a box of shells was exploding in Dakin's. When I got to the corner I saw everybody was running, everybody flying around, and the cops sprinting about. The police stopped me at Buckley's Corner.
>
> They said, "Get back, there's danger ahead."

I looked about and could see little but a G-man running up with a sub-machine gun. I couldn't tell where he came from or where he was going except that he was headed toward Dakin's and the Post Office.

Pretty soon two plain-clothes men came down the street pulling a third man between them. They took him toward the City Hall.

Then a couple of minutes more I heard a shot and I went around the corner and saw two in the street all bloodied up and a G-man standing over them with a gun.[19]

The two staff members of the *BDC* described similar scenes, although there were a couple of inconsistencies, and it is likely that they did not know that some of the men they saw were FBI agents until afterward, although if news of the impending sting was leaked, they may have had more reason for their conclusions. They both described some of the chaos in the streets, and the surprise many locals must have felt stumbling upon the scene of carnage.

Later reports would state that the gunfire had lasted about five minutes. Numerous Bangor citizens flocked into the area in spite of warnings as soon as the gunfire stopped—if not sooner. One "witness" was a former Maine governor (1925–1929). Ralph Owen Brewster was a Republican Representative at the time, and was having lunch in a nearby drugstore and along with some other people rushed into the street to see what had happened. Crowds of spectators poured into the downtown area just after the shooting, even as cleanup continued.[20]

The *BDN* printed the statements of other witnesses on October 12. Not surprisingly, one of them was from Everett "Shep" Hurd, manager of the sporting goods store. He described the events as follows, according to his "official statement":

Dalhover entered my store. I was behind the counter. I stepped out and asked him what he wanted. I didn't realize at the time that he was armed and pointing a gun at me. He said, "Have you got that stuff I ordered a few days ago from you?" A G-man stepped from behind him and made Dalhover lift his arms, pointing a machine gun at his back. The G-man asked him where his pals were, and he said, "Right behind you."

And then a flock of G-men piled into the store shooting a rain of bullets. Somebody put handcuffs on Dalhover and the battling continued out in the street. There was nobody hurt from my store, only one slight casualty. James Seeley was sweeping the street. When he heard the firing he fell to the ground. Stray glass cut him around the eyes.[21]

The following day, the newspaper would quote Hurd as stating that he did not actually see the shooting as "The boys had been told to get out of the way when the shooting started." Hurd said that after Dalhover came in to the store, however, he himself had walked by Walsh, stationed behind the counter and whispered, "There he is," not knowing if Walsh had heard him. Walsh, the *BDC* reported in a separate story, had confirmed from the hospital that he had heard the store manager's whisper and that it had served him as a warning to be ready for action. After Dalhover had asked Hurd for the "stuff" he had ordered, Walsh had ordered him to "Stick 'em up!" and then had hit Dalhover hard with his revolver, sending him sprawling across the floor, as the young crook had kept a hand on a weapon. He had then been handcuffed. Hurd had run behind the counter and up the rear stairs when the shooting started. When Hurd returned to the front of the store, he had been surprised by all that had happened and how many men had been hidden in the store by the authorities. In addition to himself and Seeley outside sweeping and the various lawmen, four women had been upstairs in the rear office working, and Silsby of Rice & Miller was in the store along with the dentist, MacDougal, who was looking for a hunting cap and was being assisted by the staff Harold Ellingwood and Al LeBrun. The paper reported that Dalhover had sported a number of bruises while in lockup at City Hall, the results of his resisting arrest, apparently. It also reported that Dalhover had told his questioners that he was prepared to kill every time that he was "out on the streets." This included Maine.[22]

Another witness had her experience of the shootings printed in the *BDC*. However, the newspaper decided it was desirable to state that she—Mrs. Grace Hardy of Bangor—"gave a *Commercial* reporter her ideas, a woman's view of the federal raid." She stated:

> I was sitting in my car in front of Dakin's sporting goods company writing a letter. A car drove up in back of me and parked. I paid no attention to it. About five minutes later a sedan bearing out of state license plates drew up in front of the store and two men got out.

About that time, the man in the car behind me yelled, "look out," and the shooting started. I dropped to the floor of my car. The burst of fire lasted about 30 seconds and when it was all over I got up and looked out of the window to see two men, the pair who were entering the store, lying in the street dead.[23]

According to the *BDC*, the female witness "finished up with, 'Gosh. Those G-men are awful good-looking, and brave, too.'"[24]

The *BDC* rushed to report, too, that the injured FBI agent shot in the sting was in "good" condition at the local hospital, and that this statement from Dr. Allen Craig "will dispel any rumor that the G-man . . . is dead."[25]

In case anyone was concerned about Dalhover's health, the *BDC* reported in a brief piece that Dr. Martin A. Vickers, city physician, had visited the prisoner at City Hall after the shootout, and reported that Dalhover "was as cool as a cucumber" in spite of the deaths of his associates that morning. The next day, October 13, the paper would report that Dalhover was a bit worse for the wear and tear of the events of the previous day, but that the authorities had brought his food in from a nearby restaurant and that he had smoked while in custody, remaining calm in spite of his being just twenty years old.[26]

As to the status of the bodies of Brady and Shaffer, the *Bangor Daily Commercial*, noted on October 13 that Dr. Herbert C. Scribner, a county medical examiner had stated, "I have been warned not to say a word." He could not speak to the autopsies performed on Brady and Shaffer, nor could hospital pathologist Dr. H. E. Thompson speak of the autopsies of October 12.[27]

The *BDC* was able to print a statement on the evening of October 12 from FBI Agent Myron Gurney, "the agent in charge of today's coupe," praising the action of the local chief-of-police and his men, stating, "Never have we had more cooperation from municipal officers than today. Chief Crowley showed that he is keeping abreast of the times by tipping us off that the Brady Gang was in this part of New England. Bangor ought to be proud that it has a man of Chief Crowley's caliber as the head of its police department."[28]

The newspaper also printed, on October 12, a Columbus, Ohio, article from the Associated Press about the gang, and the possibility of the gang having murdered Patrolman George Conn near Freeport, Ohio, on September 27. Conn's "bullet-pierced body was found in a roadside ditch Sept. 28th." The question of the gang's guilt in the murder would come again quite soon. The week before the Bangor shootout, the investigators into the Conn murder determined that the descriptions of the murder suspects matched those of the Brady Gang members. The following day, the paper ran another article about Conn's murder.[29]

Acting quickly, the *BDC* had also surmised by the afternoon of October 12 that the gangsters had been "hanging out somewhere to the West of town," as BPD inspector Frank McClay had spotted their car coming into town on Hammond Street.[30] While other people suggested that the gang had stayed near or in downtown Bangor, the *Bangor Daily Commercial* surmised otherwise, correctly as it turned out. Both local newspapers reminded readers that President FDR was to hold one of his radio chats that night.[31]

The *BDC* printed a photograph of Dalhover behind bars at City Hall on October 13, and superimposed the mug shots of the three members of the gang near the bottom of the cell photograph. The photograph of Dalhover taken in the cell did not show much of the man, but just the one-half of his stern lips, most of his nose, and one eye looking out were a bit haunting. His hands were clearly cuffed, although one of the vertical cell bars split Dalhover's picture almost right down the middle, while a horizontal bar obscured his forehead, as it did others parts of his chin and arms.[32]

The *BDC* as noted printed few photographs related to the actual shootout and its aftermath. It did, on October 13, print of collage of photographs of other newspapers' front-page coverage, which showed how widely distributed news of the shootings was in the Northeast. Under the title "Brady Killing as Viewed by Metropolitan Newspapers," the collage showed the headlines of the *Boston Herald*, the *Daily Record*, the *Boston Traveler*, the *Boston Herald*, the *Boston Post*, and the *Daily News*. These were shown layered over other newspapers. The caption included with the photograph asserted that the bold headlines and photographs published in newspapers throughout the East more than twenty-four hours after the shootout "proclaimed to the world that the Number One Enemy of America and his pals had been slain or captured. The coverage given the shootout "show[s] clearly the importance of the killing—whereas here in Bangor a person is apt to miss the actual scope and significance of the affair, because of its exciting nearness." Most of the papers ran headlines about the Brady Gang underneath or alongside their announcements of FDR's latest calls for "new power" over the economy of Congress.[33] Certainly the events in Bangor were exciting to locals, but many would indeed have realized the importance of events in the city, so perhaps the *BDC* was showing that its staff had been reticent in some ways as *it* understood the importance.

Under its collage, the *BDC* ran an article stating, "State Trooper Russell Fletcher, assigned to the Bangor-Newport Road, had a narrow escape from being shot by Dalhover." The paper reported that the trooper had stopped at the Auto Rest Park where the gang was staying for a cup of coffee. He did not know about the sting operation in Bangor, nor that the gang was in the area. He said later that he had noticed a man sitting near the door eating lunch on Monday, but thought nothing of it. After his capture, Dalhover purportedly stated that he had seen a state trooper at the motor park. Asked why he did not shoot the man, he replied, "He didn't know me and I didn't know him, but if he had made a move toward his gun, even brushed for it or reached for a handkerchief, I would have let him have it." It was during the same interview that Dalhover told the police that he and his cohorts had stayed at the Auto Rest Park on Monday night, and driven to Bangor Tuesday morning.[34]

As to the automobile the gang drove to Bangor, in addition to other inventories to be published of the gang's arsenal found in it, the *BDC* also noted in a small piece on October 13 that the car had a "trick window." To help enable the mobsters to "shoot their way out of any tight spot," the gang had had "all the screws on the rear window of their black sedan . . . removed so that the glass could be taken out in order to fire from the back seat." The paper did not clarify if the trick window was one or other of the rear side windows, or if it was the rear view window. The paper did note that according to one official, "That is no ordinary equipment on the car. It is really an armored sedan, with special medal covering to withstand any bullets."[35]

In addition to writing about the trick window in the gangsters' car, the *BDC* on October 15 noted that a hidden "trap or receptacle, obviously for the hiding of a revolver or other weapons, was discovered at the top of the back seat." (This seems to have been much like the compartment found in Baltimore, and the gang likely secreted guns in their automobiles whenever they could.) Moreover, after discovering the compartment, authorities upon further searching had found a revolver hidden away in it, one the paper surmised was "a probable reserve weapon for probable use in event of a surprise attack and seizing of guns in view." With all weapons seized, by October 15 the car had been taken to the basement of Bangor's Central Fire Station for storage.[36]

Perhaps just as important, the newspaper ran a short piece from Indianapolis in its evening paper stating that Dalhover had confessed there that the gang had killed Richard Rivers. Charles Geiseking, for whom the gang had been seeking medical aid when the murder took place, remained in the Ohio penitentiary hospital, still incapacitated from his having been shot following the gang's second jewelry store holdup in Lima, Ohio.[37]

In addition, an AP piece from Chicago stated that "several Chicago underworld characters breathed easier today upon learning federal agents had wiped out the Al Brady Gang at Bangor, Me." This might have been a bit of conjecture by the Chicago press, which additionally reported that Brady "had sworn vengeance against eight gunmen and a fence who had hijacked $50,000 from him and his associates." The hijacking had supposedly happened on April 12, 1936, the day on which the gang had been robbed of their stolen goods in the Chicago flat.[38]

The newspaper also printed a somewhat peculiar pen-and-ink drawing that day. The caption noted that "Raymond F. Prince of the R.B. Dunning Company was so moved by the grim spectre [sic] of death which struck down two gangsters" that he had made the drawing. His artwork showed one man fully dressed lying on the ground, blood pooled near him. Over the dead man stood what must have been "Justice," holding the scales of justice and wearing a cape, but Justice was a skeleton.[39]

The *Commercial* likewise ran a few editorials on the days after the shootout. On October 13, in an editorial with the lead "Touch of the Wild West," the paper commended the authorities on the job they had done. It noted, "Al Brady and his gang will plague the law no more and we expect that in the future the crooks and bandits from the middle west will remember the fate that Brady met in Bangor, Maine, and will shun this city like the pestilence. And that will be entirely satisfactory."[40] The paper had run four different editions over the past day to keep readers abreast of the developments, and noted that thousands of extra copies had been sold, with people lined up at the door to get copies, and requests for information were coming in in person and via telegraph and telephone.[41]

Meanwhile, the justice system moved forward. On October 14, the death certificate for Clarence Lee Shaffer Jr. was filed at the office of the Bangor City Clerk, Archie R. Lovett. The certificate had been signed by the Penobscot County medical examiner, Herbert C. Scribner. Shaffer's age was noted as twenty, his residence as Indianapolis, Indiana, and his place of death as: "Central Street, Bangor, Me." There was no hospital, no home, no last refuge from or during death for the young man. As to the cause of death, the medical examiner stated on the certificate: "Multiple gunshot wounds of the abdomen and chest." The death's contributory cause was "justifiable homicide." The medical examiner filed the death certificate just before Shaffer's body was loaded on a train headed for Indianapolis.[42]

Al Brady's death certificate was also placed on file in Bangor that week. His full name as listed was Alfred James Brady, his age given as twenty-six, his birthplace or residence as Indianapolis, Indiana, and his occupation as "Bandit." Brady's death certificate was filed the day after Shaffer's, and his place of death was likewise identified as "Central Street, (public highway) Bangor, Me." The official cause of death was stated as "Gun shot wound through heart," with the contributing cause "justifiable homicide" just as it had been with Shaffer's.[43]

As to the wisdom of the gang in general, the *BDN* noted just after the shootout that the men had acted in Bangor "with incredible stupidity as they all but engaged a press agent to let Bangor know they had arrived." The paper then described the first visit by the gang about ten days earlier, the follow-up visit, and their greater insistence on acquiring the desired munitions, and so forth.[44]

The conditions under which Dalhover was being held were unique. He was deemed the first "important" prisoner held in the small lockup, and he stayed there as the only prisoner. The prisoners previously at the lockup—or who would have been taken there that week—had been transferred. In the past, any "important" or dangerous criminals like Dalhover had been held at the more secure Penobscot County Jail. Moreover, in another break with tradition, soon after the arrest, Myron Gurnea, leader of the G-Men in Bangor, imposed a rule of silence upon City Hall, as the local press announced in large headlines on the 14th. He had been described the day before as being "tall, quiet and decisive.

He listened to the pleas of reporters that they be allowed to see the prisoner and replied: 'The case is not closed. The trail is not dead. There will be no statement to the press.'" He did allow reporters to take one photograph each of the prisoner, and Dalhover was described by a *BDN* reporter as "a slight young man . . . as white as death—the blood still congealed upon his weary face." He was also described as having walked into the store "smoothly shaven; neatly dressed—[the] exact opposite of the gangster of fiction and the movies."[45]

When asked again for further information, Gurnea told one reporter, "I'll get you a badge. . . . I'll make you a member of the squad. Then you can ask all the questions you please." Neither local, state, nor federal agents were to speak with the press. The federal agents grilled Dalhover both in his cell and in the police chief's office. According to Gurney, his own report would be sent to Fred Soucy, head of the FBI's New England headquarters in Boston. The initial report had been sent out just after the gunfire; others would follow. Soucy had spoken in Bangor in the past, so some Bangorites were familiar with him.[46]

A seal of silence may well have been imposed on the authorities, but the press and other individuals seemingly had no such inhibitions about telling whatever they knew about the situation or the men. The *BDN* on October 14 ran an advertisement for an article written by Chicago Police Captain John Egan and to be published in *Official Detective Magazine* on the history of the gang, advertised as being now available at all local newsstands and excerpted in part in the *BDN*. The excerpts had taken up a few pages in the newspaper on the previous day. The issue of the magazine that would hold the story was due out on October 29, however, so by then the author would have had time to finalize his story. The press seemed to be drumming up business in advance of publication.[47]

The *Bangor Daily News* and, to a lesser extent, the *Bangor Daily Commercial* continued to publish everything they could about the case. Bold headlines topped almost every page of the *BDN's* coverage, such as the inside page of one of the October 13 issues of the *BDN*, which declared, "G-Men's Guns Roar As They Get Gangster Pair," with various photographs and related articles printed on the balance of the sheet. The paper stated that the gang had robbed over $100,000 in jewelry from four Ohio stores, "had hijacked other gangs, had defied the police of many states, [and] had been hunted from coast to coast." It stated, too, that the black sedan the gang had driven to downtown Bangor "nosed its way into Central Street at 8:30 o'clock. Its sleek exterior gave no hint it was a rolling arsenal." On October 14, the *BDN* printed the wanted posters or flyers for the three men, including their numerous aliases and birth dates. The paper published all sorts of photographs, including those of the dead bodies in the streets, the places the gang and the FBI had stayed while in the Bangor area, shots of Dalhover under arrest, and so forth. The *BDC*, as noted above, was much more circumspect in its use of photographs, and had published the "Wanted Poster" or notification paper on the day of the shooting.[48]

While the trap was being set and during the aftermath of the shoot-out, one group of the G-men, according to local sources, had stayed at an apartment house at 291 Maine Street, while other federal agents stayed in downtown hotels. Elsewhere, in Bridgeport, Connecticut, reports were made that the two women who had accompanied the Brady Gang there were placed under arrest, or, at a minimum, taken into custody for questioning. The location where the Brady Gang had spent the night before the shootout was identified as the Auto Rest Park in Carmel, the men sharing a cabin there.[49]

The New York Times picked up the story of the Bangor shootout, as would most major U.S. newspapers, and had a somewhat different slant on the events in Bangor. Its header ran, "Brady Gang Is Wiped Out Planning Bangor Bank Raid." Its subtitle stated: "Leader and Chief Aid Slain in the Street, Another Captured as They Try to Buy Machine Gun—G Man Is Wounded."[50]

The reason for the planned bank heist being assumed, according to the *NYT*, was that a floor plan of the Merrill Trust Company Bank—with deposits of more than $5 million—was purportedly found in "the inside pocket of Al Brady," probably the inside pocket of his jacket. The article also stated that the two dead men had some $8,000 in cash in their pockets, and that Dalhover had had $2,000 on his person. Moreover, the *Times* stated that once the Brady Gang had been identified as having come to Maine, authorities had taken steps to protect local banks, warning bank officials to keep all money, except for limited "counter money" in their vaults. Police and Androscoggin County officials in Maine were also looking for anything that might link the gang with a robbery at the Livermore Falls Trust Company in which $25,000 was stolen. Officials of the banks would be allowed to view the bodies for possible identification.[51]

However, the local press reported on October 13 and October 14 that "unofficial sources" had stated that James Dalhover, after being taken into custody, denied having had any plans with his fellow gang-members to rob the local bank. He said that the men had come to Maine only to replenish their ammunition and firearm supplies. They had no intentions of robbing any Bangor bank; rather they had planned a payroll robbery in another state as their next heist, one that they thought would net them some $85,000. Had the G-men not put an end to the gang, they would have needed only two or three years before they would have been "on top of the world."[52]

Yet, no member of the gang was "on top of the world" after the events of October 12, 1937. Two of their number would soon be placed under the surface of the world, while two others were wounded and incarcerated, and locked away from the world.

The federal agents allowed the press access to Dalhover once just after his arrest, when Gurnea had allowed each press photographer to step forward from outside his cell one at a time and take one photograph each of the prisoner. The *BDC* printed its one such photograph the day after the shootout, with the mug shots of all three gang members included with it. Dalhover in his intense questioning by the agents, did, according to local police, confess to numerous crimes on the part of the gang.[53]

The FBI would later release a more comprehensive list of weapons seized, but the *NYT* announced the day after the shootout that the agents had recovered "seven revolvers, two machine guns, two army rifles, a supply of cartridge clips, 2,000 rounds of ammunition," plus license plates from Indiana and Wisconsin, various road maps, and clothing and blankets. The authorities would soon identify two Marlin machine guns found in the car, each with some 350 rounds of ammunition, and, as crucial to the justice system in the months that followed, the handcuffs taken from State Trooper Paul Minneman at Caley's Church on the day he was murdered. In addition, federal officials were able to show that three shells found at Caley's church had been fired from one of the machine guns found in the gang's car. So, too, were one set of plates in the car traced to those used on the gangster's car the day the Goodland, Indiana, bank had been robbed. Dalhover soon admitted that two of the rifles and one of the machine guns found in the gangster's sedan had been used by them during the bank robbery. More than a few people noted that the Brady Gang had met its end exactly a year and a day after their prison escape from Greenfield, Indiana.[54]

The perhaps more fortunate, for a time, thirty-year-old Dalhover was returned to Indiana to await trial for murder and other crimes. Twenty-year-old Shaffer, killed beside his gang leader, had his body sent home to Indianapolis for burial. No one wanted to claim the body of twenty-six-year-old Al Brady, so his remains stayed in Bangor. This presented something of a problem for the City of Bangor, for the city ultimately had to bury the gangster, initially at taxpayer expense. The municipality later recovered money (stated as being closer to $5,000 than the $8,000 earlier reported) for the burial from money found on Brady, but this, of course, may have been—one way or another—taxpayers' money from another locality.[55]

Al Brady did have an uncle, but his uncle could not or would not pay to have Brady's remains shipped home nor pay for a funeral. The city buried Brady at Mount Hope Cemetery, in the unkempt city section, without a headstone. Members of Mount Hope Cemetery staff, a member or two of the press, a few law officials, and a representative from the local funeral home attended the burial. Seemingly, no one else did. The *Bangor Daily Commercial* described the situation in its October 15 headline, "No Escort, No Mourners, No Sun as Man Who Fought Law Is Lowered into Ground Begrudged Him by Natives." The *Bangor Daily News* reported that the burial had been without flowers, mourners, crowds, and ceremony and observed that "the city that repudiated Alfred Brady in life, was forced, by ironic circumstances, to receive him in death."[56]

The *New York Times* ran a brief article on the burial, its header being: "Brady Buried as Pauper; No Mourners Attend Funeral of Gang Leader:" The Associated Press had sent out the article, which appeared in newspapers across the country. The article stated that "Al Brady's body went into a grave today, unmourned, unattended and unmarked." It referred to the events of October 12 as "a Federal machinegun coup" and said Brady "was buried in an isolated section of Mount Hope Cemetery." As opposed to its earlier statement regarding the amount of money found on the gangster, it said, "officials declined to say, but he was far from being a pauper. Police had estimated the gang had around

$5,000 in all, which was turned over to Public Administrator C. J. O'Leary, representing the State."[57]

It was the Overseers of the Poor, an institution dating back to the early history of Bangor as a city under the State of Maine as of 1834, and even before that as a town under the control of first Massachusetts and then Maine, that buried Alfred Brady. The Overseers of the Poor had long had charge of burying the poor and indigent, and although Brady was found with money on his person, it would be a fairly lengthy legal process to settle his estate as well as Shaffer's. In the meantime, another department of the City on the Penobscot became involved in the story of the Brady Gang. And, as was its custom, the man who had terrorized parts of the Midwest would have only the simplest burial available at the time, and as also the norm in Bangor, no headstone.[58]

The local press noted that it was a grim, gray day when Brady was buried. Although his was a burial by the Overseers of the Poor, he did not end up in "Strangers' Row" as the older section of paupers' graves became known, or the newer section for pauper burial just across Mount Hope Avenue from the older location.[59]

Over the following seven decades, many people would seek out Brady's interment spot, located north of Mount Hope Avenue. The story of his demise in Bangor became something of a local legend. His interment spot was often referred to as "Mount Hope's most talked about grave."[60] Decades later, in 2007, a group of citizens would purchase a small stone for his gravesite and would reenact the shootout.

At the time of his burial, the *BDN* saw the day as having "no touch of mistaken romance: it was all utterly dreary, ugly, and disillusioning under the leaden skies. In this one concrete example, at least, complete oblivion was the reward of crime."[61]

The *BDC*'s coverage of Brady's funeral included one photograph of the actual burial, its major headline being about the interment and the "Gloomy Day and Begrudged Grave," with a brief article underneath with its title simply: "Not Wanted Here." The piece was marked as an editorial and stated, "The burial was without ceremony, without tears, without a semblance of sorrow." The FBI had done a "splendid job" by ending the careers of the gang members, and they should have ended the job by "taking possession of [Brady's] body and ordering its removal back to Indiana. Had the killer been captured alive the federal men would have taken him away. Why should they not have taken his body?"[62]

No person had been allowed into the funeral parlor to mourn Brady or his fallen companion. Only federal agents, the coroner, and police had been allowed into the rooms, as the FBI secured the premises, as was its custom. Only on the day of the burial was a minister allowed to come in to offer up a prayer. Asked if it had been difficult to secure a clergyman to give the prayer, a member of the funeral parlor staff later reported, "No, the first one we approached was willing." After the prayer, Brady's body in its plain pine box, was transported to the cemetery in the parlor's hearse, accompanied by Malcolm S. Hayes and Walter A. Jellison of the firm. Harold S. Burrill, superintendent of Mount Hope Cemetery (the private section, which also contracted its services to the city for the public section), his assistant, Stanley Howatt, and a gravedigger, Eugene Meehan, plus a few newspapermen made up the attendees of the bleak burial. Photographs of the burial appeared in the local papers, the *BDN* printing a number of them, the *BDC* just one, showing the wooden box at the site and those in attendance.[63]

On October 14, 1937, the *BDC* had reported Clarence Lee "Loudmouth" Shaffer's body leaving the city in "a modest black casket" with "bronze handles and a cream silk lining," and James Dalhover's flight out of the state under the direction of FBI agent Myron Gurnea. It also ran a large hand-drawn map identifying major points involved in the shootout and its aftermath, including locations of officers, cars, stores, and so forth. With this, on the left side of the map, it printed a caricature or two of Brady: one was a sketch of a face, clearly Brady's with his eyes looking glum and angry, and the other of a dead body, hat beside it. The caption of the sketches and map was: "Farewell to Crime, Al Brady, Ex. Public Enemy No. 1." The script was one of hand-drawn letters of various sizes and styles, and once again the artwork seemed a few decades ahead of its time, the lettering looking like something out of the 1960s. At the end of one article, the paper noted that with his extradition, "this morning's episode loomed as the beginning of the end for the youthful 30-year-old Dalhover, the youngster who had defied the law since 10 years of age."[64]

The local press had exploded with the biggest news to hit the city in years. The *Bangor Daily News* had quickly issued a second edition on the day of the shooting, October 12, and devoted almost all of its regular issue to the shootout the following day—October 13, 1937—as well as issuing a second issue that day and the next. The paper printed articles written by its own staff, as well as a few pieces sent in from other states. It printed photographs of everything and everyone it could obtain related to the case, including numerous street photographs taken in the aftermath of the gun battle including those of the dead Brady and Shaffer, of Dalhover being escorted off to the local lockup, a photograph of G-man Walsh as taken several weeks before the shootout in Bangor while he was given a marksmanship demonstration at Quantico, Virginia, showing how to aim through the use of a mirror. The paper also printed a large hand-drawn map on October 14 that showed the trail the Brady Gang had taken in their deadly careers, infamous careers that ended in Maine. The *Bangor Daily Commercial* had likewise given the shootout and its aftermath close coverage, although its articles were a bit less dramatic overall and it printed fewer photographs.[65]

The *BDN* and the *BDC* both printed a Central Press photograph of Clarence Lee Shaffer's purported love child, Russell Lee Shaffer, age fourteen months, and the toddler's mother, Christine Puckett. The caption the *BDC* included stated that Puckett had not known of Shaffer's criminal activities, that she would fight on behalf of her son's property rights, and that "she had no regrets and would attend Shaffer's funeral."[66] The photograph would appear in the papers in Baltimore, Bridgeport, Indianapolis, and in other American communities, especially ones that the gang had "hit"—in one way or another.

The *BDN* wrote that in the aftermath of the shootout people were asking one major question: would three dangerous men from the Midwest travel all the way to Bangor just to buy guns? Part of the reason they might have done so, the paper posited, was that almost every state required that a person secure a police permit to purchase a gun or ammunition, and in some states merely possessing a machine gun is a felony. No such restrictions existed in Maine. There did exist a Maine law prohibiting the carrying of concealed weapons, but any adult could buy them, "and he may buy a whole arsenal of machine guns if the fancy [strikes] him." The paper did not know everything the recently arrested Dalhover had told authorities, but it did know that he had started off by saying that the men had come to Bangor "to replenish their supplies" and that Al Brady had been the killer in the group, and that he himself had never meant to kill anyone.[67]

Even Dakin store clerk James Seeley had his picture included in one of the October 13 editions of the *BDN*. It was printed under the lead of "The Story of Brady Gang's Reign of Terror," and alongside excerpts of Chicago Police Captain John Egan's story of the gang, "The Second Dillinger." Seeley was photographed in a dress shirt and tie, looking quite pleased, and holding a cigarette in his hand. The accompanying caption stated that Seeley had just escaped the bullets when the gunfire erupted by hitting the ground as fast as possible. He had been positioned outside the store sweeping the sidewalk, as if all was normal. On the 12th, in addition to calling the gang "stupid" in their actions in Maine, the newspaper had called Al Brady a "master bandit," and the gang—which the paper noted may have included more than the three men in the shootout—"masters of crime" before they came to Bangor.[68]

The *BDN* had printed photographs of the G-men in the streets, and such items as bullet holes in the window of the Singer Sewing Machine opposite the Dakin store, and a traveling salesman who was in the store when the shooting started. The staff of Dakin's store, and people inside the store on the day of the shootout, were photographed together. The newspaper anticipated that Mr. Everett S. "Shep" Hurd and his staff would receive the award money for the tip leading to the apprehension of the gang. Hurd did eventually receive a reward of $1,500 as well as a letter from the FBI's J. Edgar Hoover.[69]

In addition to the local newspaper coverage, one of Bangor's radio stations—WABI—aired a "resume" of the gang and a re-enactment of the shootout at 8:00 p.m. on October 12. Two of the radio's staff had written the script that Tuesday afternoon, which was acted out by eight people, including a couple of women. The presentation covered the gang's actions—as far as they then knew them, over the previous year. The presentation was deemed a "fine" one, and the *BDC* reported that it had drawn "much commentary about the city Wednesday."[70]

The FBI recovered an impressive—or frightening—arsenal from the Brady Gang's car and stashes. Their arsenal included thirty-five guns; their trip to Bangor was not necessary. The thirty-five guns as listed by the FBI were:

Eight .45 caliber automatic pistols
Seven .38 caliber revolvers
Three .30 caliber machine guns with 350 shot belts, 22 of these
mounted for use in an automobile
Five .32 caliber automatic pistols
Five .30 caliber rifles
One .30 caliber automatic rifle
Two 12-gauge shotguns
One .45 caliber revolver
One .32 caliber revolver
Two .22 caliber automatic pistols[71]

The FBI also found "large quantities of ammunition, extra shot clips, drums, and tear gas grenades."[72]

Although the local press would not have had full access to the weapons list, they did indeed learn that the gang had come to town heavily armed. The *BDN*'s page-wide headlines in its paper the day after the shootout read: "Bandits' Car a Regular Arsenal—Wanted More." A large photograph underneath showed some of the arsenal: a machine gun, a roll of five hundred jacketed bullets, a box of ammunition, and a few other items. The caption caught the irony of the gang being wiped out in the pursuit of even more weaponry.[73]

A later entry in the *BDN* quoted the chairman of the Bangor City Council, Benjamin W. Blanchard, as stating that the weapons found in the gangster's car would be "quite an asset to the Chinese Army." The recounting of the arsenal at this point, according to the paper, included:

Two army machine guns, each fully loaded with 500 rounds of ammunition; five revolvers—including one pearl handled weapon—all of heavy caliber and all completely loaded; five automatic pistols all with fully loaded clips; two high powered Army rifles, also completely loaded. In addition, a vicious "pocket-gun"—a heavily caliber revolver with the barrel sawed off until but a half-inch of it remained—was found. Two steel boxes, similar to those used for filing valuable papers, were found in the car. Both boxes contained extra ammunition and clips. Two powerful flashlights, a pair of imported binoculars, and two machine hammers completed the excess equipment in the machine.

Automobile registration plates taken from the bullet-battered machine included four sets from Ohio, two sets from Indiana, and one from Wisconsin.[74]

While not too dissimilar from the later listing by the FBI, the day-after accounting was a bit more descriptive. Another piece in the paper stated that all of the personal effects of the gang were confiscated and "carefully labeled." Some $5,000 in currency had been found on the men. All weaponry found on the men or in their sedan was "being crated for shipment, supposedly to the FBI headquarters in Washington."[75]

The gangsters, in addition to guns and ammunition, were also reported to have sought accurate road maps for both Bangor and Maine, or at least for Penobscot County. Daniel L. McOlay of the Bangor Public Works Department stated that the men had come into his office at City Hall to inquire if "accurate city maps were available for distribution." Herbert Leach, a Penobscot County Commissioner, said the three men had also visited his office at the Penobscot County Courthouse. He recognized the men after being shown their photographs after the shootout. He stated that the men "were quiet and taciturn" and had asked him for maps for Penobscot County showing all the roads and byways in existence.[76]

In a few amusing quips and observations, the *BDN* reported too, "It was a rather interesting fact that of Bangor's 30,000 people it seemed that at least nine-tenths of them were eye-witnesses to yesterday's killings." However, few of them could "agree on many of the important facts, and versions of what occurred differed widely."[77]

In another short article, the *BDN* printed the header: "Custom's Agent's Warm Reception." The agent in question had supposedly come to town from Vermont to start work in the Bangor area. He asked Captain L. J. Perry, "What kind of a town is this?" He then added, perhaps after being told that it was a nice quiet city, "Just a ways down the street, the road is full of bodies."[78]

In the event that anyone missed the shootout, the *BDN*—or its advertisers—included a small advertisement with the statements: "Today, In case you weren't on Central St. yesterday, you must see *Dead End*. . . . How are these killers made. . . . Where do they come from?" That day, Samuel Goldwyn's film *Dead End* was playing at Bangor's

Bijou Theater, starring Sylvia Sidney, Joel McCrea, and Humphrey Bogart. The film was based on a Broadway show that had "set records." A small separate article stated in its header, "*Dead End* Scene Very Much Like Bangor Tragedy." The film story followed the life of a gangster whose life and death, the paper observed, resembled that of Al Brady.[79] Perhaps, as Brady was still alive when the story was written and performed on stage, it was based on John Dillinger or another 1930s gangster.

Also, for anyone who might have missed the downtown events, or who wished to revisit them, the Bangor Opera House featured "motion pictures of the Brady Gang killing here," on Saturday, October 16. The pictures seemed to be primarily those taken by Shep Hurd just after the shootout. The show was first presented at 1:30 Saturday afternoon, with Hurd a guest of the manager, and Paramount News Pictures presenting the show again on Monday through Wednesday of the following week. The *BDC* ran a short article about the show, as well as printing advertising for it.[80]

Everyone had a story to tell. A local barber had shaven the gangsters a few times, he said, and had been asked by them where they might find a rooming house nearby where they could also get their meals. Howard L. Chisholm, who owned a barbershop on lower Main Street, reported that two of the Brady Gang had come to his shop the Friday before the Tuesday shooting, and asked for a shave. They also asked about nearby lodging, although overall the men spoke very little. He recommended a house nearby to the men, and stated that he had seen their car parked near his shop a number of times over the weekend. He had also seen the G-men going to a nearby apartment on Tuesday with their "equipment," and the paper lead the short article with the question, "Bandits and G-Men Neighbors?"[81] The *BDC* was the first to refute that idea.

Interactions between gang members and women were also noted. One woman, a waitress in an Exchange Street restaurant, told reporters for the *BDN* that she recognized Al Brady from his photographs, that he had come in a few times and just ordered orange juice, and that he "always flipped her a dime." (Years later, a woman who had worked at the Pine Tree Restaurant, a bit further off the main thoroughfare and so, she surmised, a favored place for the gang for dinner, stated to Richard Shaw—a *BDN* writer whose mother had seen the aftermath of the shootings on October 12, 1937—that the men were indeed good tippers, as well as being soft spoken and well dressed, punctual men she had thought were "city slickers."[82])

Another woman, the only one to see James Dalhover after he was locked up in Bangor, a municipal court stenographer, Mrs. Edgerly had gone into the cellblock accompanied by officers. Dalhover had called out to her, "Don't be afraid of me. Look me over. I'm only a human being."[83]

In an odd twist, the *BDC* ran not photographs of the gang but of Jack Dempsey, champion heavyweight boxer, stopping at their offices and reading the *BDC* in its sports department for details of the events in Bangor. Both local papers had covered Dempsey's appearance in Bangor as a referee in a wrestling match held in the city. The *BDC* printed a photograph of Dempsey holding a newspaper sitting on the edge of sports reporter Bud Levitt's desk reading the paper of the evening before, October 14, the large caption "DALHOVER GRILLED" clearly pictured. Underneath the photograph, the paper printed a signed letter from Dempsey to Frank L. Bass, the paper's managing editor, about the fine job the local police had done in aiding the capture of the Brady Gang.[84]

The car the three men brought to Maine remained in the basement of the fire station on the day Brady was buried and after Dalhover had been extradited to Indiana. Supposedly, it remained locked, and the key had been retained by the FBI. Agent Gurnea had taken the key with him when he left Bangor to help transfer Dalhover to authorities in Indiana. (The ultimate fate of the car remains unknown, but no doubt the city disposed of it once certain that it held no further evidential value. A Skowhegan insurance agent, G. Allan Wentworth, purportedly drove the car until late 1938, after acquiring it from Bangor in 1937.[85]) Rumors that additional weapons had been found in the car after the lead FBI agents left town were quickly refuted by Bangor's fire chief.[86]

Other unknowns continued to exist. Included in the inventory of items found on or with the Brady Gang was the photograph of a young woman found in Al Brady's pocket. Local journalist Richard Shaw posited that it might have been one of Alicia Frawley whom Brady had met while the gang hid out in Connecticut, but of course Brady had had many women. In addition, the city may have retained Brady's brain for scientific study after his autopsy and not buried it with Brady in the city section of Mount Hope, although the brain also might have been studied and then placed back inside Brady's skull.[87] There were indeed some odd issues to resolve.

The September before the FBI sting in Bangor, FBI Director J. Edgar Hoover had spoken about coordinating efforts between the FBI and local, state, and other law enforcement agencies. He said that as criminals viewed other criminals as their cohorts and "pals" to be aided when possible in escaping the law, all law enforcement agencies must band together in apprehending criminals. The FBI looked forward to a time when there would be complete cooperation between various law enforcement agencies, and Hoover stated that progress to that end was already being made. The *Bangor Daily Commercial* ran an editorial about the September 30, 1935, address and opined that the smooth sting operation in Bangor was a prime example of the cooperation Hoover sought, stating that in Bangor, Hoover had "received 100 percent cooperation."[88] However, the final fate of Rhuel James Dalhover remained in question. He had survived the shootout, but would he survive the judicial system?

NOTES

1. "The Brady Gang," *FBI History: Famous Cases*, FBI; Circuit of Appeals, Seventh Circuit, *United States v. Dalhover*, 18 May 1938; and local newspaper coverage; *Bangor Daily News (BDN)*, 12, 13, and 14 October 1937. The clerks names have been spelled different ways.

2. "The Brady Gang," *FBI History: Famous Cases*, FBI; and local newspaper coverage, especially *BDN* and *Bangor Daily Commercial (BDC)*, 12–18 October 1937.

3. Ibid. Also see "The Brady Gang," *FBI History: Famous Cases*, FBI, and local newspaper coverage. And note: Dalhover's name has also been spelled Delhover.

4. *NYT*, 13 October 1937.

5. *BDN*, 12–14 October 1937; Walsh obituary, *BDN*, 1 May 2014; "The Brady Gang," *FBI History: Famous Cases*, FBI.

6. *BDN*, October 12, 13 and 14, 1937, and see other newspaper coverage and FBI video on the gang's car and attire.

7. Circuit of Appeals, Seventh Circuit, *United States v. Dalhover*, 18 May 1938; "The Brady Gang," *FBI History: Famous Cases*, FBI; "Tough Customers," *Time*, 25 October 1937; and see local newspaper coverage.

8. Ibid.

9. Ibid.

10. *New York Times*, 13 October 1937.

11. *BDN*, 14 October 1937, first edition of the day.

12. *BDN*, 13 October 1937.

13. *BDN*, 13 October 1937.

14. *BDN*, 12 and, quotes, 13 October 1937.

15. *BDC*, Extra Edition, Evening, 12 and 13 October 1937.

16. "The Brady Gang," *FBI History: Famous Cases*, FBI.

17. *BDC*, Extra Edition, Evening, 12 October 1937.

18. *BDC*, Extra Edition, Evening, 12 October 1937.

19. Ibid.

20. "Tough Customers," *Time*, 25 October 1937; *BDN*, 12–14 October 1937.

21. *BDC*, Extra Edition, Evening, 12 October 1937.

22. *BDC*, 13 October 1937, combined from a few small articles as the paper tended to use small inserts as well as a front page story on the events.

23. *BDC*, Extra Edition, Evening, 12 October 1937.

24. Ibid.

25. Ibid.

26. Ibid. And see *BDC*, 13 October 1937.

27. *BDC*, 13 October 1937.

28. *BDC*, Extra Edition, Evening, 12 October 1937.

29. Ibid.

30. Ibid.

31. *BDN* and *BDC*, 12 October 1937.

32. *BDC*, 13 October 1937, Evening Edition, as are following dates.

33. *BDC*, 13 October 1937.

34. Ibid.

35. Ibid.

36. *BDC*, 15 October 1937.

37. Ibid.

38. Ibid.

39. Ibid.

40. Ibid.

41. Ibid.

42. As issued and printed in *BDN* and *BDC*, 15 October 1937.

43. As issued and printed in *BDN* and *BDC*, 16 October 1937; and Mount Hope Cemetery Archives.

44. *BDN*, 13 October 1937.

45. *BDN*, 14 October 1937, first edition of the day, and *BDN*, 13 October 1937, for quote and description of Gurney; *BDC*, also on 13 October 1937, on prisoners being taken elsewhere, but from the time of their arrests, not afterword.

46. *BDN*, 13 October 1937; for quotes and description of Gurney.

47. *BDN*, 13 and 14 October 1937, first edition of the day on the 14th; Captain John Egan with Douglas Hunt, "The Second Dillinger," 1937.

48. *BDN*, 12–16 October 1937, and *BDC*, 12–16 October 1937.

49. *BDN*, 14 October 1937, first edition of the day.

50. *NYT*, 13 October 1937.

51. *NYT*, 13 October 1937.

52. *BDC*, 13 October 1937, and *BDN*, 14 October 1937, first edition of the day.

53. *BDC* and *BDN*, 13 October 1937.

54. Circuit of Appeals, Seventh Circuit, *United States v. Dalhover*, 18 May 1938; *New York Times*, 13 October 1937; and "Tough Customers," *Time*, 25 October 1937.

55. *BDN*, 15 October 1937; and Scee, *Mount Hope Cemetery of Bangor Maine: The Complete History*.

56. Ibid.

57. "Brady Buried as Pauper," *NYT*, 16 October 1937.

58. See Scee, *City on the Penobscot* and *Mount Hope Cemetery: The Complete History*, for further information.

59. Ibid. Also see *BDN* and *BDC* for 16 October 1937.

60. Ibid. Also see *BDN*, February 1987 article by Dick Shaw, on quote on grave.

61. *BDN*, 16 October 1937.

62. *BDC*, 15 October 1937.

63. *BDN*, 16 October 1937. And Scee, *City on the Penobscot*, and *Mount Hope Cemetery: The Complete History* for further information on the cemetery and related stories and events, as well as *BDC*, 15 October 1937.

64. *BDC*, 14 October 1937.

65. *BDN*, 12–16 October 1937.

66. *BDN* and *BDC*, Central Press photograph, quote and caption from *BDC*, 16 October 1937.

67. *BDN*, 13 October 1937.

68. *BDN*, 13 October, and second editions, 12 and 14 October 1937.

69. *BDN*, 13 October 1937; and see second edition and subsequent issues of the paper, and the holdings of the Bangor Historical Society.

70. *BDC*, 13 October 1937.

71. "The Brady Gang," *FBI History: Famous Cases*, FBI.

72. Ibid.

73. *BDN*, 13 October 1937.

74. Ibid.

75. Ibid.

76. Ibid.

77. Ibid.

78. Ibid.

79. Ibid.

80. *BDC*, 16 October 1937.

81. *BDN*, 13 October 1937.

82. *BDN*, 13 October 1937; and *BDN*, 4–5 October 1997.

83. *BDN*, 13 October 1937.

84. *BDC*, 15 October 1937.

85. See Richard Shaw, *The Weekly*, Bangor, Maine, 4 October 2011, on the insurance agent's acquiring the car.

86. *BDN*, 16 October 1937.

87. See Richard Shaw, *The Weekly*, Bangor, Maine, 4 October 2011, on the photograph and brain.

88. *BDC*, 15 October 1937.

13

AND THE MAN TALKS ON

While Bangorites and others continued to ponder the events in Bangor, Maine, and the motives of the Brady Gang in going to that small—but busy—city, there remained an arraignment and possibly a trial or trials for surviving gang member Rhuel James Dalhover. Just as dawn was breaking on October 15, 1937, at 5:00 a.m., Dalhover was escorted from the Bangor city lockup by Federal Agent Myron Gurnea and Meredith Stewart—an Indiana State Police detective who had earlier traveled to Baltimore following the shootout there and had come to Bangor to aid in the sting operation—headed for the Bangor airport. Dalhover was photographed with his hands cuffed together, his face looking downward, hat on his head, and his suit seemingly still neat. A second row of G-men followed the two officers and their prisoner as they left City Hall, then Gurnea helped Dalhover into the car, also photographed by the *Bangor Daily News* to the pride of the paper, which would note more than once that it had beat all other presses in obtaining pertinent photographs of the events in Bangor as they had unfolded. Via automobile and surrounded by G-men, and accompanied by a Bangor Police Department detail, Dalhover was taken to the newly improved city airport. From there, on a small government airplane, his hands still shackled, Dalhover was extradited to Indiana.[1]

Agent Gurnea and Indiana Detective Meredith Stewart accompanied Dalhover on his long ride home. The four-seater plane was piloted off the runway at 5:22 a.m. Thursday. By late afternoon, Dalhover was incarcerated in a cell at the Indianapolis Federal Building. According to the Associated Press, when he arrived in Indianapolis, Dalhover was "manacled hand and foot," "haggard," and appeared "dazed," "unable to walk without assistance," and "rushed under heavy guard from the municipal airport to the federal building." Nonetheless, "squads of federal agents, city police, and state officers, armed with machine guns and revolvers, were on the alert from the minute he arrived." Dalhover soon "waived examination on charges of participating in three Indiana bank robberies at Farmland, Carthage, and North Madison."[2]

Newspapers carried accounts of the gangsters' shootout in Bangor and Dalhover's fate. Not just large papers like the *New York Times* did so, but also newspapers from the cities and towns that the gang had visited in their lives of crimes, such as Bridgeport, Baltimore, Chicago, Greenfield, Piqua, and Indianapolis. Such papers generally carried Associated Press articles, often originating in Indianapolis, but sometimes added their own local references to the stories, or at least to their headlines. *The Baltimore Sun*, for example, printed an account of the shootout in Bangor, and noted that Dalhover had confessed to the gang's killings of three law officers and to a store clerk, as well as their having committed numerous robberies of banks, jewelry stores, and grocery stores. The confessions came, according to Bangor Police captain Frank Foley, after lengthy questioning by FBI agents. The FBI, however, would neither confirm nor deny the police captain's assertions that Dalhover had made the confessions, confessions that the *Baltimore News-Post* and other papers also carried on October 13 and 14. The *News-Post* also printed photographs of three of the young people ensnarled in the Brady crime spree: Margaret Larson, Brady's former "sweetheart" in her jaunty hat but looking less than happy; one of the officers believed murdered by the gang—twenty-eight-year-old George Conn, in his Ohio State Police tie and cap, a small smile on his lips— and one of Dalhover. The photograph of Dalhover was one of the clearest images extant of the young man, showing him with large wide-set dark eyes, closely-cropped hair, and full lips, looking pensive—and perhaps already incarcerated. Dalhover was still jailed in Bangor when the *News-Post* and the *Sun* ran their articles, but the *Sun* reported that Indiana State Police Captain Walter Eckert had said that it was his understanding that Dalhover would soon be extradited to Indiana, where two indictments for murder already stood against him in two counties. He did not know just where the outlaw would be tried.[3]

According to Eckert, authorities were trying to discover who had helped the gang in their year of freedom since their 1936 jail break. The Bangor police said that Dalhover had claimed that the trio had made three trips to Maine—staying in tourists camps on their visits—from Connecticut to try to resupply their arsenal, "depleted when police almost caught them in Baltimore." Moreover, the Baltimore newspapers noted that the gang was suspected of killing not just the clerk and two Midwestern law officers, but also Patrolman George Conn of Freeport, Connecticut. Dalhover had apparently acknowledged these shootings—blaming just Brady for the clerk's murder—but not the November 1935 slaying of Frank Levy, the first police murder attributed to the Brady Gang. The Bangor police captain said he had heard Dalhover state that the gang had committed these four murders.[4]

Dalhover purportedly blamed Brady for much of the gang's violence, as he did a few other issues. He supposedly stated, "'Brady was the boss, but he didn't have half the guts Shaffer did. Brady was always anxious to pull his rod. We didn't like that." Of the shooting of Minneman, he stated, "The Indiana cops were on one side of the fence and we were on the other. If we didn't kill them, they [would have] killed us." He said that Brady had ordered the killing. He said of himself, "I wasn't born a killer. If I had been, I'd have bumped off Brady long ago."[5]

Dalhover was also quoted as stating that Brady "was too ritzy," and that he had had frequent arguments with Brady, but just one with Shaffer, and that was only about an hour before the two died in Bangor. Dalhover said that the argument with Shaffer had been about going into the sporting goods store in Bangor. He thought the way they had been conducting their business there "looked phony."[6] And indeed, it had.

Yet, he added, "These two guys are better off than I am. I wish I had got what they got. I've got to take it now." He said he had just been working on (not owning, he implied) a farm and making moonshine on the side when he met Brady. Shaffer had been working on the farm with him, and the two had met Brady together when they visited a neighboring farm.[7] This seems to contradict other versions of how the gang formed, but how they separated is well known. And of course, Dalhover was a liar. But so were the other men. What seems to have been true was that from their escape the year before with $12, the gangsters had stolen and saved over $5,000 by the time they dispersed.

The *Baltimore Sun* also covered the legal issues and the emotional ones tying the gang to Baltimore. Detective Captain John F. Cooney stated that if James Dalhover escaped murder charges in Indiana, Baltimore would press charges. "We will watch the outcome of any trial of Dalhover in Indiana and if he successfully defends himself from charges, we will place a detainer on him on charges of attempting to kill Patrolman Joseph Herget and Fred Fleischmann on Loch Raven Boulevard," the captain stated. However, he added, "I don't think he has any chance of beating the murder charge against him out there." (The paper also noted that the authorities had come to believe that the Brady Gang might have been planning to rob the newly opened Bel Air Race Track, which had had about $100,000 on hand on the day of the Baltimore shootout.)[8]

The AP had carried some snippets of what the women who had married two of the gangsters had said after learning of events in Bangor. The Baltimore press carried lengthier coverage. The *Sun* reported that the women heard the news of Dalhover's capture and Shaffer's death "quietly." Minnie Raimondo, who had married Shaffer, had stated, "I'm not sorry. I'm glad they have been caught. Now I know where they are. We were afraid they would come back someday—but if they had I don't believe they would have done us any harm." She stated that she and her sisters on being released from jail had initially been afraid the gangsters would return, but had then "gotten used to it." She did not plan on claiming Shaffer's body, as she did not have the money for a funeral, and the family still owed their landlord and their attorney money. Her sister Mary, who had married Dalhover, at first stated, "I don't feel sorry about it. They had it coming to them. They ought to get it after the trouble we've been through." After reflecting for a moment, she added, "In one way, I guess I'm a little sorry after all. But it had to happen sometime."[9]

For her part, Alicia Frawley in Bridgeport soon heard that FBI agents were searching for a blonde woman who had accompanied the gang around town and to the Bridgeport Airport. She contacted the FBI, who then interviewed her and asked her to accompany agents out-of-state to help them identify another woman with whom Brady or another gang member had had relations. She apparently told agents what she knew, as did Frawley's mother, the two pilots who had flown Brady around the region, and the women in whose boarding houses the gang had lived while in Connecticut. The Bridgeport police initially had little to say, but helped the FBI conduct its investigations. Authorities soon discovered the car kept in storage, and learned that it was from their last rooming house in Bridgeport that the gang had made their trips into Bangor; although if this was so, they clearly had traveled northward earlier from their first establishment, as they had brought their landlady on Washington Street the souvenir pillow from New Hampshire. When she was interviewed, she was quoted as being surprised that the men had been thieves and murderers, and said that she realized now that she could have been killed when she questioned the men about their activities.[10]

Moreover, the Bridgeport press covered, as did some of the other cities associated with the gang, possible crimes and planned crimes by Brady and his cohorts. In particular, the Bridgeport papers reported that the gang had planned to rob a Hartford bank and possibly one in Cambridge, Massachusetts, and that two of the three men had been identified as having robbed a bank in Providence, Rhode Island, that July. Their purchase of an older model car in Connecticut was viewed as a ruse to acquire state "markers." The car found after events in Bangor had its front "markers" just loosely wired on, while the rear plates were fastened on with rusty bolts. The papers found the discovery of Brady's attempts to learn to become a pilot especially onerous.[11]

Meanwhile, as the press exploded with news and theories and suppositions about the gang, federal, state, and local authorities debated exactly for which crimes—of the many, many possibilities—to charge surviving gang member Rheul James Dalhover. While the questions were examined, Federal Commissioner Howard S. Young had Dalhover held on a $50,000 bail in Indiana—which Dalhover could not raise—for one specific charge of robbery.[12] This and any other robbery charges were temporary, according to Herald Reinecke, chief of the Indianapolis office of the FBI. Indiana indictments already standing against Dalhover charged him with the murders of Richard Rivers and Paul Minneman. It was not certain yet for which murder Dalhover might be tried, and "Michael Morrisey, Indianapolis police chief, and State Police Captain Walter Eckert were equally anxious that the murders of their men be avenged."[13] They had no doubt that he would be tried for at least one of the murders, but wanted him tried for both.

Authorities continued to investigate both the history of the gang and specific crimes for which Dalhover might be charged in following days and weeks. He was initially held for arraignment in Indianapolis, as Julius J. Wichser, Chief Deputy U.S. Marshall, ordered the sheriff, Otto Ray, not to transfer or otherwise take Dalhover from the Marion County Jail while he, himself, went out of town to attend Federal Court in New Albany. While Dalhover awaited arraignment, authorities traced one of the stolen license plates found with the gang to a Clarence Watson of Flora, Indiana, stolen the previous August. Dalhover had purportedly stated to the authorities that the gang had been in the East at that time. Dalhover was already under indictment for the murder of Paul V. Minneman in Cass County, Indiana, and on October 17 the AP stated that a new indictment stood against him for the murder of Police Sargent Richard Rivers. [14]

Questions remained about Dalhover's exact status, but that he would be arraigned for murder there was no doubt. Still, Dalhover could not keep from bragging about his past, even to his jailors, even to police.

When he was placed in lockup in Indianapolis, Dalhover told Sheriff Otto Ray, "Well, I'm back home again, and I'm sure glad of it. You know I'm no stranger here." The words may have been slightly different, as they were said in semiprivate and then repeated to the press, but certainly Dalhover had been at the facility before. He, Brady, and Shaffer had been held there briefly after their arrest for the shooting of Richard Rivers. Dalhover purportedly also told Otto that the gang had planned to escape from the lockup, but had been transferred to Greenfield before they could do so. He reminded the sheriff about the key that had been found which the men had fashioned, and Otto told him that the key would not have worked. Dalhover said that the key had not yet been finished. Then, according to the press, the sheriff had told Dalhover, "If you ever tried to get out of here you'd have been riddled with bullets." To this, his prisoner had responded, "Anybody who lived the life we did expected things like that. . . . We were always willing to take a chance." [15]

Then, too, Dalhover was not willing to let the end story be that he had just been a second man to Brady. He stated that in the beginning Brady had been the gang's leader, but after they made their prison break from Greenfield that he and Shaffer had more of a say in how things happened. He would have this testimony brought to bear in his sentencing, having stated that he himself was able to lead the gang as he was able to sway Shaffer. According to Dalhover, Chief Deputy U.S. Marshall Julius Wichser told the press, Brady had made more than one mistake. It had been Brady's desire to wear dress clothes every night—something which made the men stand out from some of their surroundings—and Dalhover had said that Brady wanted the gang to operate a night club and skating rink in Baltimore. Brady started making a fool of himself when he did indeed get hold of a skating rink. The sisters that Dalhover and Shaffer married would go skating sometimes with the men. Once, Brady had fallen down while skating and had broken his nose. "We didn't like that sort of stuff. It was dangerous," the deputy reported Dalhover as stating. Both he and Shaffer, Dalhover said, were unhappy with Brady's so-called leadership at this point.[16]

However, Dalhover said that he had been outnumbered in the decision to try to purchase guns in Maine. "After we ran from Baltimore the other two voted to go to Maine. I didn't want to go, but we had decided on a two-to-one vote, so I went along, although my hunch against the move sure enough turned out right."[17] It certainly did.

While the justice system determined the best place to detain Dalhover and the charges for which he might be tried, other events unfolded. On the same day that Dalhover had been returned to Indiana, Shaffer's body had been sent back to Indiana via train. Only a few hours after the shootout on October 12, the undertakers of White & Hayes—then in custody of both Brady's and Shaffer's bodies—had received a copy of a telegram sent to the Clayton Company, requesting that Shaffer's body be prepared for "express shipment to Shirley Brothers, Indianapolis, Ind. In accordance with their instructions." Clarence Lee Shaffer Sr. had signed the telegram. The gangster's father had later wired money to cover the expenses involved. To secure the body, the Clayton Company had had to get permission from the county medical examiner and the federal agents, and pick it up at Bangor's White & Hayes funeral parlor. According to the press, problems included preparing the body "which [had been] literally filled with holes, from his neck to his heels and the shot to his neck had probably been the ultimate cause of his death." Agent Gurnea of the FBI ordered that no pictures be taken of the bodies after they were removed from the streets of the city. Hence, the only photographs of the bodies available to the press had been those taken on Central Street just after the shootout. Other gangsters, such as Bonnie and Clyde and Dillinger, had post-mortem autopsy and other photographs that eventually reached the public's eyes. On October 15, Shaffer's grandmother, Mrs. George Shaffer, told the press that funeral services for Clarence Lee Shaffer Jr. would be held that Saturday. She made the statement before the body arrived in Indianapolis.[18]

The two women who had accompanied the gang in Bridgeport, Connecticut, just before the gang hit Bangor, were reported to have been arrested there shortly after the shootout. Later reports stated that the second woman had never actually been located.[19] They were not charged, and their story remains largely unknown, although one of the two referred to in the early reports would have been Alicia Frawley, and she had come forward of her own accord.

However, while the car the three men had brought to Maine remained in the basement of the city's fire station on the day Brady was buried, and after Dalhover and Shaffer's body had been returned to Indiana, the gang's second automobile had, as a result of the shootout, been essentially abandoned. The Bridgeport police soon recovered the vehicle, and the Bridgeport Superintendent of Police, Charles A. Wheels, spent a few days tracing the gang's path through his city, aided by the FBI. The car, a ten-year-old one (an unusual choice for Alfred Brady, who generally preferred to steal new cars, perhaps he did this as part of his plan to elude police and to easily secure Connecticut plates), had been left in a parking lot, and Brady had paid for one week of its storage there.[20]

Back in Maine, after Dalhover had been extradited to Indianapolis, Brady buried, and Shaffer's body returned to Indiana for burial, Bangor Chief of Police Thomas L. Crowley formally congratulated his department for the work they had undertaken during the previous few weeks. He said of his staff, "They proved themselves good policemen. . . . They kept silent, however great may have been the temptation to speak, when silence was necessary to the course of justice; they were not afraid to do their duty when the time came. No men in any big city department could have done better."[21] (However someone, not necessarily a local police officer, may well have tipped off the press, as a few reporters and photographers from the two local papers would later say that they had spent the night before the shootout waiting in their cars for the action to break. This is not inconsistent with the authorities having had to warn at least some of the people who might otherwise been—or were—in the line of fire. Moreover, Baltimore police had warned nearby residents to vacate the immediate neighborhood of the married gangsters' home there.)[22]

Chief Crowley emphasized, "The successful ending of the case was due to one-hundred percent cooperation between representatives of the Federal Bureau of Investigation, popularly called G-men; the Maine State Police; the Indiana State Police; and the Bangor Department." He stated that there had not been any friction between the agencies, and that he was certain that the first tip to the FBI had come from Maine State Police Chief Towle from Augusta.[23]

Bangor's chief of police likewise stated, "It was a remarkable case—the most unusual ever known in Maine." Moreover, now that the pressure was off, he continued, "there is a satisfaction in knowing that the law enforcement agencies that centered here have succeeded in wiping out America's greatest individual menace to law and order—and no innocent person was harmed."[24]

Myron Gurnea, FBI agent, had likewise expressed his appreciation of the local police before he had left town, stating, "It could not have been done finer." So, too, did the Bangor City Manager state, in a letter to the chief of police, that he commended the Bangor Police Department for its part in apprehending the gang.

The *BDN*, as part of its coverage of Chief Crowley's remarks, noted that it had been fortunate that the shootout was on a holiday, such that the children were not in school, and that no officers had had to be pulled from their usual assigned duties at city school such that "curiosity would have immediately been aroused. As it was, members of the day crew were concentrated in the business section without, apparently, causing any comment." The American public, moreover, had been informed that "the murder-gang which terrorized large communities in many states met with swift retribution when it came to Bangor, Maine—and the Bangor police had a lot to do with it."[25]

Moreover, police could now relate further facts about the shootout. On the day of the shootout, an officer had been on the way to pick up the police chief—who had called in for a ride having spent long hours at the office over previous days, not knowing just when or if the gangsters would show up—and spotted the mob's car near Hammond and Fourth Streets—a few blocks away from the downtown area. The officer picked up Crowley and then drove quickly to City Hall. A report soon came in that the car was parked in the downtown section as the three gangsters—as they were believed to be—ate breakfast just across from the Bangor Opera House, at John Skoufts's restaurant. They stayed in the restaurant for close to one-half hour, speaking in quiet tones and eating leisurely what would prove the last meal for two of the men. The three men had then cruised along Central Street at least once before they parked their sedan about three doors down from Dakin's and near the entrance to the Norembega Mall and Dalhover went in to make the anticipated purchases. They may or may not have thought of using the mall as an escape route should trouble arise.[26] (The Kenduskeag Stream route, which passes under or through the small park and walkway, would have led the men down to the shores of the Penobscot River, or upstream and further out of town.)

The Bangor police had already parked a large car, an REO, directly outside the store, with the intention that it might help block any bullets being fired from the store toward the street—as it turned out it did.[27] When gunfire erupted, the car took some of the shots.

In Indiana, where the latest news was taking place as the rest of the country watched on, Dalhover eventually pled guilty to homicide and robbery. State authorities considered indicting him also for the murder of Indianapolis Police Department Sergeant Richard Rivers, but awaited federal action on the matter. Dalhover was initially jailed in Indianapolis, as noted previously, held on federal charges of robbing three Indiana banks, then the standing murder indictment against the gang was added. For a time, Cass County, Indiana, sought to obtain custody of Dalhover for the murder of Minneman. While in custody in Indianapolis, Dalhover blamed the always dressed-up Al Brady for the idea of having the gang operate a nightclub and skating rink in Baltimore. Moreover, he supposedly told authorities that he and Shaffer had once discussed killing Brady because of his "show-off antics." Their discontent with Brady's leadership had led to their agreeing to vote on future jobs, although Dalhover was outvoted on the plan to go to Maine.[28]

According to one Indiana jail source, in addition to his and Shaffer's having contemplated killing Brady, Dalhover stated in Indianapolis, "When we broke out of jail at Greenfield, all I wanted was one year of freedom, and I thought we were good for that. Well, we were out a year." He said this a day or two before Shaffer's burial.[29]

The authorities allowed Dalhover to conduct an interview while incarcerated in Indianapolis. He told an International News Service correspondent:

> If I could get out of this jail I would do the same thing all over again. I would live by the law of the heater [gun], just as we did after escaping from the Greenfield jail, robbing banks, jewelry stores, and other places with money.
>
> However, I guess it's all over now. They've got enough to hang me a couple of times. I understand in this State you must stand trial before they can sentence you to die. Well, I probably would plead guilty if I could get a life sentence, but I guess they won't listen to it. [30]

As to how he liked life on the road, and marriage, Dalhover had a number of things to say. He said:

> A lot of people want to know how I liked a life roaming to avoid the law. Well, to tell the truth, the only moving about we did was when we raided banks. Outside of that we lived in Baltimore from October 3, 1936, until August of this year. Three days after we escaped from the Greenfield jail we went to Baltimore, and after getting married to the Raimondo sisters, Shaffer and I settled down pretty much.
>
> We sort of became domesticated, and only left on occasion to do our work. The Raimondo sisters were fine girls, and didn't know what we did. They thought we were lumber men from New England. [31]

Dalhover seemingly did not mention reading about their crimes in the newspapers, or about the experiences of the Raimondo family after the gang left Baltimore.

As to the blame for the gang's downfall, Dalhover seems to have revised his thinking some. He stated:

> Women are the downfall of all criminals according to the coppers. I guess we were no exceptions, although they were responsible only indirectly for our being caught.
>
> You see, Brady took unnecessary chances. He appeared in every conceivable public place with girls, and Shaffer and I had to jump him for it. It was this that led him to tell the Raimondo sisters we

were from Bangor, Maine, because we had been there several times.[32]

Dalhover did not elaborate on this last statement. Perhaps the time line in the article which quoted him was a bit off. But, he said:

> Well, the girls told the G-men—and here I am. And they are dead. I warned Brady to stay away from Bangor, because he had told the girls, but he wouldn't listen to me. Guess I would have been better off if the coppers had clipped me also.[33]

Dalhover, however, did have a few regrets about his life:

> While I have no regrets for the life I have lived, I hope my two boys do not follow in my footsteps. If I could again have a chance to supervise their bringing up, I would see that they had enough spending money, especially in their high school days. Boys with a reasonable allowance do not steal or get into trouble.[34]

Dalhover's social commentary may have been a bit off, but he did see the gang members poor upbringings and the harsh economy as having been part of his life of crime. He continued: "If you want to stop having gangs like Dillinger's and ours, get rid of the slums. I bet that more crime is bred in those parts of large cities than anywhere else."[35]

Dalhover's concluding interview words were: "All in all, I have no regrets. I had my fun while it lasted, although it didn't last long."[36] No, it did not last long, and it came at the cost of serious injury to other people.

Not long after giving his interview, Dalhover was indicted in South Bend, Indiana, on October 28, 1937, for the murder of Paul V. Minneman and for robbing $2,668 from the Goodland State Bank in Indiana. A federal grand jury indicted him.[37]

On November 14, 1937, Dalhover waited in his cell to be taken to Hammond for his arraignment at 10:00 a.m. the following morning. The local FBI agent in charge, Herald Reinecke, refused to tell the public just how and when the prisoner would be moved, but did say that he would be arraigned for both robbery and murder.[38]

Shackled hand and foot, his voice just above a whisper, Dalhover was arraigned on Monday, November 15, 1937, in federal court at Hammond, Indiana, for the murder of Indiana State Police Officer Paul V.

Minneman, the officer who had died from an ambush by the Brady Gang on May 25, 1937, from behind a small church. He was charged by a grand jury indictment in the District Court for the Northern District of Indiana. The indictment charged "that on May 25, 1937, at White County, Indiana, within the Hammond Division of said court, did 'unlawfully, feloniously, willfully, deliberately, maliciously, and with premeditation and malice aforethought kill and murder Paul Minneman, a human being, with a dangerous and deadly firearm; that the murder was committed by appellant while acting jointly with Alfred J. Brady and Clarence Lee Shaffer, Jr., in avoiding and attempting to avoid apprehension for the commission of the crime of robbery" of the Goodland bank, a bank insured under federal regulations. The crimes were punishable by not less than ten years of incarceration or death for murder in the attempt to escape apprehension for robbing the bank, plus fines of up to $5,000 and up to twenty years in prison for the robbery itself.[39]

According to Assistant Attorney General Brien McMahon, the plan before the arraignment was for Dalhover's trial to follow "as speedily as possible after the arraignment." He had been confined in Indiana since a few days after the shootout in Maine, and had been the subject of ongoing discussions between federal and state authorities to determine who should try him and on exactly which charges.[40]

Dalhover pled guilty, however. Judge Thomas W. Slick, accepting the gangster's plea, appointed two attorneys to represent Dalhover after Dalhover stated that the only money or property he possessed was the $2,600 taken from him after his arrest. The prisoner produced a government receipt pertaining to the same. Judge Slick also set December 6 for a jury hearing to determine if Dalhover should be put to death in the electric chair or be imprisoned for life. The option of a fixed term of no less than ten years in jail was also an option.[41]

On December 6, 1937, a federal jury was impaneled at Hammond, Indiana. The jury was composed of eight farmers, a painter, a real estate salesperson, a store manager, and a heating contractor. In questioning the prospective jurors, defense attorney C. B. Tinkham emphasized that "the minimum penalty for Dalhover's admitted crime—murder in flight from robbery of the Goodland State Bank—[was] ten years' imprisonment." He stated that he and his co-counsel, Timothy P. Galvin, sought to obtain a life sentence for Dalhover. Before the lunch break,

Judge Slick dismissed prospective jurors and spectators from the court-room, and asked news reporters to report the case factually and "with-out any editorializing." He wanted to be certain that nothing be printed that could cause a mistrial.[42]

Dalhover had admitted to a federal officer that he aided Brady and Shaffer in the robbery of the Goodland Bank, and that he was with them during the shootout at the church. Dalhover had also told officers that he himself had removed the murdered officer's gun and belt as Minneman lay wounded in the road, and that he may have fired off three four shots himself, but that he was not certain if he had actually fired any shots at all. This was the only murder for which a Brady Gang member was ultimately "convicted," and Dalhover would soon contest the evidence given the jury charged with sentencing him. Dalhover's admission that he and the gang had robbed some 150 stores—four jewelry stores specifically—plus three banks before they robbed the Goodland Bank was also submitted. He had also told agents that the gang had been implicated in two other murders. He had stated, too, that Brady was in charge prior to October 1936, but after he and Shaffer married the sisters, he himself had come to dominate the gang. He had also told a government agent about how he himself had rebuilt their machine guns, and how the men would test them, practicing on rocks, trees, and small stones.[43]

The impaneled jury of the Northern Indiana Federal Court, in Hammond, heard the evidence submitted, and, after hearing instructions given by court and by counsel, sentenced Dalhover to death. The defense asked for mercy for their client, in "consideration of the background of this man's life." Galvin stated, "Perhaps if consideration had been shown Jim Dalhover at age eleven we would not be here today." He referred to Dalhover's sentencing to reform school after he and his brother George had robbed a grocery store. He argued that Dalhover had had no one to guide him, "to put any moral fiber in him."[44]

In response, the prosecution, via U.S. District Attorney James Fleming, strode to the table where numerous weapons of the Brady Gang had been placed, "ripped several feet of machine gun bullets from a belt," and said, "This is not a case for mercy. . . . Think of that broken-hearted wife in Lafayette who is soon to become a mother, and I might ask you to go with me to that snowy mound in Logansport cemetery."

He then pointed to Dalhover and asked, "Did this defendant show mercy to that wife and Paul Minneman?"[45]

When the prosecutor pointed at Dalhover and demanded that he had not shown mercy, Paul Minneman's father, who had sat through the proceedings, broke into sobs, while Dalhover stared straight ahead.[46] The prosecution would carry the day.

The jury deliberated for only two hours and seventeen minutes. Dalhover was not pleased by the sentence. He had probably hoped to serve a limited time in prison, and, if he had not hoped that just after his arrest, he certainly did so before sentencing. However, he was found guilty and sentenced to the maximum punishment. The jury's death sentence was found consistent with the verdict of guilt.[47]

Judge Thomas Slick deferred the pronouncement of sentence formally, in spite of the jury's verdict. He deferred the sentencing until he could meet with the attorneys involved to determine procedures to follow and set a date for the pronouncement.[48]

Dalhover was identified in the press as the "trigger man" of the Brady Gang, in part because of his own boasting. Dalhover appealed his sentence first to the U.S. Circuit Court of Appeals and later the U.S. Supreme Court. He lost both appeals, as well as a request for executive clemency to President Franklin Delano Roosevelt—the president whose New Deal programs had done so much to aid the city that finally brought the gang down, as well as the towns and cities the gang had robbed and terrorized.[49]

Dalhover based his appeals—argued by C. B. Tinkham and Timothy P. Galvin, both of Hammond, Indiana—on the admission of various pieces of evidence. His attorneys argued that, essentially, too much of his and the gang's career in crime had been revealed to the jury, that as Dalhover had confessed to the crime they should have been told much less than they were, that the evidence presented for a person who pled guilty should be more limited than that presented when the government had to prove guilt. All that the jury had heard about Dalhover's role in the gang, about other shootings by the gang, about things he had said, his motivations behind certain acts, and so forth should not have been submitted to the jury, only the "cold facts" of the case at hand. They did not need to know about all the robberies, possible other murders (although the court had struck out the "implications" with other murders), and so forth. The defense also asserted that the bloody shirt removed from Paul Minneman should not have been shown the jury, nor should various guns and other weaponry uncovered by the government including two large machine guns seized in Bangor. A federal agent, moreover, should not have been allowed to testify about the shootout in Bangor, and issues surrounding Dalhover's arrest.[50]

With James R. Fleming, Luther M. Swygert (both of Hammond), and Assistant U.S. Attorney Alexander M. Campbell (of Fort Wayne, Indiana), presenting for the United States, in considering the decisions of Thomas W. Slick, judge for the Northern District of Indiana, the Seventh Circuit Court of Appeals majority—Circuit Judges Sparks and Treanor—found that the original court had not erred in the vast majority of its admissions of evidence and rulings, especially as most of the information had come from Dalhover himself, and he had not recanted those admissions and statements, and the court had used its latitude generally within its limits. As the majority stated it:

> We hold that all the pertinent facts and circumstances with respect to the robbery, the shooting at the church, the flight, the pursuit, the attempted capture at Baltimore, the bandits' property there recovered, the arrest of the appellant and his associates at Bangor, the killing of Brady and Shaffer, the actions of each of the bandits at Bangor and all the property in their possession, were competent not only to establish guilt if it had been denied, but to be considered by the jury in fixing punishment. It may be that this evidence would establish other specific crimes, such as shooting with intent to kill both at Baltimore and at Bangor, yet that would not render the evidence inadmissible, because those crimes could not be considered as unrelated to the murder of Minneman. At Baltimore and Bangor the bandits were merely trying to escape arrest for the robbery and murder, and what they did at that time and what they had with them was clearly admissible not only as bearing upon their guilt of the robbery and the murder, but also in disclosing a lack of contrition, and a continuity of similar and unrelated criminal tendencies which were quite proper for the jury to consider in fixing the penalty.[51]

The court likewise upheld the admission of Minneman's blood-soaked shirt, the guns, the federal agent's testimony of what Dalhover had told him in October 1937 about the gangsters' careers, and so forth. It also supported the admission of Dalhover's statement that the gang had robbed another bank after the Goodland, the one at Thorp, Wisconsin, with Brady, Shaffer, and Dalhover committing the crime.[52]

The appeals court did, however, determine that the statement made by Minneman in the hours before his death about being kicked when he was already down and related statements should have been left out of the permitted evidence. However, the officer had not stated that Dalhover specifically had shot or kicked him, "and we cannot conceive of its admission having any harmful effect upon the verdict. We think the error was harmless." The appeals court found no issue with instructions given or not given to the jury by the original court: "We find no fault with them. Judgment affirmed."[53]

And so Dalhover lost his case, although the circuit judge—Major—writing the minority or dissenting finding had a few additional statements to make. He did not agree with the "form of verdict which was submitted to the jury." He believed that the jury should only had been asked, "whether the defendant shall suffer the punishment of death" and not other possible terms or punishments. The judge also stated:

> I am unable, by any process of reasoning, to conclude that a person charged with crime, who confesses his guilt, should have his punishment determined under circumstances more unfavorable to him than one that, by denial of his guilt, forces the government to establish the same. Of course, it is said in some cases such a standard would operate to the benefit of the accused, but that is not the situation here, and it does not mitigate the harm done the accused in this case to say that in some other case the accused might be benefited.[54]

The minority judge did agree that all presented evidence was properly submitted. He primarily objected to the admission of Minneman's near death statements (although he took a more critical view of its importance, stating that with other case issues it would require a reversal of the court's judgment), and statements and admissions made by Dalhover after his arrest in Bangor, even though the presiding judge at the sentencing hearing had objected to the admission to the information regarding two other murders, although the judge had objected not because it was "immaterial or improper, but for the reason it was not responsive to the question propounded. Without doubt, such evidence under a plea of not guilty would have constituted a reversible error." Summing up his findings, Judge Major stated:

> That this record discloses a crime brutal in the extreme is obvious, which is not difficult to believe justifies the extreme penalty. Notwithstanding this situation, however, appellant was entitled to have the only issue submitted to the jury [if the death penalty should be imposed] determined upon competent evidence and to have the penalty determined for the offense charged.[55]

The only judge dissenting from the original court proceedings and the majority decision at the May 1938 rehearing decision would still have deemed Dalhover a proper defendant for execution; he simply would have had some of the evidence or testimony thrown out. Were Dalhover to be granted a new trial, seemingly all the judges believed he would again be sentenced to death.

On June 24, 1938, James Dalhover was moved from St. Joseph's County Jail in Indiana to the Federal Detention Farm in Milan, Michigan, for "safekeeping." He had lost his appeal to the circuit court, and was scheduled for execution that fall.[56] Dalhover, however, was not yet ready to give up his pleas for clemency or a stay of execution.

The Supreme Court refused a stay of execution. On November 18, 1938, James Dalhover died in the electric chair at the Indiana State Penitentiary (also called the Michigan City State Prison) in Michigan City, Indiana. He was thirty-two years old.[57]

The *Milwaukee Sentinel*, like other papers, carried news of the execution. "Dalhover Put to Death; 'Trigger Man' of Brady Gang Dies in Indiana Chair," ran the newspaper's header in its report from Michigan City, dated November 18. The paper reported that on Friday, that same morning, "James Dalhover, tiny red haired trigger man of the Al Brady Gang, died in the electric chair at Michigan [City] State Prison here early today for the slaying of a state policeman."[58]

Dalhover, stiff-legged and heavy footed, was "taken from the death cell by two guards at two minutes past midnight and strapped in the chair."[59] Another paper reported that Dalhover "wore an old brown shirt and black pants" as he walked the "13 steps to the chair." He also wore a "triangle-shaped black mask as he was brought into the death chamber." Fifteen people witnessed the execution, including slain officer Minneman's former partner, Loren Ayres of Delphi, Indiana.[60]

Only about 1½ minutes after Dalhover reached the chamber, "the current was turned on." The execution was quick. "Dalhover was taken out of the death seat at 12:09. Dr. P. H. Weeks, prison physician, and Dr. J. E. McMeet, physician for the federal government, pronounced him dead at 12:11 a.m."[61]

Dalhover was executed for the murder of Paul Minneman on May 25, 1937, following his gang's robbery of the Goodland bank. Moreover, the *Sentinel* reported, "He confessed two other killings following the capture in Bangor, Me. where Brady and Clarence Lee Shaffer, Jr, were slain in a G-man trap."[62]

Dalhover had then changed his mind about his plea, apparently, and "Federal Judge Thomas W. Stark, in a two-hour night session of the Northern Indiana Federal District Court at Hammond, overruled a petition alleging Dalhover had plead guilty to the Minneman killing in South Bend federal court on November 15, 1937, because he feared mob violence. The petition asked a writ of error *coram nobis* to necessitate new legal proceedings for Dalhover."[63]

"Along with the petition for the error," Dalhover's (or his mother's) attorney Mansiel Hagerty sent petitions for an appeal in the Chicago Federal Court of Appeals in event his petition was denied and for a stay of execution pending this appeal. Judge Slick denied these also. On October 17, 1938, the U.S. Supreme Court denied Dalhover's plea for a review of his case.[64] So, like his fellow gangsters' deaths in Bangor, Dalhover's death was, to a large extent, a public one with his confessions, hearings, and appeals followed closely by the press. Unlike the others', however, he had had a mother who fought for him.

Dalhover's mother, Bertha Dalhover Craig of Madison, Indiana, traveled to Washington, DC, to seek clemency for her son just two days before his execution, and was photographed by the Associated Press with attorney Mansiel Hagerty, of South Bend, Indiana, leaving the Department of Justice building in Washington. The press stated, in what would see a rather odd last-minute twist to the case—that she wanted "to save her son from the disgrace of the electric chair. If he must die, she wants him to realize his desire to be infected with deadly germs in the interest of science." She was wearing a dark dress or suit and a long dark coat with dark shoes. Her request was not to save her son's life, but rather to allow scientists to study him as "his life ebbed" away from the effects of some fatal disease, according to another source.[65]

While awaiting the results of his last appeals, authorities had transferred Dalhover from the federal detention farm near Milan, where he had been held since he had been sentenced to death a year previously, to "the Michigan City prison of electrocution," as identified by the press. The trip, depending on the route taken was about 175 to 200 miles, about four hours by automobile. The transfer took place on November 17.[66]

His mother's plea was submitted to Attorney General Homer Cummings. As reported, "The petition bore Dalhover's signature which was pasted to it on another piece of paper."[67]

The *Bangor Daily Commercial* carried an Associated Press article on the legal proceedings from Washington, DC, on November 17 in its evening paper. It used the headline "Dalhover Loses Last Hope Today" and stated that the U.S. Supreme Court had refused to stay Dalhover's execution, referring to him as a "convicted killer of an Indiana state policeman." It stated, "Dalhover's lawyer, Mansiel Hagarty, asked the court to stay the execution and to reconsider his previous action [of October 17] in refusing to review the Seventh Circuit Court affirmance of the death sentence. The court denied both requests." In a second article, the *BDC* noted that the refusal to stay the execution came before the president actually had a chance to rule for executive clemency, should he have been so inclined.[68]

The *BDC* ran both its short AP article from Washington on November 17, 1938, and a longer article on the events scheduled for that night, researched and written it seems by its own staff, with excerpts from the Associated Press, entitled: "Dalhover Dies Tonight; Gangster Captured in Bangor taken in Secrecy Over 'Last Mile' Today." It noted that Dalhover had been transferred to Michigan City, and that that night six men would "line up in front of six switches at the Michigan [City] State prison" soon after midnight, and once the order was given they would "cut strings dropping weights on the switches, one of which will send a current through the electric chair to wipe out the last of the Al Brady Gang."[69] The person who cut the fatal string would not know his was the killing cut.

On November 18, the Associated Press in Chicago noted that a U.S. Circuit Court of Appeals had just "denied a petition for postponement of the execution of Rhuel James Dalhover, member of the Brady Gang condemned to die next Friday in the electric chair in Michigan City, Ind." As noted by the *Milwaukee Sentinel*, in addition to the appeal, "a delay had been requested pending the outcome of an appeal for executive clemency sent to President Roosevelt earlier in the day." As another AP article from Michigan City printed in the San Diego *Evening Tribune* described the last minute appeals, "The United States Supreme Court at Washington had turned down another plea, and President Roosevelt spurned Dalhover's offer to become a human medical 'guinea pig.'" "A similar plea was denied by the same court last week."[70]

Moreover, an AP release from Fort Wayne, Indiana, reported that District Attorney James R. Flemming had announced there that Federal Judge Thomas A. Slick had just that night—that scheduled for the execution it seems—denied the two last-minute appeals to save Dalhover's life at the Northern Indiana District Court at Hammond. These included the aforementioned petition for a writ of error *coram nobis* and Dalhover's appeal to the Chicago federal court. And as the San Diego *Evening Tribune* reported, Judge Slick denied Dalhover's final appeal "a scant few minutes before midnight," while earlier that day the Supreme Court and Roosevelt had turned him down. Nothing the *Evening Tribune* had to say about Dalhover's last attempts to save himself (which the paper noted had lasted for over a year) or his last minutes was flattering.[71]

The San Diego paper reported that the "midget triggerman" of the gang had not gone bravely to his end. Instead, "The erstwhile tough guy who once boasted that he would take it sitting down in the electric chair had to be half carried to it." It stated that Dalhover was "half led, half carried into the death chamber by guards." Moreover, it titled its article "U.S. Pays $130 to Rid Society of Brady Gang," stating that Dalhover's exit from humanity cost just "$130 to rid society of this latest Public Enemy No. 1." It noted, too, that Dalhover had three children but had never "seen the last one of his children," as "it was born to his second wife, Mary Raimondo Dalhover, of Baltimore, after the gangster was captured."[72]

The Associated Press kept the cities of America informed about Dalhover's status, including Bangor, Maine, where citizens had seen the deaths of the two other long-term gang members, Baltimore where the men had lived for most of a year, and the other cities where shoot-outs and fatalities had occurred involving the gang. The local papers printed news of his attempts to stay his execution, as well as the final results, although now most of the news came via the AP instead of their own reporters. As the Associated Press stated it, albeit in something of a mix of day and night: "The federal government threw an electric switch tonight to complete extermination of the Al Brady Gang, which Head G-Man J. Edgar Hoover once called the 'most vicious' criminal group in the United States." The execution of the "diminutive trigger-man of the gang" in the Indiana penitentiary finished "the job that federal agents started when they killed his two pals in Bangor, Me. a little more than a year ago." Dalhover was sentenced to death for the death of Minneman following the $2,500 bank robbery in Goodland, Indiana. This, the new article added, in a new vantage, resulted in the federal government becoming involved because "the bank had federal insurance," with the end result that "the federal government took jurisdiction and pressed anew the hunt for the Brady Gang." Moreover, during Dalhover's execution, the "federal jurisdiction of the case gave U.S. Marshall Al Hosinaki the unaccustomed role of executioner." To date, the earliest records of the group operating as a gang and committing a crime was the Robinston, Illinois, robbery of $320 from a store. The article also noted that the government at present knew of robberies of banks, jewelry stores, grocery stores, and theaters in both the Midwest and the East.[73]

The *Evening Tribune* of San Diego, meanwhile, noted that the man the government spent just $130 to rid society of, had had no money of his own at the end. It reported that Dalhover died broke, not seeing his children again—if ever in the case of his youngest—and that the many holdups and bank robberies of the gang in Indiana, Wisconsin, and Ohio had "left him nothing."[74]

The *Bangor Daily News*, in addition to following and printing some excerpts from the AP from the Midwest coverage, reprinted a photograph of Dalhover on November 18, following his electrocution. It appears to have been a cropped photograph from when Dalhover was escorted from his cell in Bangor to be extradited to Indiana the year before. Under the long, narrow, photograph of Dalhover, its caption simply stated: "Dalhover, whose death in the electric chair at midnight wrote the final chapter to the Brady Gang." The article moreover stated that Dalhover had confessed not just to the Minneman murder, but also to the gang having killed Edward Lindsey, the grocery store clerk in the robbery in Piqua, Ohio, in March 1936 and Police Sergeant Richard Rivers in April 1936. A *BDC* article reiterated these statements, calling the gangster "little red-haired James Dalhover, 32-year old gunman for the gang," and noted that Dalhover had given up bootlegging and farming "in the Southern Indiana hills" to join the gang.[75]

Just after Dalhover's execution, the *BDN* noted that the "Mystery Why Gang Was Here" remained, as the article's title stated. Dalhover's death did not truly answer the questions left unresolved about why the gang had come to Bangor. A number of "pertinent questions" were "unanswered." After noting that "the diminutive but venomous gangster was never wounded—at least not by the flying lead," in Bangor, the newspaper printed parts of earlier writings in the November article, and then pondered why the gang had picked Bangor specifically, as "there are many sporting goods stores between here and the New Hampshire Border." Maine might have had laxer gun laws than many states, but Bangor was rather far up in the state. The paper posited, "Possibly they wanted to get deep into the 'country.' Contrary to many fantastic stories published at the time, they had no intention whatever of holding up a local bank."[76]

The paper had refuted this earlier idea soon after Dalhover's extradition, and had noted that he had stated while in custody that, "our 'rotten roads' might have been fatal to a getaway" should they have ever considered pulling a bank heist in Maine, especially eastern Maine. He had also stated that they had come to Bangor three times, staying along the way at roadside camps. Moreover, "the police believed this too, and discounted utterly the stories of those who thought the three took rooms on lower Main Street" near downtown Bangor. As to why they came, he had stated that they thought it would arouse no suspicions to try to buy guns in a place like Bangor where it was legal to buy them openly, and when asked by two police inspectors, "But didn't you know they would be suspicious when you wanted a machine gun," Dalhover had "shrugged his shoulders slightly and said, 'I guess that was our mistake.'"[77] A mistake it was indeed.

Dalhover had given Bangor as his place of birth on his marriage license when he married one of the Raimondo sisters, but this had obviously been a fabrication. He had also made references to Bangor to the Raimondo family. "Why? Had he been here—and, if so, in what capacity? It would be interesting to know: but it's unlikely now that anyone ever will." So concluded the newspaper that had so closely followed the events surrounding Bangor, and had exploded its paper with images and stories about the gang. The reporters from both Bangor newspapers would perhaps have asked such questions about Dalhover had they been allowed to question him while he was being held in Bangor, but they had not. Dalhover's death had taken a year and a month to come after the gang's final shootout, primarily because of the delays in his trial and his several appeals, so at least that question, as to why it had taken so long for Dalhover to die, could be answered. Now, Dalhover awaited burial, Shaffer had been buried in Indianapolis, and Brady had been buried with money found on his person but his grave remained unmarked. "The lot [is] in a remote part of the cemetery, is overgrown with tall grass; few know its location. No stone was ever erected," the paper wrote of Brady's gravesite site in 1938.[78]

There were no more stones to uncover to answer the remaining mysteries about the gang—except, perhaps, one. Later that year, Ohio authorities charged five men with the September 1936 death of Ohio State Trooper George Conn. The Brady Gang had not killed him. One of the men convicted of his death was sent to the Ohio State Penitentiary, where George Geiseking was still incarcerated.[79]

Geiseking remained alive but would not directly speak to the November 1935 death of Frank Levy, the one remaining murder directly associated with the gang that Dalhover seemingly had denied up to the day of his electrocution. But there had been earlier testimony that the gang had been responsible. Perhaps the Brady Gang killed Frank Levy, perhaps they did not. But kill they did, and rob, and steal, and lie. And now their time as America's No. 1 "public enemies" and "public rats" was over.

NOTES

1. *BDN*, 15 October 1937. Also see AP article as printed in *BDN* and other papers the same day and on the following one, including the *Baltimore News-Post*, 14 October 1937.

2. *BDN*, 15 October 1937. AP article from Indianapolis, printed in *BDN*, 15 October 1937, for quotes; *BDC*, 15 and 16 October 1937.

3. *Baltimore News-Post*, 13 October 1937; and *Baltimore Sun*, 14 October 1937.

4. Ibid.

5. *Baltimore News-Post*, 13 October 1937.

6. Ibid.

7. Ibid.

8. *Baltimore Sun*, 13 October 1937.

9. *Baltimore Sun*, 13 October 1937.

10. *Bridgeport Press*, 14 and 15 October 1937; *[Bridgeport] Herald City*, 17 October 1937; and *Bridgeport Times Star*, 13–18 October 1937.

11. Ibid. Especially see *Bridgeport Times Star*, 14 October 1937.

12. *BDN*, 15 October 1937.

13. AP article from Indianapolis, printed in *BDN*, 15 October 1937.

14. Associated Press Article, Indianapolis, as printed in *BDN*, 18 October 1937.

15. AP article from Indianapolis, printed in *BDN*, 15 October 1937.

16. Circuit of Appeals, Seventh Circuit, *United States v. Dalhover*, 18 May 1938; quotes and such from AP article from Indianapolis, printed in *BDN*, 15 October 1937.

17. AP article from Indianapolis, printed in *BDN*, 15 October 1937.

18. Telegram as printed in *BDN*, 15 October 1937, as well as other information. Also AP from Indianapolis, 14 October 1937, as printed in *BDN*, 15 October 1937.

19. *BDN*, 14 October 1937, two articles sent from Bridgeport, Connecticut.

20. Bridgeport, Connecticut Press and the Associated Press, 13 October 1937; and *BDN*, 14 October 1937.

21. As printed in the *BDN*, 18 October 1937.

22. See Richard Shaw, *The Weekly*, Bangor, Maine, 4 October 2011, on John O'Connell, Bud Leavitt, and Dan Mahar saying that they waited in cars for events to unfold. And, as discussed with a neighbor of the Raimondo sisters in Baltimore, authorities had warned people there about an impending raid on the gang's hideout.

23. *BDN* and *BDC*, 18–20 October 1937. Also see *Baltimore Daily Sun* and *Baltimore News-Post* for these days.

24. Ibid.

25. Ibid.

26. Ibid.

27. Ibid.

28. Ibid.

29. *BDC*, 16 October 1937.

30. *Baltimore News-Post*, 15 October 1937, INS article from Indianapolis.

31. Ibid.

32. Ibid.

33. Ibid.

34. Ibid.

35. Ibid.

36. Ibid.

37. *BDN*, AP article from Indianapolis, 15 November 1937.

38. Ibid.

39. Ibid. And, more importantly, and quoted from, Circuit of Appeals, Seventh Circuit, *United States v. Dalhover*, 18 May 1938. Also see AP article from Washington, DC, of 9 November printed in the *Baltimore Sun*, 10 November 1937. The arraignment was to be on the next Monday.

40. Ibid. Also see AP article in *BDN*, 16 November 1937.

41. Ibid. Also see AP article from Indianapolis in *BDN*, 7 December 1937.

42. AP article from Indianapolis in *BDN*, 7 December 1937.

43. Circuit of Appeals, Seventh Circuit, *United States v. Dalhover*, 18 May 1938; *The Indianapolis Star*, 17–18 November 1938; "Dalhover Put to Death; 'Trigger Man' of Brady Gang Dies in Indiana Chair," *NYT*, AP article from Michigan City; and "The Brady Gang," *FBI History: Famous Case*, FBI.

44. Ibid. Also see AP from Hammond, Indiana, article in *BDN*, 16 November 1937.

45. AP article from Hammond, Indiana, in *BDN*, 16 November 1937.

46. Ibid.

47. Circuit of Appeals, Seventh Circuit, *United States v. Dalhover*, 18 May 1938; *The Indianapolis Star*, 17–18 November 1938; "Dalhover Put to Death; 'Trigger Man' of Brady Gang Dies in Indiana Chair," *NYT*, AP article from Michigan City.

48. Ibid. Also see AP article in *BDN*, 16 November 1937.

49. Ibid.

50. Circuit of Appeals, Seventh Circuit, *United States v. Dalhover*, 18 May 1938.

51. Ibid.

52. Ibid.

53. Ibid.

54. Ibid.

55. Ibid.

56. *Baltimore Sun,* 25 June 1938.

57. *The Indianapolis Star*, 17–18 November 1938; "Dalhover Put to Death; 'Trigger Man' of Brady Gang Dies in Indiana Chair," *NYT*, AP article from Michigan City; and "The Brady Gang," *FBI History: Famous Cases*, FBI.

58. *Milwaukee Sentinel*, Special to the paper from Michigan City, Indiana. "Last of Brady Gang, Executed: Last Minute Pleas Fail to Prevent Death in Chair," 18 November 1938.

59. Ibid.

60. See AP article as printed in *BDC*, 18 November 1938, for second set of quotes on his clothing and the steps.

61. Ibid. And see *Milwaukee Sentinel*, Special to the paper from Michigan City, Indiana. "Last of Brady Gang, Executed: Last Minute Pleas Fail to Prevent Death in Chair," 18 November 1938.

62. *Milwaukee Sentinel*, Special to the paper from Michigan City, Indiana. "Last of Brady Gang, Executed: Last Minute Pleas Fail to Prevent Death in Chair," 18 November 1938.

63. Ibid. And see *BDC*, 17 November 1938.

64. Ibid.

65. AP article as reprinted in the *BDN*, 17 November 1938, and AP article from Washington, DC, as printed in *BDC*, 17 November 1938.

66. *BDC*, 17 November 1938.

67. AP article as reprinted in the *BDN*, 17 November 1938.

68. *BDC*, 17 November 1938, two articles.

69. *BDC*, 17 November 1938.

70. AP from Chicago, as printed in *BDN*, 17 October 1938; and San Diego *Evening Tribune*, 18 November 1938.

71. AP release from Fort Wayne, Indiana, 17 November 1938; and San Diego *Evening Tribune*, 18 November 1938.

72. San Diego *Evening Tribune*, 18 November 1938.

73. AP article as printed in *BDN*, 18 November 1938.

74. San Diego *Evening Tribune*, 18 November 1938.

75. *BDN*, 18 October 1938, and *BDC*, 18 October 1938.

76. *BDN*, 18 November 1938.

77. *BDN*, 15 October 1937.

78. *BDN*, 18 October 1938.

79. Ohio State Highway Patrol, "Seventy-Fifth Anniversary History, 1930," website posting of 2015.

AFTERWORD

Those Who Died and Those Who Remained

The core of the Brady Gang all died young. Ironically, and justly, one of the men who shot Alfred Brady dead in the streets of Bangor, Walter R. Walsh, lived to be almost 107 years old, missing his 107th birthday by just five days in 2014. He had been a "legendary marksmen" of world-class skills, a World War II veteran, a Marine colonel, an Olympian who competed in marksmanship in 1948 at the games in London, and an FBI agent, as well having had five children. At the time of his death, he was both the oldest living Olympian, and the oldest living retired FBI agent. In addition to the Brady case, Walsh had made his name as a federal agent first by discovering the body of George "Baby Face" Nelson in 1934 following Nelson's shooting by other federal agents, and in helping capture Arthur "Doc" Barker, son of the infamous Kate "Ma" Barker, who was wanted like the Brady Gang for bank robberies, murder, and a jailbreak—as well as for kidnapping. Walsh traced Doc Barker to a New Jersey apartment, and on an icy January day in 1935 caught the gangster unarmed, causing Barker to slip on the ice. He had asked Barker, referring to his gun, "Where's your heater, Doc?" Barker had responded, "It's up in the apartment." Walsh responded, "Ain't that a Hell of a place for it?" Walsh was ready to shoot the mobster if he tried to run for it, but Barker did not.[1]

Walsh is credited with killing at least ten gangsters during his career with the FBI, as well as participating in competitive shooting until late in life and helping to train snipers and competitive shooters. However, it was purportedly his role in the shooting and capture of the Brady Gang that cemented his legacy. Walsh had been the agent stationed in the store as a clerk who had helped apprehend James Dalhover, and had first engaged Shaffer in gunfire. Then, already wounded in his chest, shoulder, and his right hand, he had been the agent who fired the final shot that killed Alfred Brady. He spent the night after the shoot-out in a Bangor hospital, Eastern Maine General Hospital as it was then called. He returned to Bangor in 1987 as the guest of honor at a fiftieth-year anniversary ceremony marking the shoot-out in downtown Bangor, and was given a key to the city.[2] Other lawmen across the nation were rewarded or recognized for their roles in battling the Brady Gang. Some would bear lasting scars from those battles.

Matt Leach of the Indiana State Police, by having some of his men go to Baltimore and then to Maine, did get his man. And the Baltimore Police had no need to get theirs: Dalhover did not escape his murder charge in Indiana, and, in addition, no further evidence surfaced to connect the Brady Gang with the shootings they were once suspected of in Baltimore. Moreover, the two Baltimore officers who had chased the gang on August 7 had their actions recognized and were vindicated by subsequent events.

However, even after Shaffer's and Brady's deaths, when some money and goods had been recovered, and during Dalhover's period of incarceration in Indiana, issues remained concerning what might still be recovered of the jewelry, cars, money, and other items the gang had stolen. Just before Dalhover's arraignment in November 1937, on November 10 the *Baltimore Sun* had announced that property seized after the trio escaped that city had been put into trust, with a trustee appointed by the Second Circuit Court "for the known worldly goods of the erstwhile Brady Gang." The goods consisted of one automobile, one speedboat, and three bags of firearms. The United States Fidelity and Guaranty Company had requested the action, as it argued that it had paid more than $10,000 in burglary insurance to the Lima, Ohio, bank that the gang had robbed. The petitioner also stated that it had "reason to believe that there are cached in some other bank or other place in Baltimore large sums of money, securities, or valuables." The issue remained complicated as the Brady Gang had done business under assumed names, taken fraudulent actions, and so forth, making it difficult to ascertain just what assets they might have had, or where those assets or stolen goods might be. Brady had no legal address at the time of his death (nor had the other men), and so they might reasonably have held some goods elsewhere. This might be especially possible in Chicago and Indianapolis. Moreover, the 1931 automobile in question was not even securely held; it was being driven by a person, seemingly a male, who had no legal claim to the car.[3]

Some of the goods the original gang of four had stolen had been recovered in Baltimore, some in Bangor, and some in Chicago and Indianapolis following the arrests of the men in 1936 in Illinois, Indiana, and Kentucky. They included jewelry and gems, pens and silverware (although not listed in the above legal action), guns, ammunition, cars, and money, the last of which seems to have largely dissipated. Items like some of the arsenal, the Baltimore speedboat, and various cars were no doubt purchased through the gains of their many heists. Stores, theaters, gas stations, banks, jewelry stores, and security companies could not hope to recover all of their losses.

More importantly, in addition to having amassed a huge arsenal for just three or four men, as well as thousands and thousands of stolen dollars and a fortune in jewelry, the Brady Gang stole the lives of at least three men, injured numerous others, and, perhaps, in the case of Dalhover, even stole a marriage. They destroyed the trust of many people who had at one time cared for them, and wrought havoc throughout the Midwest, and to some extent the East Coast, where they may well have continued to commit crimes had they not been stopped in Maine, as well as, no doubt, in other states through which they passed in their careers of crime including a few in the Southwest. They had previously spent time in prison, but they did not learn their lessons. Had Al Brady truly have wanted to outdo John Dillinger, he might have avoided being shot to death like Dillinger; he could have learned during his various incarcerations and turned his life around. Instead, he continued his villainy and helped take the life of a man, for which he and his cohorts in the crime would die: Brady and Shaffer in the streets of Bangor, Dalhover in the electric chair. And that left still others dead and "unavenged," some might argue.

The *Bangor Daily News* had noted its in-depth coverage of events and the special work of its photographers, especially Dan Maher, who had been one of only two press members to have waited through the long night and early hours outside City Hall on November 15 for Dal-hover to be removed from lockup and flown away. The newspaper noted that day of its photographs, "They will be priceless some day, for they illustrate the last scene in a drama that will have its place in America's criminal history."[4] The newspaper was correct, in that several of the photographs taken by its staff and those of the *Bangor Daily Commercial*, by Dakin store proprietor Shep Hurd, as well as a few by city police remain historical images. Moreover, Hurd received the award money from the government, a letter from J. Edgar Hoover, and a $200 award and thank-you from the sheriff of Cass County, Indiana.[5]

Like Walsh, the victims of the Brady Gang's murderous assaults were honored for their work and remembered by their communities with pride. The officers whose lives the Brady Gang took, as well as the one they are presumed to have taken, did not live to go on to such honors, as did the man who fired the final shot that killed the already bullet-ridden Brady. But, they, too, were not forgotten.

Mrs. Dorothy Rivers, widow of the fallen officer Richard Rivers, killed in April 1936, told the Associated Press following the events in Maine that she found some satisfaction that the death of her husband had been "avenged."[6]

In a similar vein, Mrs. Margaret Minneman, widow of the murdered Paul Minneman of the May 1937 shootout, stated that the end of the Brady Gang revived thoughts of her husband and "brought a measure of satisfaction." She said, "I am glad that the killings by the Brady Gang are ended. But most of all I'm glad that no more police officers were killed capturing them."[7]

Minnemen and Rivers have been recognized as clear murder victims of the gang. There were witnesses to these deaths, people who clearly knew the Brady Gang members' identities. So, too did the gang bear responsibility for the death of young Edward Lindsay at the grocery store robbery in March 1936, and quite likely for that of Frank Levy in November 1935. As there was no true trial or prosecution for any of the murders, the facts remain murky, especially in the case of Frank Levy. And of course, the gang caused numerous severe injuries as well as the three, or perhaps more, deaths.

Deputy Sheriff Elmer Craig sustained serious injuries the day he saw Paul Minneman murdered when the two men confronted the gangsters at Caley's Crossing. Officer Edward C. Swaney, who had been in the car chase after the death of Richard Rivers at Dr. Rose's home in Indianapolis following the second Lima, Ohio, heist, was hospitalized for months with his spinal injuries. Jesse Ford, who had been driving the police vehicle, had suffered numerous fractures in the accident when he tried to avoid a "huge interstate truck" passing through the Public Square in front of them after leaving a side street, while giving pursuit, having tried to avoid first the truck and then a mother and child on the sidewalk, the child just a baby and in a "baggy buggy" or pram.[8] Both officers perhaps felt the impacts of their injuries for the rest of their lives, while people caught in the crossfires of the gang's shoot-outs and chases, like the mother with her baby, or the truck driver who almost crashed into a police car, or vice versa, no doubt remembered the gang for the remainder of their lives.

So too, did Sheriff Clarence Watson bear lasting injuries from the escape the Brady trio made from the Greenfield, Indiana, jail. His son, Melville Page Watson, later stated that he believed that the fight with Al Brady for the iron bar with which Brady had hit him numerous times had hastened his father's death.[9]

Edger Ridlen and his wife Lottie, who had stopped to aid the sheriff and given up their car to end the battle, survived the events of that day for decades, and a 1971 photograph of the two shows them as a seemingly happy elderly couple, smiling in a backyard with a child's metal slide behind them; Edger wearing a plaid shirt, pants, and glasses, and sitting in a webbed-lawn chair with a fedora resting on one knee, Lottie standing beside him, still slender but with her hair now waved and cut short, smiling with her hand on Edger's shoulder and wearing her eyeglasses, a strand of pearls and fancy earrings, a printed dress, and white sandals. An empty lawn chair of the same aluminum and plastic or fabric webbing as the one Edger was seated in stands empty near the couple; perhaps Lottie's chair to enjoy when they sat together in the fenced backyard. This couple at least seemed to have weathered the storms of life and the Brady Gang violence quite well, and were happily remembered by their family years later.[10]

The fight and escape in Greenfield affected those involved in various ways, and it also brought yet more people in a small community to the realization of how dangerous life could become in an instant when one encountered the wrong person or persons. This awareness came to other communities over the course of the gang's violence and threats, including Baltimore, Maryland, where two patrolmen were cut from flying glass during their encounter with the gang, and to Bangor, Maine, where an FBI agent suffered a minor injury also from an encounter with the deadly trio. Other people had sustained other injuries from the gang members, some even before the men "officially" formed their gang with Charles Geiseking in 1935. The four men who formed the core of the gang were violent thugs and thieves, liars and con artists, and began their lives of crime while still quite young. They stole from banks, but they also stole from people who had much less to give or to lose during the grim years of the Great Depression. Perhaps having miserable starts in life, they brought that misery to the lives of others. They may have had their charms, but they could be merciless.

And of course, the Brady Gang was composed of young men, and they left behind parents and other family members, wives, and consorts, and seemingly at least four children. After the shootout in Bangor, Clarence Lee Shaffer Jr.'s mother—who had pleaded with him to give up criminal activities just the year or so before—stated that she was sad to hear that her son had been killed, but that she had expected it, and she had read accounts of the shootout with her husband, John Bailey, in their farmhouse. Neighbors of the couple had brought them the news. The couple looked grim in a photograph taken of them in their Noblesville, Indiana, home following the shootout. According to the Associated Press, when interviewed just after the news broke, his stepfather had said, "We expected the end would come just as it did. In a way it was a shock to us and in another way it was not a surprise." Clarence Lee Shaffer Jr.'s biological father also survived him, and paid to have his body shipped home.[11]

Shaffer's grandfather, George W. Schaffer, then aged seventy and living with his wife Sally, aged sixty-nine, said that, "We've been expecting it," when they learned that their grandson had been killed in Bangor by federal agents.[12]

Clarence Lee Shaffer Jr. also left behind a young wife, Minnie, as did James Dalhover. Dalhover—in addition to Minnie's sister Mary, also left behind an earlier wife and his two children with her. His Baltimore wife also apparently bore him a child before his execution, but he did not see the baby. Shaffer had also left behind his young girlfriend Christine—she said she had been his fiancée and that he had given her a ring and introduced her as his wife—and their young son,

Russell Lee Puckett. According to the Associated Press, after she learned of Shaffer's death, she had said, "It is probably for the best for him for his folks, for me, and for the little boy." She said she had heard nothing of Shaffer from the time she told him they needed to get married until his arrest for the murder of Richard Rivers. She had not known the type of man he was in the outside world.[13]

Al Brady left behind his beloved Margaret, who had earlier left behind her husband and child to be with him. He seems to have abandoned or left behind other women also along the way. Some, like Alicia Frawley, did not express any great regret over the loss. Brady's uncle, Charles Courtwood of Brook, Indiana, said that the death of his nephew who "went bad" saddened him, but both of his nephew's parents were dead, and, Brady's uncle replied, "I haven't any money to bury the man," when he was asked if he would claim Brady's body.[14]

The sisters who had married Dalhover and Shaffer stated that they were "'relieved and 'not sorry' when they learned that G-men had wiped out the Brady Gang," according to a statement reported by the Associated Press, although one sister then expressed that indeed she was a bit sorry. After his arrest in Bangor, Dalhover purportedly stated that he thought that it was the two sisters who had tipped off the police as to the gang's whereabouts, although he did not state that the young women actually knew their "true professions." He did say that Brady had told them that they were all from Bangor, Maine. He said that the gang had been to Bangor several times, but their having been in Maine previous to autumn 1937 is unsubstantiated. Dalhover also apparently blamed Brady's former girlfriend, Margaret Larson, for having brought the law down on them in Chicago. But, she, too, had been arrested, and she, too, had been tricked by the Brady Gang, as was her friend from New Orleans who dated Shaffer for a time. These were not the only women fooled—although in truth they may have known or suspected more than they admitted—and like the judge in Baltimore told the Raimondo sisters, the members of the gang could have had "half a dozen wives" and no one might be the wiser.[15]

Dalhover's mother and Dalhover himself had something to say about his capture, his mother's statement perhaps the most damning. Or, perhaps, just the fears of a mother that her son would suffer more in the long run by the way things occurred in Bangor. Now going as Mrs. Bertha Craig and living in Madison, Indiana, in an interview with the

Associated Press just after the Bangor shootout, she was quoted as saying that he, too, should have been "killed suddenly like the rest of them." The local papers, however, ran with the headline: "Too Bad He Wasn't Killed, Says Dalhover's Mother." Subsequent months had shown her fighting for the life of her son. And after she made the longer 1937 statement, which indicated that she did not want to see her son undergo prolonged suffering, Mrs. Craig purportedly fell to the floor in a faint.[16]

While still retained in Bangor, James Dalhover told officers that he would rather have fought it out with his friends and died with them. Guards at the lockup reported he spoke fairly often with them when not under interrogation, and that he did not speak of having any remorse over the fate of his co-thugs Brady and Shaffer, rather he seemed to regret that he himself was taken alive, while Brady, who had—apparently after the gang's escape from their Indiana jail cells—sworn that he would never be recaptured was not captured, or rather, not captured alive.[17] But then, when his time came to die, Dalhover fought his death penalty and purportedly had to be half-dragged to the electric chair.

The gangsters also left behind a few former associates, including former gang member Charles Geiseking, who remained in jail in Ohio after the shootout. He stated after learning of the Bangor deaths and capture that "Brady was a squealer." Geiseking was still under medical care for the bullet wounds he had received in the shootout in Lima, Ohio, after the gang had robbed a jewelry store there. He was photographed in his prison bed lying down, still bandaged. The following year, Dalhover went to the electric chair, while Charles Geiseking remained in prison.[18]

In 1938, the year Rhuel James Dalhover met his death in the electric chair, work began in Bangor on a new, stronger, police station. The police station would remain in the same location into the early twenty-first century, at which time the city would construct a new one—one better suited to the needs of that century. However, the 1930s had demonstrated a need for a stronger jail in Bangor, just as the escapes of the Brady Gang and several other gangsters in other locations had shown a need for stronger prisons or strengthened security elsewhere.

In addition, 1938 also saw reclamation work begin on the Mount Hope Municipal Cemetery in Bangor—which adjoins Mount Hope Cemetery proper. The relief project aimed to repair and beautify the city-owned section, the private section already being recognized as a place of great beauty and tranquility. According to municipal records, the city section had fallen into a "deplorable condition" over recent years. Stones had cracked and fallen over, grass was overgrown, and weeds ran rampant. The project undertook to fill in the swampiest areas of the property, as well grading some sections and laying out new roads, constructing bridges, and widening the brook. This was a project that took a few years to complete.[19]

In the meantime, Al Brady rotted away there. It did not truly matter if his gang had "out-Dillingered Dillinger, or made "Dillinger look like a piker." They were all dead, all except Geiseking, who had not been at the scenes of most of the gang's worst crimes. But Brady would not be remembered the way Dillinger was, nor the way Bonnie and Clyde were, nor as were some other notorious gangsters of the era like Pretty Boy Floyd or Ma and Doc Barker. Even FBI Director J. Edgar Hoover only included the Brady Gang in one sentence in a long book on American Crime in 1938. Certainly the people and communities who had had the misfortune of encountering the Brady Gang remembered them, but to date they have not reverberated in American history the way so many other gangsters of their era have. A later generation might have labeled Brady a sociopath, any generation would have labeled him a failure, for overall, as a human being, he failed miserably. He brought darkness, not light, to the world.

And so ended what some consider the last of the Depression Era gangs, all three core members dead, with very few mourners left behind, and the surviving one-time member in prison. As Dalhover had quipped on more than one occasion and with varying wording, "It was fun while it lasted." Perhaps, but for whom? Not even for them, in the end.

NOTES

1. Video and transcript of FBI anniversary presentation, "Ex-Agent [Walter Walsh] Recalls Role in Gangster Era," FBI website. Also Obituary, *BDN*, 1 May 2014; also see *NYT* obituary.

2. Ibid. Also see *BDN*, 13–16 October 1937; *NYT*, 13 October 1937; and "The Brady Gang," *FBI History: Famous Cases*, FBI.

3. *Baltimore Sun*, 10 November 1937.

4. *BDN*, 15 October 1937.

5. Letter from J. Edgar Hoover, 1938, and Cass County Sheriff, Robert D. Schmit to Everett Hurd, 12 October 1938.

6. As printed in the *BDN*, 13 October 1937.

7. Ibid.

8. Egan and Hunt, "The Second Dillinger"; and see other Indiana press reports.

9. Williams and Williams, *A History of Hancock County, Indiana, in the Twentieth Century*.

10. Letter and photograph supplied by Joyce Miller, niece of the couple.

11. *BDN*, 14 October 1937, 2nd edition, and *BDN*, 15 October 1937, on Shaffer's father paying for the body transport to Indianapolis; and quotes from Associated Press interview as printed in the *BDN*, 13 October 1937.

12. As printed in the *BDN*, 13 October 1937.

13. As quoted and covered by the Associated Press and printed in the *BDN*, 14 October 1937, 2nd edition, and in other newspapers; and her statement as printed in the *BDN*, 13 October 1937, and *Baltimore News-Post*, 15 October 1937; and see the *Baltimore News-Post* and *Baltimore Sun* for August 1937–November 1938.

14. As printed in the *BDN*, 13 October 1937.

15. As quoted and covered by the Associated Press and printed in the *BDN*, 14 October 1937, 2nd edition, and in other newspapers. Also see *BDN*, 18 October 1937, on Dalhover's statements about the sisters and *Baltimore News-Post*, 15 October 1937.

16. As printed in the *BDN*, 13 October 1937. On the child see San Diego *Evening Tribune*, 18 November 1938.

17. *BDN*, 13 October 1937.

18. As quoted and covered by the Associated Press and printed in the *BDN*, 14 October 1937, 2nd edition, and in other newspapers. AP, as printed in *BDN*, November 1938.

19. Ibid.

ACKNOWLEDGMENTS

Like always, I first wish to thank my family and friends. Nothing seems to change here, except for more books and papers scattered around the house, and more creatures demanding pets—but these are not really changes. I remain fortunate to have an at least somewhat understanding family, who continue to put up with my scribbling life, so thank you Mariah, Mom, Bub, Juanita, Donna, Vishnu, Basil, Wendell, Peter, Stephen, Jono, Josh, Shelby, Stephie, Brandon, and all those mates and babies!

And to my friends, too, thank you. If you are gone, thank you just the same. You have helped make me who I am, for better or for worse, for saner or for not. And for those who are still here, well, you know what I mean. And Colleen, I hope I do not blow your cover, but, writing this book, I could not help thinking how funny, and not violent like the Brady Gang's, was the jailbreak you made with Michelle. Of course, you two both had to break into the jail first! My only question is: Why didn't you invite me?

And, this book has been different from any other I have written. I generally drive all over the place to research a topic, but in part due to a bad winter, an extensive geographical course followed by the Brady Gang, and some difficulty getting documents from various governmental agencies, I have been aided by more people along the way than usual, and relied on some different sources than I had anticipated.

I wish to thank Linda Oliver at the Bangor Public Library for writing numerous letters on my behalf to various other reference librarians, and to say thank you to the staff at the Bangor Public Library in general, seemingly one of my homes away from home, and to Bill Cook for keeping the archives, and thank you to the folks at Mount Hope Cemetery for the same and allowing me to use some of your photographs, and to the Bangor Police Department. Also, I must say that I owe my gratitude to the University of Maine also, for the many hours I spent there researching microfilm and microfiche newspaper and journal articles. Thank you to everyone along the way.

I also wish to thank Mark at the National Archives, Paul at the Hancock County Public Library, Vickie at the Anderson Public Library, Meg at the Enoch Pratt Free Library, Dagny at the Indianapolis Public Library, and Elizabeth at the Bridgeport History Center and Public Library for digging out documents and newspaper articles that I could not have otherwise accessed; at least, not in a timely fashion. Writing this book was more like solving a jigsaw puzzle than has been any of my previous works. And the fact that I think a few pieces are still missing does not make it any less so, perhaps it only adds to the work—I hope. For the Brady Gang was ruthless much of the time, interesting some of the time, and its members still remain in some ways enigmas. But thank you all for supplying so many pieces to the puzzle!

And I wish to thank Michael Steere at Down East Books for asking me to write this book and for his support along the way. I also want to acknowledge the rest of the staff at Down East Books and at Rowman & Littlefield. For like a Beatle now, it seems, I am "a paperback writer." Hopefully, I shall become a better one. I do not seem to have any choice in the matter of writing. I think it owns me more than I own it.

Trudy Irene Scee
On the River in Brewer, Maine
April 2015

SELECTED BIBLIOGRAPHY

BOOKS

(Note: Most of these general books do not include more than a sentence or two about the Brady Gang, if the gang is included at all, an exception being Scee's history of Bangor, Maine. They do, however, help set the stage for the era, and most discuss a number of the other gang and mobster histories included in this work.)

Beverly, William. *On the Lam: Narratives of Flight in J. Edgar Hoover's America*. Jackson: University Press of Mississippi, 2003.

Block, Lawrence. *Gangsters, Swindlers, Killers, and Thieves: The Lives and Crimes of Fifty American Villains*. Oxford: Oxford University Press, 2004.

Burrough, Bryan. *Public Enemies: America's Greatest Crime Wave and the Birth of the FBI, 1933–1934*. New York: Penguin Press, 2009.

Cooper, Courtney Ryley, with a foreword by J. Edgar Hoover. *Ten Thousand Public Enemies*. Boston: Little, Brown, & Company, 1935.

The editors of *Look Magazine*, with a foreword by J. Edgar Hoover. *The Story of the FBI*. New York: E. P. Dutton and Co., Inc. 1947, 1954 revised edition.

Helmer, William J., and Mattix, Rick. *Public Enemies: America's Criminal Past, 1919–1940*. New York City: Facts on File, 1998.

J. Edgar Hoover. In addition to his books, several documents and writings and of Hoover are included in the National Archives Collection.

Jensen, Richard J. *Illinois, A History*. New York: W. W. Norton & Company, Inc., 1978.

Johnson, Judith R. "A Mighty Fortress Is the Pen: The Development of the New Mexico Penitentiary." In Judith Boyce DeMark, ed., *Essays in Twentieth-Century New Mexico History*. Albuquerque: University of New Mexico Press, 1994.

Leibowitz, Irving. *My Indiana*. Englewood Cliffs, NJ: Prentice Hall, Inc., 1964.

Peckham, Howard H. *Indiana, A History*. Nashville, TN: W. W. Norton & Company, Inc., 1978.

Scee, Trudy Irene. *City on the Penobscot; A Comprehensive History of Bangor, Maine*. Charleston, SC: The History Press, 2010.

Scee, Trudy Irene. *Mount Hope Cemetery of Bangor, Maine: The Complete History*. Charleston, SC: The History Press, 2012.

Scee, Trudy Irene. *Rogues, Rascals, and Other Villainous Mainers*. Camden, ME: Down East Books, 2014.

Williams, Dorothy June, and Thomas E. Williams. *A History of Hancock County, Indiana, in the Twentieth Century*. Greenfield, IN: Coiny Press, 1995. The document is typewritten and available at the Hancock County Library, Indiana.

NEWSPAPERS

Alliance [Ohio] Review, 5 March 1936.

Anderson Daily Bulletin, Indiana, November 1935–November 1938.

Baltimore News-Post, Maryland, 7 August–20 October 1937, and November 1938.

Baltimore Sun, Maryland, 7 August–20 October 1937, and November 1938.

Bangor Daily Commercial, Maine, 12–22 October 1937 and October–November 1938.

Bangor Daily News, 12–22 October 1937, October–November 1938, February 1987, 4–5 October 1997, and 1 May 2014.

[Bridgeport] City Herald, Connecticut, 17 October 1937.

Bridgeport Post, Connecticut, 14–15 October 1937.

Bridgeport Times Star, Connecticut, 13–20 October 1937.

Daily Times Tribune of Alexandria, Indiana, 19 May 1936.

Dayton Journal, 10 April 1936–June 1936.

The Gleaner, Henderson, Kentucky, 13 September 1936.

Greenfield Daily Reporter, Indiana, October 1936–November 1938.

Greenville Daily Advocate, Ohio, 5 March 1936–November 1938.

Indiana Wire Service, Logansport, 18–19 July 1937, and various dates in 1936–1938.

Indianapolis Star, 28 April–4 May 1936.

Kokomo [Indiana] Tribune, 26 May 1937–October 1937.

Milwaukee Journal, 6–10 October 1937.

Milwaukee Sentinel, 18 November 1938.

Pharos Tribune [Logansport, Indiana], 25 May 1937–June 1937.

Rushville [Indiana] Republication, 4 October 1937.

San Diego *Evening Tribune*, 18 November 1938.

Tipton [Indiana] Daily Tribune, Evening Edition, 23 May 1937–June 1937.

Toledo Blade, 5–10 March 1936.

World Herald, Omaha, 11 August 1937.

COLLECTIONS

Anderson Public Library, Indiana

Bangor Public Library, Bangor, Maine

Bangor Historical Society, Bangor, Maine

Bangor Police Department, Bangor, Maine

Bridgeport History Center and Public Library, Bridgeport, Connecticut

Enoch Pratt Free Library, Baltimore, Maryland

Federal Bureau of Investigation, FBI websites under "Famous Cases." See individual sites as noted. Also FOIA collections as now held at the National Archives.

Hancock County Public Library, Indiana

Indianapolis Public Library, Indianapolis, Indiana

Indianapolis Metropolitan Police Department reports on Sergeant Richard Rivers

New Mexico Corrections Department

United States National Archives, FBI Collection, Brady Gang, Archives Case Records 87–257, National Archives at College Park, Maryland.

Transcript of Arraignment, James Dalhover, November 1937, District Court for the Northern District of Indiana.

Circuit of Appeals, Seventh Circuit, *United States v. Dalhover*, 96 F.2d 355 (7th cir. 1938), 16 April 1938. Rehearing Denied May 18, 1938.

"Mayors Annual Reports" of 1920—1941, Bangor, Maine.

ARTICLES AND MISCELLANEOUS

"Brady Gang." *Time*, June 7, 1937.

"Tough Customers." *Time*, October 25, 1937.

"Brady Gang Is Wiped out Planning Bangor Bank Raid." *NYT*, 13 October 1937.

"Brady Buried as Pauper." *NYT*, 16 October 1937.

"Dalhover Put to Death." *NYT*, 18 November 1938.

Obituary, Walter R. Walsh. *NYT*, 1 May 2014.

"A Byte out of History, Closing in on the Barker/Karpis Gang." *FBI History: Famous Cases*. Federal Bureau of Investigation, FBI website, 2012 posting.

"Bonnie and Clyde." *FBI History: Famous Cases*. Federal Bureau of Investigation, FBI website, 2015.

"The Brady Gang." *FBI History: Famous Cases*. Federal Bureau of Investigation, FBI website as posted in 2014.

"John Dillinger." *FBI History: Famous Cases*. Federal Bureau of Investigation, FBI website, 2015.

"Pretty Boy Floyd: The Kansas City Massacre." *FBI History: Famous Cases*. Federal Bureau of Investigation, FBI website, 2105

"Al Capone." *FBI History: Famous Cases*, FBI.

Discussions with Steve Bissell, Baltimore, Maryland, Spring 2015.

Junior Welfare League. "Bangor, Maine: A Community Study," 1933.

Letter from J. Edgar Hoover to Everett Hurd, 1938.

Letter from Cass County Sheriff, Robert D. Schmit to Everett Hurd, 12 October 1938.

"Officer Down." Web Sites, for the murders of Anderson, Indiana, Police Officer Frank Levy; Indianapolis Police Sargent Richard Rivers; and Indiana State Trooper Paul V. Minneman.

Ohio State Highway Patrol, "Seventy-Fifth Anniversary History, 1930," website posting of 2015.

Richard Shaw. "Last Days of the Brady Gang." *BDN*, 4–5 October 1997, and related article in *The Weekly*, Bangor, Maine, 4 October 2011.

Video and transcript of FBI anniversary presentation, "Ex-Agent [Walter Walsh] Recalls Role in Gangster Era," FBI website.

Wisconsin State Police History website, "The 1930s," as posted in 2014.

Captain John Egan as told to Douglas Hunt, Chicago Police Department, "The Second Dillinger," written for *Official Detective Magazine* for November 1937 publication. Excerpts printed in the *Bangor Daily News*, Maine, 13 October 1937.

INDEX